BRYAN NELSON

GALAPAGOS
CRUSOES

A YEAR ALONE
WITH THE BIRDS

Bradt GUIDES

First edition published April 2022; hardback published January 2022
Bradt Guides Ltd
31a High Street, Chesham, HP5 1BW, England
www.bradtguides.com

Print edition published in the USA by The Globe Pequot Press Inc,
PO Box 480, Guilford, Connecticut 06437-0480

Text copyright © Bryan Nelson (1968) and June Nelson (2022)
Maps copyright © 2022 Bradt Guides
Photos © Bryan Nelson

Edited by James Lowen
Cover design by Ian Spick
Layout and typesetting by Ian Spick
Author photo page v © Roger Lever
Map by David McCutcheon FBCart.S
Line drawings by John Busby
Production managed by Sue Cooper, Bradt Guides & Jellyfish Print Solutions

ISBN: 9781784778859 (paperback), 9781784779320 (hardback)

British Library Cataloguing in Publication Data
A catalogue record for this book is available from the British Library

Digital conversion by www.dataworks.co.in
Printed in the UK by Jellyfish Print Solutions

To Bryan Nelson (1932–2015)

I dedicate this book to Bryan, friend and husband for 61 years. We shared so much: a sense of humour, zany in different ways; a deep love of life and the earth; a need to explore, in all senses; fascinating friendships; an enjoyment of words; and a horror of cruelty and bigotry. And we shared the creation of *Galapagos: Islands of Birds*, his lyrical 1968 book which has been the springboard for this joint one. Bryan was loved by many people; I was privileged to have so much of him. Thank you, Bryan.

Bryan Nelson honed his perversity and argumentative skills with an elder sister, which stood him in good stead as local preacher and lecturer. He left school at 16 and earned a qualification in sewage purification while simultaneously studying for university entrance. After  Bryan obtained a 1st in zoology from St Andrews, he and June married in 1960, studied gannet behaviour and ecology from a garden shed on the Bass Rock for Bryan's D. Phil., then the rest of the Sulidae family on the Galapagos, Peruvian Guano Islands, Christmas Island and New Zealand. They enjoyed 18 months trying to establish a desert research station at a wonderful oasis in Jordan, but the Israeli/Palestine conflict scuppered that. Bryan's lectureship at Aberdeen followed and he eventually became a Reader. Early retirement to Galloway allowed him to add several books (including large tomes on the Sulidae and Pelicaniformes) and papers to his prolific output. More general books showed his versatility: *The Atlantic Gannet*; *Galapagos: Islands of Birds*; *Azraq: Desert Oasis*; *Living with Seabirds* and *On The Rocks*. He became a Fellow of the Royal Society of Edinburgh, and received an MBE from the Queen, when she expressed her regret about never visiting the Galapagos.

With Prince Philip's intervention, their work on Christmas Island helped save the rare Abbott's booby. Bryan became a founder board member of the Scottish Seabird Centre and on its tenth anniversary engaged with the Queen and Prince Philip, who exclaimed: 'You must be at least a hundred.' Later Bryan showed Prince Charles round the Bass Rock. Many folk, especially students, were inspired by Bryan's amusing lectures and talks, and zany wit.

Other interests included writing, birding, hillwalking, cycling, sailing and tennis. He died in 2015 aged 83.

June Nelson began work in a London tax office, in revolt against studying and being denied a university place to study English literature because she had never taken Latin. Following family tradition she loved the outdoors and camping. Aged 11, she began birding with her  godmother, and, through her, met Bryan birding at Spurn Point (June gloated about having ringed a gannet before Bryan did). Their first significant meeting was sheltering from the rain under an abandoned table on Spurn Peninsula, when June insisted that Bryan should share her apple.

In their late thirties, the couple settled in Aberdeenshire, had twins and acquired pets, embraced gardening, cycling and tamer travelling. Later June became a relationship counsellor with Couple Counselling, worked in a wholefood shop and cooked in a wholefood café long before they were fashionable. She then began working with adults with a learning disability, and later became secretary of the Sutherland Trust. Into her eighties she still cycled, played tennis and walked hills, but hip and knee replacements latterly curtailed such activities and, now 85, she gardens and writes. Writing days with friend Margaret, who soon became a professor of English, led to enthusiastic contributions to Margaret's book about life during COVID-19, and the subsequent monthly writing group. A student film by George Pretty on climate change and seabirds, which June narrated, has recently won numerous festival awards. She believes vehemently in 'keeping going'. This is her first 'big' book.

A NOTE ON AUTHORSHIP

This book blends an edited version of Bryan's text from *Galapagos: Islands of Birds* (in places updated or tailored where judged appropriate) with June's fresh observations, written nearly 50 years later and thus from an entirely modern perspective. Rather than indicate precisely who wrote which words, which would prove rather cumbersome, each chapter has a byline identifying one or both authors. Occasional clarifications are also given within the text, where needed.

CONTENTS

FOREWORD TO
GALAPAGOS: ISLANDS OF BIRDS

HRH THE DUKE OF EDINBURGH

In *Galapagos: Islands of Birds* Bryan Nelson has achieved a rare combination; he has written a book full of important information and valuable scientific discussion in a lively and entertaining style.

I found the book particularly interesting as I had the pleasure of visiting Tower and Hood and meeting the Nelsons at their camp on Hood Island, albeit on the last day of its occupation. Although the author makes light of their long period of isolated existence, it ranks as a major achievement in itself. I think he is also particularly fortunate to have found a wife and helper willing and able to put up with that kind of life, and at the end of it all to appear as neat and tidy as the day she left civilisation.

If, on occasions, his descriptions of life sound almost idyllic, I would strongly advise anyone who has ideas about rushing off to live on a desert island to think three and preferably four times about it and then to consult June Nelson.

The Galapagos Islands hold a special fascination for all naturalists. I suppose it is partly because of their association with Darwin and because of their extraordinary list of animal populations that they inevitably prompt speculation about the 'hows' and 'whys' of evolution. Dr Nelson has quite a lot to say about this fascinating subject as a result of watching and recording many of the islands' inhabitants. It is books of this kind which emphasise what a fundamental redirection of human thought was initiated by Darwin with the publication of *On the Origin of Species*.

The objective study of wild populations within their environment is yielding more and more remarkable information. However, I find it difficult to believe that every feature of structure and behaviour is important for the purposes of survival. In some species quite wide margins of difference in physical features or behaviour patterns seem to be tolerated, whereas in other cases a very slight difference or aberration can spell greater success or complete extinction in a particular environment. The difficulty seems to be to assess the relative survival value of any particular feature without an exact knowledge of all the environmental changes through which a particular species has developed, and without being able to distinguish accurately which features of colour and habit have given rise to greater breeding success.

There seems to be one hangover from the pre-Darwinian days which still recurs to haunt many ethologists today. It was not unnatural for the philosophers of old to make a sharp distinction in humans between the purely physical processes of life and the apparently totally different operation of the brain; the growth of a fingernail and the ability to invent a limerick were considered to be two quite unrelated processes. They probably are, but in animals, without the same ability of conscious and deliberate thought, the processes of the brain must surely form an integral part of the physical process as a whole. To a large extent the animal brain must resemble a 'printed circuit', in that a particular combination of inputs produces a given output every time. The answer to the questions 'Why does a bird grow feathers?' and 'Why does a bird have a migratory instinct?' is the same: it is part of the whole physical process of a successful species. Without both these features it would have become another failure or, at any rate, a different sort of bird. This to me is the wonder and fascination of the evolutionary concept, that the process of natural selection has controlled the very minutest details of every feature of the whole individual and the group to which it belongs.

This book, and a more specialist one, *The Sulidae*, will provide many new pieces for the giant jigsaw puzzle of life which the natural sciences are slowly putting together; Dr Bryan Nelson has made a valuable contribution and I am sure he would consider that ample reward for all his discomforts, painstaking observations and detailed records.

Philip
Buckingham Palace 1968 (reproduced with permission and updated in 1984)

FOREWORD TO
GALAPAGOS CRUSOES

TUI DE ROY

I vividly recall, when I was just ten years old, briefly meeting a lanky young couple at the Charles Darwin Research Station in Galapagos, tanned chocolate-brown, their hair sun-bleached. June and Bryan Nelson had just returned from months living alone on an outlying island that I'd never been to. They were studying seabirds, I was told. And they made me dream. A few years later I got my first camera, and soon set out to photograph all the wild species and places in Galapagos, a job still ongoing over half a century later. I also got a copy of Bryan Nelson's eloquent book, part science, part narrative of a Robinson Crusoe life. It became my bible.

The decades passed, and so did Bryan. But the birds are still there, flying in from the ocean on their flights of freedom, their raucous calls giving life to the wind. And I'm still fascinated. Tour guides showing visitors around Genovesa still quote the Nelsons' observations on population and behaviour of boobies and frigatebirds.

It seems remarkably fitting that the late Prince Philip should pen the introduction to Bryan Nelson's original volume, as both men shared inquiring minds that were way ahead of their time. Writing more than half a century ago, the Prince spoke of the connectivity between animals and their environment, of needing to understand the wholeness of these interrelationships, even before the term 'ecosystem' had been widely adopted. He alluded to the process of evolution at work on the brains and bodies of animals, to make them what they are as species. Both men questioned simple dogma, Bryan going as far as ascribing *individuality* to particular birds he came to know well.

Science has moved on and we now recognise – at long last – that animal minds can be as fertile as our own. What differentiates us most is not our respective abilities to think, but the human capacity to store accumulated knowledge in writing, thereby letting others build upon our own thoughts long after we've passed. In this, both Prince Philip's and Bryan's legacies live on, still fresh and timeless, replete with fascination. And June's recollections of island life are as vivid as were the young couple's adventures nearly 60 years ago, when life on a desert island was far more remote and disconnected than a stint on the International Space Station is today.

PREFACE

THE EVOLUTION OF THIS BOOK
HILARY BRADT

On my first date with my husband George in 1971 we discovered a mutual desire to visit the Galapagos Islands. We had each read a book about this little-known archipelago and they had sparked our interest. Sparked is the wrong word – they had set us alight with enthusiasm. Mine was *Galapagos: Islands of Birds* by Bryan Nelson. We duly visited the islands, by boat from Guayaquil, in 1973 when visitors were few and far between and there was no supervision of those that did make it there. We stayed for two weeks, camped in the highlands of Santa Cruz with our tent nibbled by a giant tortoise, took a fishing boat to visit South Plaza to gape at the land iguanas and *Opuntia* cacti, and most memorably, and extraordinarily, were dropped on Daphne Major (now closed to tourists) to spend a day marvelling at the blue-footed boobies scattered 'like currants' on the crater bottom, with Nazca boobies nesting along the edges – an experience evocatively described by Bryan in *Chapter 3*. Because I had read Bryan's book I knew a lot about boobies and the other seabirds, and that visit is one of the very best – possibly the best – in a lifetime of wonderful wildlife encounters.

We should never have been allowed to wander unsupervised. By the time I started leading trips to the island in the 1980s visitors were strictly regulated, thank goodness, and even with the huge growth in tourism in recent years, the environmental impact from all these people has not been disastrous and their hard currency has been well used for conservation. But I can rejoice in my good fortune to experience some of the islands only a few years after the Nelsons' epic studies, and to continue to visit them another six times as well as publishing the first tourist map of the islands and one of our first wildlife guides. Right from the start, however, I have wanted to reprint Bryan's book, given that it sparked my interest in the first place. It's taken 40 years and several attempts, but thanks to June, Bryan's widow, here it is. As June's memories of their extraordinary year returned and as she blossomed as a writer, this version is less about the science than the experience of living on uninhabited islands. At 85 she lists one of her hobbies as 'keeping going' – fortunately for us.

JUNE NELSON

This book began with a request from Hilary Bradt. Would I add my recollections of our 1964 year in the Galapagos as part of a rewrite to make Bryan's eloquent book, published in 1968, accessible to a more general audience? That sounded unexpected but interesting; I was shackled by a worn-out knee and COVID-19 restrictions. It continued with the suggestion that, as I had worked alongside Bryan, maybe it would make sense if I edited the sections meant for scientists and also updated some of our findings. Even more unexpected, but I like a challenge.

Bryan was gung-ho, believing anything was possible. Four years younger, without a degree, I began as his Sancho Panza. Writing this book began with me still as Sancho Panza. The first thing I did was copy out one of Bryan's scintillating paragraphs, close my iPad and retire disheartened. My English-professor friend, Margaret, suggested I close Bryan's book and find my own voice.

It took a long time, with me dutifully adding, as usual, to Bryan's perspective. I think Hilary despaired at my initially slightly leaden, quasi-scientific prose – after all, I had spent a lifetime editing the real thing for Bryan – but soon I began to enjoy the writing.

Reading old letters and diaries I began to realise that a lot of our life on those Galapagos beaches had escaped Bryan's book. Scientists were peering over his shoulder, he wanted to write about our research and he had always maintained that domestic life had no place in a worthwhile conversation.

As a feminist the idea of writing two chapters with 'housekeeping' in the title or as the main theme appalled me, yet I kept wanting to do it. I assured myself that it was impossible to be a housewife on a desert island. I wanted to write about planning what to take, about eating as well as possible, keeping us sane and alive, being a rock and sharing Bryan's fun. I also wanted to correct Bryan's picture of me as 'helper'; somebody much appreciated and thanked profusely, but a Sancho Panza. I suppose Sancho Panza probably would have piggybacked Don Quixote across our creek. Sancho was the strong, practical one.

Yes, I was a typical 1960s housewife. We had to live, and Bryan was older with a doctorate, but added to 'housework' I shared his work completely. Sometimes I even did it alone, whilst he applied poultices to his sores and read Churchill. It's beginning to sound more like most 2020s women.

I had fun writing about 'housekeeping'. It turned out to be not much about housekeeping. Mostly, from my perspective, it describes life on a desert island: the joys, the frustration, the humdrum, the absorbing scientific research, the challenging minutiae, the delight in trusting Galapagos creatures, being outdoors in idyllic surroundings, and the highlights and the misery. After a long day battling boobies, we recovered in the lagoon. Somewhat refreshed,

I tried to think up something interesting for supper, then we spent the evening, with Radio Belize in the background, repairing equipment, writing up the day's work, typing, analysing and planning more of the same for the morrow.

We shared most things.

I have enjoyed sifting out Bryan's science. It felt good to reveal his lyrical best. But I also enjoyed leaving in the fascinating information about how our Galapagos subjects lived. Bryan describes that so well and accessibly. Perhaps most of all, although it often felt like an impossible chore, I felt genuine excitement at piecing together a layman's account of how boobies talk to each other and manage, sometimes, to rear offspring in unpredictable Galapagos conditions. I didn't want this to be smart, scientific English, written by a man. I wrote as a woman, with no scientific training.

Also, it has felt exciting slowly moving away from that quasi-scientific style. Huge chunks read like an abstract for a scientific paper. Writing for a book felt like a serious undertaking, and out came detached prose, as from a mincer, as I fed in our information. I have had to step back from each paragraph and try to relive the experience it describes. I would love to start the book again. It has an awful lot of paragraphs about many unique experiences.

Although we added another fascinating booby piece to the jigsaw, our often miserable time when we moved to a demanding Peruvian guano island proved a watershed. Once back in Scotland Bryan expected our relationship to continue in Galapagos mode, despite lecturing 20 miles away in Aberdeen. He was astonished when I accepted an invitation to meet the women of our nearest village. He was working hard. I should be analysing Galapagos data, typing up results, starting our new garden, continuing barrowing out broken-up cement ready for a wooden floor in our new house, ensuring that a meal awaited his return…

Eventually I pursued my interest in wholefoods and counselling, and worked with adults with a disability. Bryan and I were no longer joined at the hip.

Sometimes, in the last few weeks, I have felt ambivalent about discovering that this 'new writing voice' was in fact the one I have used for most of my life. Chatty letters, and later emails to distant friends, have revelled in my exciting experiences in distant places. Or, latterly, they have offered a wry look at being 85, with a worn knee, in a time of COVID. I am in training to reach 100.

A note on names

In 1964 there was some toing and froing about what English name to use for the seabird then known as *Sula dactylatra*. In *Galapagos: Islands of Birds* Bryan referred to it as 'white booby'. It had already been called blue-faced booby and masked booby. Then in 2002 it was decided that the bird that occurred in the eastern Pacific and on the Galapagos was sufficiently different in genetics and behaviour to be deemed a separate species, and it was named the Nazca booby, *S. granti*.

Some other bird names have changed over the intervening decades, as ornithologists' understanding of taxonomy has evolved. For example, the bird that we knew as 'Madeiran storm petrel' *Oceanodroma castro* (and referred to as such in *Galapagos: Islands of Birds*) has become band-rumped storm-petrel *Hydrobates castro*, its English name also gaining a hyphen and complemented by a change in genus. Reptile taxonomy also ebbs and flows over time, so the number of species of lava lizard and giant tortoise, for example, evolve. For the current English and scientific names of Galapagos animals mentioned in the book, see *Appendix 2*.

In 1964 several of the Galapagos Islands were still known by their English names. For some years we knew our two islands as Tower (Spanish: Genovesa) and Hood (Española). These islands should be known by their Spanish names. However, as this present book is about 1964 and we knew them by their English names, I have continued, apologetically, to use the English.

ACKNOWLEDGEMENTS

Foremost I must express huge gratitude to Hilary Bradt, for this book was her vision, and without her persistence, humour, encouragement and positivity it would never have fledged.

James Lowen gathered the manuscript from Hilary and with a remarkable bird's-eye view sorted the disparate strands into a more coherent story. His dogged detective work has added immeasurably by updating 1960s science. James applied his green pen with wise sensitivity.

I owe a special debt to my writing friend, Prof. Margaret Elphinstone, for encouraging me to write and gently pushing me to discover a more authentic voice.

Several scientists have good-humouredly answered my pesky questions about ancient times and recent work. Above all, Prof. Dave Anderson must have given hours of his precious time vetting accounts of the frigatebird, albatross and boobies, with great good humour. Thank you, Dave. I am also grateful for help from Prof. Mike Harris, Prof. Sarah Wanless and Dr Tony Diamond.

Gustavo Jimenez at the Charles Darwin Research Station so patiently answered my queries, in a foreign language.

Tui de Roy responded warmly to requests for a Foreword, with anecdotes about the Galapagos, our meeting there when she was ten years old and a spot-on 2020s response to Prince Philip's Foreword.

Monty Halls gave inspiration for the crowdfunding appeal and contributed enthusiastically to the video.

At Bradt I have had more cheerful and speedy help from Anna Moores, Claire Strange, Ian Spick, Ross Dickinson, Hugh Brune and Simon Willmore.

Revive Studios did an unbelievable job in resuscitating negatives that had been in careless store for over 50 years.

Lastly I will throw my arms round the neck of Roger Lever, for endless patience behind his camera for the crowdfunding video. Four days he laboured over numerous aborted attempts, with a final-day 'take eleven'. He had already produced several 'portraits of the author' and revived the ancient print of a booby on my head.

A heartfelt 'Thank You' to everybody, for adding cheer to the whole experience of working on this book.

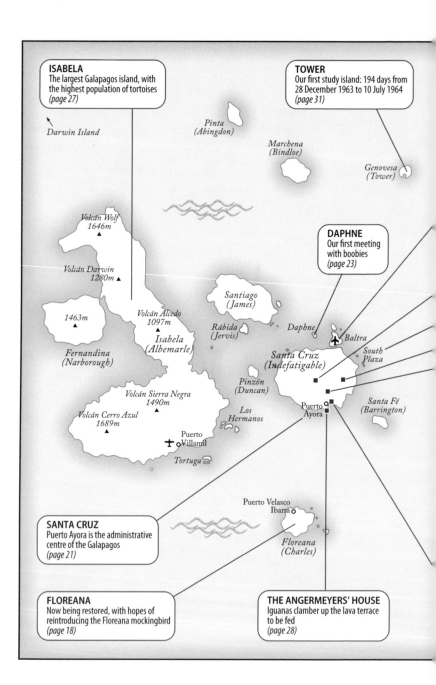

ISABELA
The largest Galapagos island, with the highest population of tortoises
(page 27)

TOWER
Our first study island: 194 days from 28 December 1963 to 10 July 1964
(page 31)

Darwin Island

Pinta
(Abingdon)

Marchena
(Bindloe)

Genovesa
(Tower)

Volcán Wolf
1646m

DAPHNE
Our first meeting with boobies
(page 23)

Volcán Darwin
1280m

Santiago
(James)

1463m

Volcán Alcedo
1097m

Rábida
(Jervis)

Daphne

Baltra

Isabela
(Albemarle)

South
Plaza

Fernandina
(Narborough)

Santa Cruz
(Indefatigable)

Pinzón
(Duncan)

Santa Fé
(Barrington)

Volcán Sierra Negra
1490m

Los
Hermanos

Puerto
Ayora

Volcán Cerro Azul
1689m

Puerto
Villamil

Tortuga

Puerto Velasco
Ibarra

SANTA CRUZ
Puerto Ayora is the administrative centre of the Galapagos
(page 21)

Floreana
(Charles)

FLOREANA
Now being restored, with hopes of reintroducing the Floreana mockingbird
(page 18)

THE ANGERMEYERS' HOUSE
Iguanas clamber up the lava terrace to be fed
(page 28)

xxii

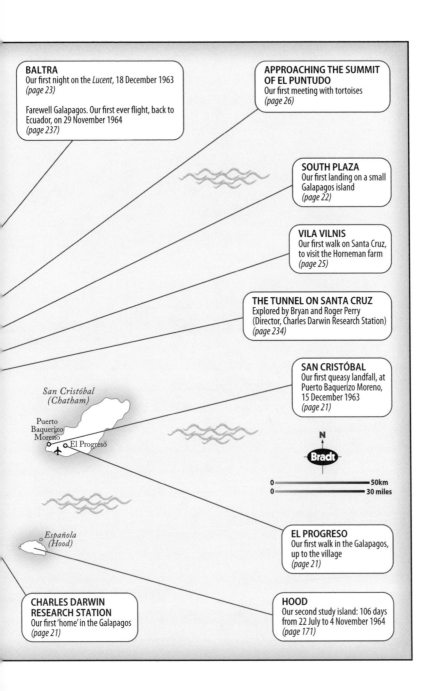

BALTRA
Our first night on the *Lucent*, 18 December 1963
(page 23)

Farewell Galapagos. Our first ever flight, back to Ecuador, on 29 November 1964
(page 237)

APPROACHING THE SUMMIT OF EL PUNTUDO
Our first meeting with tortoises
(page 26)

SOUTH PLAZA
Our first landing on a small Galapagos island
(page 22)

VILA VILNIS
Our first walk on Santa Cruz, to visit the Horneman farm
(page 25)

THE TUNNEL ON SANTA CRUZ
Explored by Bryan and Roger Perry (Director, Charles Darwin Research Station)
(page 234)

SAN CRISTÓBAL
Our first queasy landfall, at Puerto Baquerizo Moreno, 15 December 1963
(page 21)

San Cristóbal (Chatham)

Puerto Baquerizo Moreno

El Progreso

N

Bradt

0 ——————— 50km
0 ——————— 30 miles

Española (Hood)

EL PROGRESO
Our first walk in the Galapagos, up to the village
(page 21)

CHARLES DARWIN RESEARCH STATION
Our first 'home' in the Galapagos
(page 21)

HOOD
Our second study island: 106 days from 22 July to 4 November 1964
(page 171)

1

BEGINNINGS

JUNE

From our arrival on the Galapagos island of Tower, on 27 December 1963, the trusting neighbours viewed us as objects of curiosity. Before we had hammered in a guy rope, doves pottered in our tent. Mockingbirds ran from the hinterland to share our lunch. A small black finch, later named Poppet, inspected our boxes of food. To capture and mark our first booby we wandered a few yards from the tent, barefoot, in shorts and sun hats, merely lifted the red-footed booby from its bushy nest, clamped on the rings, and replaced the mildly surprised bird.

A few months earlier, on the Bass Rock in Scotland's Firth of Forth, to ring a northern relative of the boobies – the gannet – we had donned stout boots against the mud, thick trousers and jackets against battling beaks and clutching claws, slithered slowly on our bottoms over stinking ancient fish remains, warded off the assaults of irate neighbours and spent several breathless moments trying to manoeuvre a noose at the end of a long pole in a brisk wind over the head of a wildly jabbing gannet. And that was just the beginning.

Gannets are surely Scots: serious, strong, weighty, maybe a little dour but with plenty to say in a sonorous voice, good communicators, raised in demanding cool and wet climes, seemly in dress, with a cold blue eye, and fierce fighters reluctant to back off.

Boobies – the gannet's smaller, tropical cousins – are an altogether lighter proposition in their mostly dry and hot living conditions, with the male voice in some species even reduced to a mere whistling. They are given to gaudy adornments, bright colours and flashy gestures, but the comical little blue-footed booby is a comedian, a fool ('booby' comes from the Spanish *bobo*) that has taken this to ridiculous lengths with its entertaining antics, sprightly dancing, and flinging about its garish feet, even whilst landing.

It was all because of boobies that we came to be in the Galapagos. After a frustrating first year of his thesis, studying blackbirds, my zoologist husband Bryan transferred his doctoral attention to the behaviour and ecology of the gannets that formed a huge breeding colony on the Bass Rock. Extra money to finish his research came on condition that he spent another year on something to widen his study. Condition agreed. Here we had an opportunity to compare the gannet with some of its eight relatives. After three years looking at gannets, we wanted to know whether their booby cousins led a similar life or something very different. Where could we find the most species of booby in one place?

The Line Islands of the central Pacific Ocean – atolls south of the Hawaiian Islands – looked good with three species found together on several islands, but no women were allowed. The Galapagos had boobies but we would have to stay on two islands (Tower and Hood) to see three species: Nazca, blue-footed and red-footed. In truth, this sounded no hardship – and if we then travelled the short distance south to Peru we could add the Peruvian booby, which nested nowhere else in the world. After three cold and windy years on a rock off the Scottish east coast, we eagerly anticipated some tropical warmth.

Studying gannets was not for the faint-hearted. On the cold, wet Bass Rock, where gannets were packed tightly in their breeding colony, we spent many an hour in a windy hide, or crouched in deep, fish-stinking mud doing battle with indignant birds – fitting uniquely numbered rings on their legs to enable individual lives to be tracked, and weighing and measuring them. The work involved creeping about in slow motion. With care we could manage not to cause chaos and the colony remained warily on their nests, but alert and ready to inflict a stab wound in response to any sudden movement from us.

Nevertheless, the experience made its mark, literally. After our years on the Bass, a conspicuous scar lined Bryan's cheek (at a conference in Austria it was automatically assumed that this long white line was a duelling scar). Meanwhile I had neat claw holes in my skull where a gannet had thrust away in alarm; not for a gannet a peaceful sojourn on my head. Bryan reckoned that, while I was crouched ringing a chick, this particular gannet mistook my topknot for its nest and was horrified to realise its dreadful mistake. We both exhibited numerous white scars on our arms and legs from the seabirds' slashing serrated beaks and grappling feet.

But this whole adventure began with our wedding on the last day of December 1960 and, a few weeks later, Bryan's departure for the Bass. His first job was to help the skilled head lighthouse keeper, George, assemble our 14x8 foot garden shed in the remains of St Baldred's Chapel. Once a thick wire hawser secured the roof, I joined him.

For three years, with the gannets nesting from February to November, we mostly worked on the behaviour and ecology of the gannet. Food arrived fortnightly, and we carried drinking water up from the lighthouse, brought washing water down from a well, and washed clothes and ourselves in an algae-green hole beside our hut.

Three copies of Bryan's thesis, compiled on an ancient manual typewriter by a non-typist, appeared far too slowly. One of many horrendous gales had Bryan spreadeagled across the sheaf of papers in case the hut's flimsy roof blew off. The manuscript was just missed by an abandoned gannet egg that rolled off its shaking shelf and splattered stinking contents across the hut. On deadline day, Fred the boatman anchored offshore, anxiously fearing that he would miss the tide and the post. Bryan dictated the table of contents, then sprinted down the many steps still tying up the three copies with string.

Getting set for take-off to the Galapagos, 5,000 miles away, began by rounding off an overflowing 1963 that perhaps accounted for Bryan's fragile state once we arrived. Bryan's diary records it as the busiest and most successful year of his career to date. Alongside preparing to move continent, there was a full field season on the Bass, a D. Phil. thesis submitted after much trauma, three scientific papers accepted for publication, laborious organisation and departure to the Galapagos, a talk at the British Ornithologists' Union conference, a TV appearance, three short broadcasts, an article in *The Field* and another ready for *Natural History* magazine. Most of these had involved me contributing an enormous amount of work without receiving much kudos. Bryan's examiners said he had written the equivalent of two theses, so perhaps I could have had one!

It took two lighthouse keepers and Bryan two weeks to turn a pile of cheap planks into nine large chests plus one gigantic one, each with metal corners fashioned from Tate & Lyle syrup tins. The keepers valued weight and strength but failed to imagine the narrow, sloping gangplank and skinny porter that would materialise at our destination on the other side of the world.

The contents of these chests symbolised our self-contained life: notebooks, cameras, film, clothes, tools, tents, cooking and eating equipment, materials for a solar still (a device to distill fresh water from seawater), tinned and dried food with gaps for 60lb of butter, 70lb of margarine and lard, 20lb of bacon – all from Selfridges. Then we heard of good tinned butter not only in Ecuador but actually on the Galapagos island of Santa Cruz. However, when we got there, we found everybody smearing oil on their bread, and no butter within 600 miles. That British butter cheered many a dreary meal.

Lists proliferated, amidst calculations of how much dried yeast, dried egg, dried vegetables and spaghetti were necessary for a year's camping. Large items like flour were easy; we made a rough calculation on the basis of our Bass experience and doubled it. Foolishly we added the result to our list of items to buy in Guayaquil. Ordering a year's supply of anything, particularly from a tropical country, proved a bad mistake. There were no sell-by dates back then.

Knowing that replacements would be entirely out of the question we took plenty of spare parts for lamps, Primus stoves and our oven, plus twine, canvas, rope, sailmaking needles, darning needles, solder, tools and so on. We planned accurately but failed to allow for dirty paraffin, some dried food keeping badly, items we hadn't ordered proving disgusting or fizzing with age, and having our one precious box of treats stolen during the final stages of the journey.

The Carnegie Trust, a charity benefiting Scottish universities, provided £600 (about £10,500 in today's money), a living grant meant for one year that we eked out for nearly two, to cover both costs in the Galapagos and a short spell for writing up. The American Frank M. Chapman Memorial Fund paid for our fares, some film and equipment.

By the time we found ourselves leaving Southampton on the *Queen Elizabeth*, bound for New York, we were exhausted but exhilarated. Two days later, on 17 November 1963, Bryan's diary recalls 'a red letter day': just the second time in its history that the liner had logged 'dangerous seas' and a force 11 gale. Most passengers remained in their bunks, with the swimming pool drained and retaining edges placed around the dining tables. But we climbed to the top deck with dry biscuits to watch waves 40–50 feet high and admire the kittiwakes still effortlessly skimming the surface in between. The wind screamed and the gigantic ship rose to a towering height then, leaving our stomachs behind, plunged into a yawning trough.

Inevitably we arrived late into New York and saw the city's magnificent skyline to full effect in the darkness: incandescent great blocks, pinnacles and towers, and every ship blazing with light. Landing formalities took a long time, ending with the customs official puzzling over the list of contents of our numerous large boxes but stopping short of inspecting them. The porters looked amazed too, and a cooper put metal straps on the broken chests for a dollar, while giving us all possible details of his two corneal grafts. It cost £27.6s to transport our hefty baggage across the Atlantic to New York; and then $58 to transfer it to the *Santa Mariana* for our onward journey south and west. Just five months old, the Grace Line's banana cargo boat was a mere baby weighing 14,000 tons, way less than the *Queen Elizabeth*'s 83,000.

Helene Jordan at *Natural History* magazine had booked us a three-room suite at the Colonial hotel. Although well located, it was stiflingly hot, dirty and featured cockroaches in the bathroom; we escaped to Central Park. Eventually, in the Natural History

Museum, we found Dean Amadon, who had helped with funding our trip, and 'Jamie' Jordan, who was considering Bryan's article for her magazine. Jamie had sent generous advance funding, observing that she hated 'to think of emergencies arising when our friends are shoestringing it on a grant'. We were looking forward to marking our last full day in New York with dinner at Jamie's house. Then, at 1.30pm on Friday 22 November, President J. F. Kennedy was shot.

The whole of New York, the United States and the world was devastated. Folk still remember where they were that day. We couldn't forget. New York shut down, and we ate a subdued, delayed farewell dinner at Jamie's house. Preparations stumbled along as our hostess sat frequently to weep and drink whiskey. It seemed best just to let her cry, and we watched dimming lights on the street below and New York traffic thinning to a gurgle.

The city collapsed into mourning, its streets empty and its residents in tears. Having lost their much-loved president, the longshoremen refused to load our Ecuador-bound ship. Life paused.

Two days after the catastrophe, many seatainers, cars and general cargo, plus a few passengers, came aboard the *Santa Mariana*. We set sail. With sun and a soft southerly wind, the journey passed delightfully in the ship's pool, at its wonderful buffet or in our luxurious cabin. I escaped the traditional ducking as we crossed the Equator but Bryan was rigged in fancy dress, covered in paint, egg and ketchup, then tipped into the pool before receiving his fancy certificate.

Bryan described our time on the *Mariana* as 'soft' but admitted: 'I suppose we will think wistfully of that softness in the coming year.' Six months later he added a heartfelt 'yes' to this diary entry. Personally, I had no objection to 'softness' and delighted in the pool. With all our baggage in the hold, I'm not sure what I did for a swimming costume but made one for Bryan by sewing coloured hankies over a pair of underpants. The warm water reminded me of film star Esther Williams swimming sidestroke and I began to cultivate my version. So much more elegant than puffing breaststroke.

More serendipity and my posing secured us a painless exit through customs upon arrival in Guayaquil. Dr Roberto Gilbert had spent the journey from New York lounging lazily while watching the pool. Grandson of an English captain and Ecuadorian grandmother, he owned Ecuador's best medical clinic and had even removed the appendix of the chief customs officer. Roberto adopted us, got us waved through customs with a charming speech from the chief, stored our ten green chests near his clinic and supplied us with large containers for water, medicines, kerosene for our fridge, lamps and cooker, and alcohol for preheating equipment (or drinking, in desperation). He, or his intern, took us for meals at the tennis club and his captivating family entertained us at their home. We have received similar kindness from strangers all over the world, but this had both of us feeling uneasy. Bryan wrote: 'I wished he would be a little less prodigal. I thought that he would commit himself to do and provide things and then find it irksome. He is completely unstoppable.'

With the help of the British Consul, John Lacey, we found Elias Mayorga, a ships' chandler. After many sickly, warm bottles of local pilsner, in the stifling heat of a marketplace seething with the usual indescribable, dirty, but fascinating throng of human life, we reached an amiable understanding that cost us 17,000 sucres (£300) and Elias Mayorga 49 boxes of very mixed food (*Appendix 1*).

The *Cristobal Carrier*, an ancient landing barge with what looked like a cricket pavilion tacked on top, wallowed in the muddy Guayas River, connected to the wharf by a sideways-sloping gangplank. We began loading early one December morning and finally boarded after 9pm. The first job was to see safely into the cockroach-ridden hold Mayorga's food boxes, which had 'Nelson' scrawled haphazardly on any side. Once complete, we moved on to the biggest job. The Consul helped us hire a lorry that shifted hand luggage from our *pension*, called at Dr Gilbert's clinic for his large and miscellaneous contribution, then finally loaded our ten green wooden chests. As the lorry reached the quay, a second such vehicle appeared with an ironwood rowing boat that Roberto had organised for us. The *Carrier* teemed, the quay teemed, the tilted gangplank teemed and the cacophony roared on a steamingly hot day. Our heavy boxes, apart from the giant one, were carried across by a single skinny, barefoot porter.

That done, we bought a shotgun, for which Dr Gilbert insisted we needed a permit from the Ministry of Defence. Together we all, including a lieutenant colonel (the doctor of radiology from Roberto's clinic), piled into a car belonging to an intern. Shepherded by the lieutenant colonel, we passed several armed guards at the Ministry, got the permit, then bumped into the Minister himself. Our doctor thereupon dictated an impressive document requesting 'all civil and military help for the Nelsons', took us to the town hall, then led us past more armed guards and into a conference room where the Minister of the Interior signed it. We were exhausted, leaving Roberto to be exuberant on our behalf. We started our roll down the Guayas at 10.20pm that evening.

Six hundred miles in such an unstable vessel seemed a long way. The knowledge that storms were rare didn't help with the rolling. We first-class passengers lived on the top deck, looking over a rail at those less fortunate, animals and topsy-turvy baggage down below.

A stem of bananas, just for us, hung below an awning and, apart from the rolling and dirty food on dirty plates, we enjoyed the skuas, albatrosses, petrels (one landed on board in darkness), boobies, frigatebirds, gulls, sharks and flying fish. A cockroach sailed off on the Pacific as I shook out my bedding.

2

THE GALAPAGOS

BRYAN AND JUNE

Some spots in the Galapagos are just like their counterparts on any of a thousand tropical islands. But the name Galapagos, though it actually refers to the giant tortoises, means to most people a weird, fire-seared landscape like the moon, where crested dragons (marine and Galapagos land iguanas) festoon the tortured black outcrops and millions of red crabs scuttle over the algae-slimed, wave-beaten shores. The Galapagos have always had, and it is fervently to be hoped will always have, this aura of magic, of unreality. Crazy things happen there, and it is still possible to feel a strong emotional kinship with animals because of their trust and curiosity.

Straddling the Equator, the 13–16 islands and some 55 islets stretch around 300 miles from Darwin Island in the north to Hood in the south. Less than 3,000 square miles of land, they lie scattered over 23,000 square miles of ocean.

The islands sit on a raised platform, 1,000 fathoms or more above the surrounding ocean bed. Around 600 miles separate them from the coast of Ecuador to the east and 1,000 miles from Central America to the northeast. The intervening sea is deep, and the consensus is that the islands were never connected to the mainland.

All the islands are volcanic but because they vary considerably in age, size, height and position their lava looks very different. Tower, the first island on which we spent time, and one of the northern, young ones at a mere 700,000 years old, has shoe-shredding lava.

Hood, our later destination and the southernmost island, with its smooth, large boulders, could be more than three million years old.

In the grimmer reaches of the Galapagos one could hardly imagine a more desolate landscape; cinders, ash and mournful lava streams recreate the beginnings of the earth. There is plenty of fresh-looking evidence of molten lava and ash storms on all islands. Even on faraway Tower our canvas was in no time thickly coated with fine black ash, doubtless windborne.

The most recent volcanic eruptions have occurred on two of the younger islands. In 2018 La Cumbre, on uninhabited Fernandina, started belching fire. Two weeks later, Sierra Negra on Isabela followed suit, forcing the evacuation of some of the 2,000 or so inhabitants. In 2020 La Cumbre again sprang into life. Overall, 13 of the 21 Galapagos volcanoes are considered active. Tower has two craters, but we didn't fear for our lives from that direction. One has tilted sideways and sunk, to form the beautiful Darwin Bay. The other, near the highest point of the island, looks very benign with its green crater lake.

It seems clear that the present plant and animal life of the islands can be accounted for by supposing that they drifted, swam or flew there. It is surprising what mixed cargoes of plants and animals can survive such a journey among the branches of trees and other debris swept out to sea. Charles Darwin himself demonstrated that many plants are capable of germinating after prolonged immersion in seawater. Norwegian adventurer Thor Heyerdahl, with his balsa-wood rafts, proved that the currents favour such an assisted passage. So the islands' by no means hospitable shores received, as they still receive, birds with seeds and small organisms on their feet, and floating detritus with its cargo of insects, spiders, resistant seeds of all kinds and occasionally an ancestor or two of the rodents that gave rise to the endemic species later largely eliminated by their imported competitor, the highly successful house (or black) rat.

The two main sources of current-assisted invaders seem to have been Central America, from which the Panamanian current sets south, and the areas of Chile and Peru washed by the Humboldt before it turns westward into the Pacific, carving its way through the warm equatorial seas with its vast volume of colder water before lapping the shores of the southern Galapagos. The cold-loving Galapagos fur seal and Galapagos penguin must have travelled north with the cold water. The penguin still strongly resembles the Humboldt penguin from which it is probably descended. The fur seal is smaller than the South American fur seal, its presumed ancestor. Plants in the Galapagos are related to ones from Central America, although two cacti have their nearest relatives on Punta Salinas in Ecuador. Many of the invertebrates probably originated in Central America.

Considerable changes in sea levels could explain the complicated evolutionary history of land iguanas, lava lizards, geckos and snakes. Maybe they began life in the Galapagos on one of the larger islands but after smaller islands broke away they became adapted to the particular circumstances on their own small island.

Once all this life arrived natural selection got to work. Slowly the size, shape, colours and habits of the animals were changed by complex interactions between them and their environment, and gradually the unique Galapagos fauna and flora arose. At the time we visited, 86 per cent of Galapagos bird species or subspecies were considered endemic to the islands (ie: occur nowhere else); peculiar Galapagos forms evolved in their own miniature world. Galapagos wildlife is neither drastically new nor exceptionally primitive but contains many examples of small adaptive changes evolved in isolation. So this remote and sombre collection of defunct volcanoes had been steadily evolving its wonderful fauna for thousands or perhaps millions of years, undisturbed by man.

From earliest times visitors have remarked on the extreme trustingness of Galapagos creatures. But is this surprising? The islands are remote and, in the past, little visited because of their lack of water and difficult terrain. Now, on the smaller islands, with few predators, no cars or noise and empathetic visitors, why would birds not treat people with the same fearlessness they bestow on cattle? We often forget how quickly animals respond to their environment. Many elderly folk have established a rapport with wildlife in their quiet gardens. The COVID-19 lockdowns demonstrated that without cars, planes, noise and pollution, animals became bolder – and there are many accounts of 'eccentric' folk living with wildlife.

Although the Galapagos Islands are situated on the Equator, their climate is subtropical. An oceanic position, bathed by the cold Humboldt Current, means that they are uncharacteristically dry and moderate. There are two main seasons. It is typically warm and wet between December and June. March and April, the hottest and wettest months, usually have daily afternoon showers. Coastal temperatures can be around 77F (25°C) compared with 72F (22°C) in the cooler season. The cooler, drier weather usually arrives between June and December. That is the season of the *garúa* on the higher islands, when the sky suddenly becomes overcast and mist sweeps down from the hills. The higher, wetter parts of the four large islands have a totally different vegetation from the coastal lowlands, with a hugely fertile forest and the highest habitats – grass, sedge and fern *pampa* – sometimes receiving about 180 inches of rain in a year. Lower areas receive only limited amounts of rain, especially the small, low-lying islands in the north, which are less influenced by the Humboldt Current.

This cold oceanic water sweeps up from the south, bathing the southerly islands but veering away from the northern ones, and makes an enormous contribution to the life of the islands. The Humboldt provides the vast quantities of food which supports not only the Galapagos sea life but also the millions of seabirds and the resultant guano industry just over 1,000 miles south in Peru. Every two to seven years, however, a warm current flows south, significantly raising the sea temperature. Because these events usually begin around Christmas, they are known as *El Niño* (the child). The warmer water forces the vast quantities of anchovies and the marine soup on which they feed to either move or die. This in turn has a huge effect on all marine life. The El Niño of 1982–3 proved a particularly disastrous year when even 70 per cent of marine iguanas starved to death. Similar events in 1997–8 and 2014–16 also caused devastation. It is heart-rending to watch young seabirds starve to death on their nests. By contrast, with increased rainfall, life on land thrives and some landbirds can raise considerably more young.

Inevitably people eventually reached the Galapagos. Heyerdahl demonstrated that visits to these islands were well within the range of balsa rafts belonging to prehistoric men. A species of cotton found in the Galapagos had been grown by aboriginal cultures on the north coast of Peru. Heyerdahl's expedition discovered ancient sites on Santiago, Santa Cruz and Floreana; the remains of 131 aboriginal pots suggested that the Galapagos were visited repeatedly in pre-European times, though not continuously settled.

Legend, however, attributes the first successful exploration of the Galapagos to the Inca Túpac Yupanqui, grandfather of the unfortunate Atahualpa whose treacherous execution by the Spaniard Francisco Pizarro in 1533 ended the Incan empire. Ostensibly travelling around 1480, Túpac Yupanqui rather confuses things by having returned with black people and copper, neither of which he could have obtained in the Galapagos – so he must at least have been elsewhere, whether or not he ever reached the islands. In 1535 Tomás de Berlanga, the Bishop of Panama, made history by (accidentally) reaching the archipelago and committing his impressions both to the King of Spain and to posterity. To de Berlanga belongs the inspired comment: 'It seems as though God had sometimes showered stones.'

The Galapagos mostly escaped intrusion until relatively recently, first appearing on a simple map in 1570. With the arrival of better maps and larger vessels the decline of these unique islands began under successive waves of buccaneers, whalers and adventurers. Live goats were probably put ashore in 1684–85, and the Viceroy of Peru subsequently sent out dogs to kill off the goats. The *Bachelor's Delight*, a pirate ship, had trouble locating the 'Galipoloes' in 1684 for precisely the reason that gave the islands the centuries-old name 'Las Islas Encantadas' ('Enchanted Islands'); collectively, calms and currents regularly threw vessels off course, creating an optical illusion whereby the islands appeared to float on the ocean surface. Even sailors trying to leave the islands found themselves confusingly thrown off course. James Bay (Santiago) was a favourite resort of buccaneers and whalers with drinking water available and the *Bachelor's Delight* put ashore, among other things, eight tons of quince marmalade purloined from Spanish merchant vessels. More valuable treasure is supposed to have been looted from the Viceroy of Peru and buried in the Galapagos. The Incas are reputed to have removed vast quantities of gold and jewels to the Galapagos before they fell to Pizarro's conquering, avaricious hands. If so, the treasure is yet hiding its glitter beneath the dull lava.

In 1789 Alonso de Torres sailed to the Galapagos under the auspices of Charles III of Spain and renamed all the islands in Spanish. They became a refuge for pirates and in 1793 one of the world's first post offices was established on Floreana. Passing fishermen called for a supply of tortoises and collected mail from a barrel in Post Office Bay; even today thousands of letters still pass through that system. An Irishman, Patrick Watkins, became the first known resident when he was marooned on Floreana from 1807–09. The first organised attempt at colonisation came in 1832 when General Jose Villamil took possession in the name of Ecuador, renaming the group 'Archipélago de Colón'.

The islands seem to have been a popular place for penal colonies, with one established on Floreana in the 19th century and another on San Cristóbal in 1880, while Isabela acquired one after World War II. Frequent visits by pirates and fishermen made substantial inroads into several Galapagos species, notably the tortoises, land iguanas, flamingos and fur seals. A whaling ship took 2,000 barrels of sperm whale oil from Galapagos waters back to the US. When Darwin paid his famous visit in 1835 the islands had already gone through severe exploitation, mainly of tortoises and seals. He found no tortoises left on Floreana.

Then came the settlers, whose introduced animals became the main threat to the unique Galapagos habitats, exacerbated by 700 introduced plant species competing with a mere 500 native/endemic ones. Much of the *Scalesia* forest has been cleared to farm the fertile soil.

Isabela was first settled by Antonio Gill in 1897 and his descendants still live there. A Norwegian colony started on Santa Cruz in 1926 whilst the Wittmers arrived on Floreana in 1929. The Angermeyer brothers arrived on Santa Cruz in 1937, and both Wittmer and Angermeyer descendants still live on the Galapagos.

The 'Enchanted Islands', however, weren't satisfied by attracting normal colonists and settlers. The most bizarre incomers were two sets of Germans arriving on Floreana in the late 1920s and early 1930s. First came Dr Friedrich Ritter and his lover Dora Strauch. They had planned meticulously for their colonisation of this island by having all their teeth removed, instead sharing a set of stainless-steel dentures. A few years later they were joined by 'The Baroness'. Eloise Wagner de Bousquet brought with her three lovers, an invented title, and a level of chaos and intrigue which has never been surpassed in the Galapagos. She and her favourite lover disappeared – their bodies never found – and another washed up on a far-flung island. Shortly afterwards Dr Ritter died of food poisoning after eating chicken – a surprising death for a strict vegetarian.

Other settlers came and went, often dying tragically. Several were lost at sea. Few remained permanently and several commercial enterprises seemed to fail quite quickly. Before World War II several countries expressed interest in the Galapagos Islands as a military outpost, and eventually the Americans built airstrips and a naval base.

In 1954 Irenäus Eibl-Eibesfeldt, who carried out research in the Galapagos over many years, expressed deep concern about the alarming destruction and exploitation of wildlife evidently being openly pursued. His subsequent appeal to the International Union for Conservation of Nature and Natural Resources (IUCN) bore considerable fruit. A national park was declared in 1959 and a research centre built in 1960: of about 7,500 research projects so far undertaken, ours in 1964 was one of the earliest. In 1986 the area around the Galapagos became a marine reserve.

A few tourists made it to the islands during the 1960s and 1970s, but it was only from 1990 that tourism and migration increased exponentially. In 2007 UNESCO classed the Galapagos Islands as an endangered World Heritage Site (although it is no longer considered so threatened) and from 2011 comprehensive tourist management was introduced. Before COVID-19 curtailed travel, tourist numbers had reached around 200,000 each year.

Just four of the Galapagos islands have permanent inhabitants, with a total population in 2020 of over 33,000. This is a huge increase from the mere 2,400 we found in 1964. With more human lives dependent on Galapagos resources, tension became inevitable. An influx to the Galapagos of poorer settlers reliant on fishing, especially sea cucumbers, has caused serious conflict with the Charles Darwin Research Station. Things were simpler during 'our' era. Although it may not have seemed that way as we neared the end of our journey from mainland Ecuador.

3

ARRIVALS

BRYAN AND JUNE

With three raucous blasts at 5am, the *Cristobal Carrier* rolled into the bay of San Cristóbal, the first island to greet you by sea when arriving from mainland Ecuador. Here at Puerto Baquerizo Moreno, on 15 December 1963, we put our first foot on Galapagos sand, still swaying after our queasy ocean journey. San Cristóbal has the Galapagos Islands' main permanent source of fresh water, and the second largest population, approaching 10,000 in 2020. In the 1960s, an attractive scattering of bleached pink and brown wooden houses, with not a hint of concrete or smear of tarmac, spread on to the sand around Wreck Bay, backed by cloudy hills. Needing a walk, we set off in a wetting drizzle to climb the five-mile track to the village of Progreso, nearly 1,000 feet up in the hills, through silver-barked *palo santo* trees amongst the chocolate lichen-covered rocks and trailing pale green lichen. Many small, juicy oranges from the trees edging our way spurred us upwards.

With huge relief, the following day we finally left the *Carrier* to land on Santa Cruz. With over 20,000 inhabitants, this island now has the largest population in the Galapagos. It also boasts the largest town, Puerto Ayora, and has become the Islands' administrative centre. With the tide too low to unload our cargo, we went straight to the nearby Charles Darwin Research Station with its new director, David Snow, whose study of Oxford blackbirds had been developed then abandoned by Bryan, when all his nests were robbed. New gravel paths connected the Station's attractive, low buildings and pleasant surroundings with what was then a village. It provided good accommodation for visitors – we were given a small house – though relatively little equipment.

Even with the right tide, Station staff, a boat and a raft, it took three trips to unload our gear from the *Carrier*. We nearly had heart failure with every seemingly endless journey that our heavy boxes took atop the raft amid a rolling Pacific swell, but nothing was lost.

In the evening we ate at the nearby excellent hotel belonging to Forrest Nelson, who had sailed to the Galapagos several times during the 1950s and finally settled there in 1960. The modern, spacious hotel not only looked attractive, but also served good, clean food; such a relief after the grime of the *Carrier*.

Taking time to sort our gear and repack the tattered boxes of food from Guayaquil, which took all morning, we needed our first swim to restore equilibrium. We took time also to explore the village, and buy basics such as a rope, bucket, soap powder, loo rolls and other such boring items, but also to order fresh fruit and vegetables to be delivered by the relief boat to our future island home of Tower.

That evening the island's *comandante* promoted the port captain and threw a party at the hotel. It was our first experience of the busy social life, and we left early!

Following a hasty breakfast, the *Lucent* – a beautifully converted Cornish fishing boat more than half a century old, ironwood heavy and straight-stemmed – took us first to South Plaza island. Skippered by Dave Balfour in the Galapagos, the *Lucent* was actually owned by his friend Roger Jamieson. Dave, Roger and the *Lucent* had left Britain en route for Australia and called in at Santa Cruz, but there Roger was speedily commissioned to return to Britain to find and fit out a boat suitable as a workhorse for the Charles

Darwin Research Station. Dave and the *Lucent* remained behind to fill that role until a replacement arrived. Dave had a lively crew of hens and two cats, and was taking David Snow and Miguel Castro (a Station researcher) for their regular check of swallow-tailed gull nests. We also found six pairs of Galapagos shearwater wings (a species that we knew then as 'Audubon's shearwater'); the results of a bit of night prowling by Galapagos short-eared owls. With low cliffs on one side, sloping gently to the sea at the other, South Plaza epitomised Galapagos small islands. Hot, with no sand, but lava covered in cacti, thorny shrubs and a glowing red succulent, with the improbable, red-marbled Galapagos land iguanas crawling all over it. And everywhere Galapagos sea lions, the bulls patrolling offshore, roaring incessantly.

After a day exploring South Plaza, we sailed peacefully to anchor off Baltra, gazing towards Daphne Major and Daphne Minor silhouetted on the horizon. Bryan wrote that: 'At last, we had time to drink deeply from the Galapagos spirit; the creak of block and tackle, slap of waves, skimming shearwaters, cavorting dolphins and good companions.'

For us, the small island of Daphne Major proved one of the most exciting spots in the Galapagos. Here we properly met our first boobies, and in a thrilling setting. The precipitous slopes of the island were riddled with the holes of tropicbirds whilst Nazca boobies objected to our trespass by, in Bryan's words, 'vehement whistling or shouting, hair standing on end and orange bills flashing'.

The thrilling aspect appeared at the top of the climb, where we were standing on a rim encircling a giant volcanic crater with two tiers, separated by a steep scarp and bounded by walls with a few scattered shrubs holding magnificent frigatebirds. The totally flat, sandy bottoms looked to be strewn with currants; hundreds of pairs of blue-footed boobies, rocking back on their heels and fluttering their throats to dissipate some of the stifling heat. Without exception they faced away from the sun. It seemed that the hot air rose, allowing cooler air to be siphoned in through a notch in the crater rim. The nesting area may have been cooler than elsewhere, but the chicks in their thick white down still panted. No Nazca boobies nested down there and it is the blue-foots' agility that allowed them to use such a site. Their nests were sufficiently widely spaced for them to land easily and perform their aerial circuiting, 'parading' and agile displays.

Fascinatingly, following our stay on Hood, where the blue-foots had offspring at all stages, we returned to Daphne and saw nothing but fully feathered youngsters; a few nests with three young ones. The ones in the lower crater were, on average, about three weeks older. This seemed to clearly demonstrate the synchronising effect of social interactions. On Hood, terrain and vegetation had effectively separated the boobies into distinct groups; most pairs of one group having eggs, while another group had fluffy young and yet another had free-flying dependents. Without barriers, apart from the scarp, the Daphne birds had become two fairly synchronised groups.

Following lunch on board, the two of us returned to Daphne. After some time behind the camera we realised the sea had become choppy and June, at least, dreaded negotiating the dinghy from the only landing spot, a spur of rock. This time we managed to get tripod, cameras and one unstable person back on the *Lucent* without a ducking. Bryan returned pleased that his short meeting with the blue-foot had confirmed his expectations of their behaviour. They showed less aggression, meaning the chicks could be left unattended and wander, and the juveniles could safely resemble their parents. Unlike aggressive gannets, females did not suffer an attacking mate nor did the pair need a special site-ownership display or meeting ceremony.

We sailed slowly back to sociable Santa Cruz just in time for a *fiesta*, to be held at the Research Station and billed to start at 8pm. We obediently arrived at the designated time and handed over our ten sucres for two tickets. Over an hour later, with the place packed, the concert began with the national anthem. After another 15 minutes pause the priest gave a long and excited address in Spanish. At 9.30pm a play started – with nothing but dialogue from characters resolutely sitting around a table. About halfway through, one of the audience benches collapsed with a loud crack. We left after the second act; the loud crack and laughter about the only things we had understood. Apparently the main part started around 11.30pm and we heard the audience straggling home at 4.30am.

After such excitement we took to the hills, following a five-mile track that climbed 600 feet, mostly over large boulders but with the upper reaches ankle deep in mud. It steadily became greener and more luxuriant, like walking through a huge hothouse. The constant traffic of horses and donkeys with varied loads passed the bleached skeletons of their compatriots fallen by the wayside. Eventually we reached our destination, Vila Vilnis, a wooden house imported from Norway in the 1920s by the Hornemans. Surrounded by 90 acres, the mostly riotous vegetation was interspersed with many fruits and vegetables, together with hens, pigs, cows, donkeys and horses. Mrs Horneman seemed to be a required port of call for all visiting scientists, and we recognised several of the famous names in her visitors' book. The house felt old, its age somehow exemplified by its enormous spiders, which caught moths in their webs. Of special note was an ancient coffee grinder screwed to the wall, perpetually in use to fortify the stream of visitors with the farm's coffee. Anybody arriving at this house would be traumatised by their journey, so the inevitable coffee, cake and fruit would go a long way to restoring them.

The following day, guided by Sigvart, the Hornemans' son, we began a steady climb, through early morning drizzle and thick vegetation, to tortoise country. The drizzle soon turned to heavy rain and quickly we were soaked, with additional water from the vegetation dripping down our necks. Our ascent took two hours, slipping and slithering through deep mud, fallen branches and eventually stinging nettles. June became so numb that she no longer cared. But Bryan grew ever more annoyed at each trip, scratch, snag and sting. Boringly, the jungle prevented us from seeing more than our feet.

Suddenly we emerged into open country at the foot of El Puntudo, where two small ponds were covered in a sort of red sphagnum moss. Nine giant tortoises, with the largest, we estimated, weighing around 200lb, ambled through grass and low scrub over the uneven surface. A steep climb took us up the impressive crater, around 600 feet deep and a mile across, with a grassy bottom. The grey, lichen-covered rocks reminded us of the limestone of Yorkshire's Malham Cove. Several goats browsed the slopes, we heard pigs squealing and had a worrying encounter with a huge, one-horned bull as it stepped towards us – but it thought better of it and turned away. We each had insufferably itchy anklets of mud, seeds and ants.

Fifteen separate species of giant tortoise have been described from the Galapagos, each inhabiting a different island; following intense exploitation, just 11 remain. The demise of the giant tortoises began with the whalers, who ransacked the islands following the publication of Colnett's map of the Galapagos in 1798. Whalers regularly stowed 100 tons or more of live tortoises into their holds to ensure many weeks' worth of fresh (and delicious) meat, since these reptiles, to their downfall, can endure long periods without food and water.

Nobody knows how many thousands of tortoises met their end this way and they have since been further exploited by visitors and colonists, and perhaps particularly by the introduced pigs and dogs. Goats and donkeys add their bit by destroying cover and exposing the young. And trade is an ongoing threat. Tortoises were still openly for sale in the Galapagos within the last decade. In 2021, a police officer was jailed for three years for trying to smuggle out baby tortoises in a suitcase.

One of the most important jobs of the Charles Darwin Research Station is the conservation of all forms of wildlife – but particularly the rarest animals that are vanishing the fastest. The Station has been actively restoring tortoise populations, for example. Following a release of 191 captive-bred youngsters on the island of Santa Fe, the population there has quite quickly increased to more than 700. A survey of tortoises on the actively volcanic, seahorse-shaped island of Isabela revealed the archipelago's healthiest tortoise population, the 12–15,000 animals being quadruple or quintuple the island's human population.

Optimism about tortoises was soon replaced by our first ever Christmas away from home. On Christmas Eve Bryan sang a few carols to himself. David Snow and wife Barbara eased us into our new life with Christmas lunch then an introduction to the folk who would make such a difference to our year in the Galapagos: the Angermeyers, Potts and Rambecks.

On Boxing Day we loaded 60 gallons of water and 25 of paraffin on to the *Lucent*, then went for tea with Margo Angermeyer, wife of Karl, later to be joined by Carmen and husband Fritz, Karl's brother. The five Angermeyer brothers left Germany in the 1930s and established a farm in the Highlands. This they continued to work but eventually built lava houses right on the coast and started fishing. Karl and Margo, with a beautiful house on a point, had iguanas instead of dogs, which crawled on to their lava-shelf veranda to be fed. This incredibly generous family loved parties or gatherings of any kind, and we came to expect invitations whenever we landed on Santa Cruz. We were constantly humbled by their hospitality and generosity, with many a cuppa, feast, party or delivery of glowing fruit, vegetables, honey or eggs to cheer the spartan meals on our spartan islands.

'Our' first such island, pinpointed on the map long before we set out from Britain and returned to in fancy ever since we left, was Tower, which, with Wenman (now known as Isla Wolf) and Marchena, forms the northernmost group in the archipelago. Towards dusk on 27 December, we slipped past Karl Angermeyer's veranda with its tame iguanas, along the east shore of Santa Cruz and northwards towards Tower. We were away.

There was plenty of life around the *Lucent*. A spectacular shoal of yellow-tailed mullet thrashed into motion a large patch of the ocean's surface and attracted several brown pelicans, which threw themselves clumsily into the sea, jabbing and scooping with their enormous mandibles. All around vast numbers of phalaropes (shorebirds that swim buoyantly and are entirely at ease on the ocean) flitted over the surface, continuously alighting and taking off, a 'stippling of living creatures' as American naturalist William Beebe described them. On board, the ship's grey-striped cats prowled and climbed. Behind, like a frisky colt, bounded a Galapagos-built, flat-bottomed dinghy holding our paraffin refrigerator. New Zealander Sandy was crewing on the *Lucent* for this trip. On his way home from the North African campaign in 1943, he had called in on the Galapagos and was still there in 1963. We all sat in the well chatting and drinking coffee whilst the light faded.

Bryan's diary remarked on our silence for much of the journey to Tower, worrying that maybe I was having second thoughts about a year in such a remote place. The Rock we had just left in Britain had lighthouse keepers, regular visitors, fresh supplies once a fortnight and a boatman just two miles away, willing to retrieve us and play postman. The uninhabited island of Tower, 72 miles from Santa Cruz, had intervening hills that made reliable radio contact impossible. Two matching radio sets would have eaten into our meagre funds. And, anyway, how many times would a boat have set out to rescue us just because signals failed?

But I was actually quietly pondering my privilege in travelling to conduct fascinating research on a desert island with a beloved man. Reflecting on how I'd jumped from a London tax office, via the Bass Rock, to the tropics. Watching stars in a blue-black sky with a warm breeze. Anticipating our first desert island. And I love silence.

Unlike Bryan, I was not a stoic, nor a former Methodist local preacher who revelled in hardship, in non-stop work, in pitting himself against foul weather on rugged terrain and invariably wanting to reach the tops. I had enjoyed the challenge of the Bass, experiencing a totally different life with a new husband, providing good meals with limited resources, sharing virtually all aspects of Bryan's research. After three years I was ready for change, an exciting new adventure, somewhere warm, and the Galapagos answered that.

We both knew from the Bass that our research would be all-consuming. We expected that the inevitable chores of washing, cooking, maintenance would be different in a tent. Warm swimming and crazy outdoor games would never pall. Bryan had good cameras and developed his own film. The evenings would fly by with reading, our small transistor radio and all that writing – a book, scientific papers, diary, letters. Apart from a bad accident, I had no qualms about the year ahead.

Soon the moon rose, shedding a beautiful silver light over the sea, and the whole venture became alive again. Six weeks of intermittent travel, organising and hanging around had taken the edge off it. Our aim was to arrive at Tower with the dawn; we were travelling by dead reckoning, and Tower is low and easily missed. Currents are dangerously strong in Galapagos waters and the next landfall on a northerly heading was the coast of Mexico; northwest it was somewhere off the Russian coast, if we missed the Aleutian Islands. In the grey dawn, it was a relief to see the faint line of Tower breaking a nondescript sea. But it didn't look at all exciting. We tried to pierce the greyness and make out more details; there was only a blackish line of cliffs, broken in places, and fringed on top by the thinnest fuzz of dry scrub. Seven months in such a place suddenly seemed rather a long time. Meanwhile an outward-bound stream of red-footed boobies appeared overhead, stationing themselves on winnowing wings and peering down curiously; they were going fishing.

Two hours later we dropped anchor in the calm of beautiful Darwin Bay, about a mile across and girded by cliffs on all sides but the south where the sea enters what is actually a volcanic crater with the southern wall broken down. Dried scrub silvered the tops of the igneous cliffs and stretched away inland. Colour was muted, even drab: black, browns, buffs and silver. At the head of the bay and quite invisible from outside lay a dazzling little coral beach backed by a small patch of dense green shrub. This beach, no more than 60 yards long, about 30 yards wide and hardly clear of high tide, was to be our campsite for seven months.

In that period the world could have erupted into nuclear war, the pound been devalued or the trade unions learnt some sense, and we might never have known. It all seemed quite irrelevant. We savoured that moment. There lay our beach, imagined a thousand times, the improbable attainment of a long-held desire to live on, not just visit, a deserted bird island in the tropics, and of all islands for the biologist, the Galapagos. Bryan recalled Beebe's emotions when he first anchored off Indefatigable: 'In my turn I had come to the Galapagos and another dream of my boyhood had become real.' When he visited Tower, Beebe pitched his tent in the exact spot on which we lived for half a year. His photograph shows that only extremely small changes had taken place in the vegetation in the ensuing 40 years.

But even though we could never again sail up to live on our first desert island, there was no time to daydream. Everybody was bustling as we prepared to land. The eastern half of Darwin Bay is an abyss whose depths are still unplumbed. Towards the beach, probably above a shelf near the rim of the crater, the water suddenly becomes shallow, with one or two nasty reefs just clear of low tide. For a few hundred yards off the beach the bottom is mixed sand and rock, at an average around four to six fathoms, often much less. Dave Balfour anchored the *Lucent* 400–500 yards out, leaving enough leeway to manoeuvre if it dragged anchor towards the cliffs. We breakfasted in bright sunlight, to the screaming of the red-billed tropicbirds ('bosun birds') performing their aerial courtship and the frantic screeches of red-footed boobies attacked by the great frigatebirds which piratically forced them to regurgitate their fish. These special envoys were to become the background to everyday life.

Now and then Dave looked doubtfully at the beach, guarded by breakers that roared in before smashing against the jumble of boulders at the cliff base. Bryan's landing luck, famous among the keepers of the Bass, had stuck to him across half the world. As we later found, such days were extremely few and far between. We took a trial run with the 'fridge' and a few odds and ends. On this very first run the dinghy's outboard went on strike and for seven grilling hours we toiled back and forth with one oar and a piece of driftwood lashed to a thick bamboo pole. Getting the heavy stuff from the yacht down on to the bobbing dinghy was hair-raising. Dave prophesied disaster on every trip and with such heavy loads we might easily have been swamped, but he read each 'big un' right. I was thankful to stay ashore stacking boxes and helping to repeatedly drag the boat up the shelving beach, a painful exercise when the roiling undertow flung sand and pebbles over feet and ankles.

Operations began about 8am and by 4pm we were through. Dave and Sandy, in haste to get away before dark, shook our hands, wished us luck and departed. We strained our ears for the rattle of the anchor chain then the strong note of the diesel. There it was; they were away. It was a moment of strongly contrasting emotions; that dwindling speck, now finally beyond recall, was our last link with human beings probably for months. We had no radio communication; no boat till February; we were not an official expedition with several members and an expedition doctor; we were on our own.

Having waved away the *Lucent* and finished stacking, we watched with horror as a small, tattered fishing boat chugged into the bay and anchored within a stone's throw of the beach. All set and weary for our first night on a desert island and here were seven scruffy men to share it with us. With the shotgun loaded, we put up the store tent, filled it with our few valuables and settled down for an uneasy first night on Tower.

4

LIFE ON A DESERT ISLAND

BRYAN

It is first light; all is quiet. Suddenly there is a violent clattering outside the tent, as though somebody has kicked over a pile of pots and pans. Somebody has. The mockingbirds are cleaning up the remains of yesterday's supper. June stirs on her worn and patched old safari bed; it gives a tired creak and, if it is that kind of a day, collapses. The scraping and pecking noises continue, mingling with the loud chirps of an inferior bird being persecuted. There is a scratching on the canvas and a small black finch with an enormous beak like a hawfinch squeezes in through any hole he can find and hops up boldly on to my face. Inches behind the tent, among the coral shingle, a swallow-tailed gull makes the funny combination of choking and squeaking by which the male precedes his courtship feeding of the female, probably on the squid he caught last night in the darkened sea. A loud, harsh *arrk-ar*, full of despair, tells us that another red-footed booby is being victimised by frigatebirds. Nostalgic Galapagos sounds.

I would open my eyes and peer suspiciously around, looking for giant centipedes that came into the tent at night, clanking their crusty skins among our store of tins and bringing us instantly wide awake. Of course, by now, they were all back in their hiding places under boulders, behind bark or beneath our groundsheet. An inquisitive watcher would see the tent flap move and a shaggy head peer out. Each morning I looked to see if the dinghy had been washed away or beached and whether we were still alone on our desert island or a yacht had crept into the bay. The swallow-tails drew themselves up thinly and screeched their alarm whenever we first emerged; they never got used to it.

Our personal appearance, apart from the vagaries of nature, depended on several variables, chiefly the weather and the state of the wash. We were not fussy about our looks. If we ran out of shorts and shirts, we went without – a natural state to which even inhibited north Britons quickly become accustomed. I drew the sartorial line at wearing just boots; nothing or shoes and at least shorts was my firm principle. June lacked such fine feelings and often did one of our routine checks in a straw hat, sunglasses, tennis shoes and a neck scarf. The scarf was not for elegance, merely to stop sunburn on the collarbone.

The first chore was to milk the 'cow': the solar still, which we nicknamed 'Solly' and which produced, drip by tardy drip, half to three quarters of a gallon of fresh water daily.

The next job was the naturalists' early-morning walk. Off we went lurching over the lava and threading through the scrub, with attendance sheets, canvas weighing bag, spring balances, dividers, ruler, notebooks, camera, binoculars and a certain lack of enthusiasm. We tried to do the most tiring work, such as detailed checks of 200 red-footed booby nests, involving the weighing of chicks, before 10am or after 4pm, when it was cooler. Pushing through dense scrub, cumbered with paraphernalia, with a million small flies tickling and scrambling into eyes, ears and nose, was trying enough without frying in the midday sun.

Research sounds impressive, but involves drudgery. However interesting and wide-ranging the conclusions may be (but rarely are) the work that supports them is almost always repetitive, boring or even irksome. Observations on animal behaviour are less tedious, since there is always great pleasure simply in watching. Even then, it is essential to make detailed notes and constantly question one's observational accuracy. Postures used in bird displays seem obvious in a drawing or photograph, but are frequently fleeting and difficult to recognise. Often it seems necessary to prick oneself awake to make even trivial advances in interpretation and to keep the boundary between mere ideas and facts in good repair. Many biases can be introduced by careless methods of gathering information, much more subtle than the apparent tendency for frogs to spawn and birds to migrate at weekends. My approach to gathering information on behaviour is laborious, but fairly safe, since I do not usually begin with a hunch and select the range of enquiry accordingly. I try to look at the total range of behaviour in a certain situation, say the breeding colony, and by gathering quantitative information acquire the pieces with which the jigsaw can ultimately be more or less assembled. This is particularly rewarding when trying to relate behaviour and ecology in a whole group of species.

After the checks came the pleasantest meal of the day, breakfast under the tent veranda, often in warm sunshine. We took half a hundredweight of milk powder and plenty of oats; tinned bacon was strictly rationed but bread was not. Bread making became a ritual; the deities invoked in animistic rituals are basically hostile and unpredictable and so was our bread god. I don't think the bread turned out twice alike. The paraffin oven performed badly, partly owing to the dirty paraffin – and when the flour became extra weevily, the bread emerged even more dejectedly. Flour weevils are known to secrete a substance which lowers reproductive rate in other weevils and so limits the population in the flour bag; no-one knows what its effect is on man!

As an undergraduate I once did summer work in a large modern bakery. I remember the relentless ascent of rows of tines bearing empty bread tins, and the conveyor belt bearing lumps of dough that moved from right to left. As the belt moved along the operator simply took from his left a lump of dough already cut to size, twisted it into a certain shape and plonked it into the left-hand tin on the ascending row. Seizing the next lump, by then in front of him, he plonked it into the tin second from the left and so on till the row was filled. Things were so timed that he just managed to fill the right-hand tin before it rose out of reach. Grab, twist, plonk; grab, twist, plonk. The work was so monotonous until suddenly you had to move a little further to the left for the next bit of dough, then further still. Soon you were dashing down the conveyor belt, chasing the dough before it fell off at the end, rushing back and with a frantic leap filling the inexorably rising tin. You couldn't win once it had you on the hop. Somehow, though, you always thought you would overtake the system. The pile of dough on the floor and the rows of tins coming out of the oven destitute of golden loaf showed otherwise. I never criticised our small, sunken loaves coming from the battered oven.

A small colony of Galapagos fur seals flourished in one corner on the east side of Darwin Bay and a magnificent colony of white-vented storm-petrels inhabited the eastern horn. Both these rarities attracted us, and with our rowing boat, the *Plus Ultra*, were just a pleasantly long row away instead of an exhausting grind over difficult terrain. Near the fur seals on the east side we chanced upon a negotiable crack in the cliffs leading to a flat, ashy area, strewn with whitened blocks of lava and dotted with shrubs.

Here Nazca boobies were scattered about, and a few frigatebirds and red-footed boobies looked down from their superior nests in the bushes. The remnants of wooden huts set up by the last American oceanographical survey lay about. Just around the corner one suddenly emerges from shirt-tearing scrub into an astonishing plain of scoriae and other lava, absolutely bare of any vegetation and almost perfectly flat. It looks like the efforts of some town council in a mining area to make a huge car park out of ashes and slag. The deep reddish-brown surface is seamed and fissured, there are lava bubbles everywhere and in places one crashes through the thin surface crust into cavities up to two feet deep.

Nothing could look more dreary, yet beneath the lava crust there is a teeming city of at least 5,000 petrels inhabiting a maze of cavities and tunnels. They flit about like a cloud of midges. Training your glasses on one, it apparently follows the bird in front but then turns aside. This is obviously not a pair-formation display flight; there are just so many individuals that they sometimes collide with an audible bump. Now our bird runs its beak over the lava and moves its mandibles as though feeding. Next it suddenly pops into a crevice, seemingly house-hunting. But that can't be true for the majority, as birds fly round for long periods, incidentally rendering them vulnerable to the partly diurnal Galapagos short-eared owl.

During the day the petrels must endure terrific temperatures. We found many fresh, broken eggs. Although mockingbirds are egg thieves, they could hardly be expected to go pot-holing for their booty, which would in any case be protected by the incubating petrel. Researcher Mike Harris later showed that whilst there are two species of storm-petrels breeding on Tower; the wedge-rumped (formerly Galapagos) storm-petrel flies in vast numbers around the colony during the day and feeds at night while the band-rumped storm-petrel flies around at night. The two species nest at different times and in different areas.

On this particular day, my thoughts were brusquely dispelled when we returned to the crack. It was getting late and ahead of us was a long row back to camp. But there was no boat. From the clifftop we could just see its outline beneath the surface. It had dragged the anchoring boulder, grounded on a submerged rock and then filled with the tide. It was far too late to return to camp overland; the deep fissures and jagged lava would have been suicidally dangerous in the dark. A night out on the lava with no food or drink and very little clothing also seemed unattractive, so we leapt into the sea and by furious hand-baling managed to raise the boat. The oars had floated away, but one was visible just out in the bay. A boat seat furnished a rough paddle; hastening out we retrieved both oars and thankfully set off back across the darkening bay.

Evening on Tower was always peaceful, except when a Galapagos short-eared owl sat on the tent ridge and laughed its weird, cackling old man's laugh. To us, of course, the owls looked quite appealing with their large, blinking golden eyes and knock-kneed stance, but no wonder the swallow-tailed gull chicks crouched motionless in cracks or between boulders. The owl's strong talons found every single one around our camp. But even peaceful evenings can be rather dreary. There were always plans to be chewed over in minute detail – most of which had to be ditched when it came to the point – diaries to write and, if one felt energetic enough, field notebooks to pore over and get into some sort of order prior to the long job of transformation into a reasoned account.

But these things don't make much of a change. Conversation became threadbare, reading ran out and the age of meditation dawned, but I, for one, tend to belong not to those who sit and think, but to those who just sit. During full moons we ate our spaghetti and sardines out in the warm night air, watching the late incoming red-foots etching the sky. On dark nights the evening flight of insects made it impossible to take a lamp outside. Beetles, flies, mosquitoes, dragonflies and moths swarmed round the lamp inside the tent, not only immolating themselves but in so doing wrecking another of our fast-dwindling stock of mantles.

Some of these insects are now in the British Museum, where at least one has the honour of forming a 'first ever' for this monumental institution. Our most beautiful visitor was a huge brown saturnid moth, measuring precisely seven and a quarter inches across, with a double-banded eye spot on each hindwing; at first I thought it was a bat. During April and May several more came to us, but none so large as the first.

I could not have lived and worked on Tower for seven months in complete isolation without severe depression. Doubtless there are many who could, and in less restricted, desolate and frustrating terrain it would be fairly easy. We often discussed whether we would have liked somebody else there. It might have been pleasant to have had another couple on the other side of the island – far enough away to provide elbow space but near enough to see and talk with every other month. In particular I would have enjoyed talking to a Beebe or a Tinbergen [Professor Nikolaas Tinbergen, the Nobel Prize-winning founding father of ethology and Bryan's supervisor at the University of Oxford] about our work. Since continuous and fairly long-term fieldwork of this sort is so hard to organise and carry out it is a great pity to miss useful evidence simply through lack of foresight; discussion helps here. But the wrong people would have been disastrous, and we could well imagine why the advertised attempt of an American party to colonise a Galapagos island was a dismal flop. Imagine living with the answer to an advertisement. Some of them never even landed on the islands – one look was enough.

Before we had done much after supper, it was time to turn in. Out for some seawater for teeth-cleaning and a lick with seawater soap, then the rigmarole of putting up the beds and battening down the hatches against centipedes – a sock to stuff up this hole and a shoe to wedge that flap. Routine was both helpful and extremely irksome. The very knowledge that certain chores were inescapable every day irritated when superimposed on the larger restrictions of a very basic camp life, where activity is limited and diversions more so. Romantics who have never experienced genuine and prolonged isolation may find this hard to believe, hearing only the lazy murmur of the surf and the wind-rustled palms.

In small, primitive and self-contained communities the practical man is both more valuable and probably, despite his grumbles, usually more at home than the intellectual idealist. Yet it is probably the latter who dreams of desert islands but fortunately rarely gets there. A blend of practical ability and matter-of-fact outlook with artistic sensitivity would be ideal but, failing that, Beebe's set-up on the yacht *Noma* had much to commend it: 'We gathered at last, all telling of the new and unexpected things seen and collected, all sensible of the spirit of weird isolation of this land. At dusk we climbed the companion-way to our home of orderliness and electricity, a land of linen and cut glass, of delicious food and drink, easy chairs, music and absorbing books. Each made the other so much more worthwhile.'

We, for our part, stepped from the beach outside to the beach inside the tent – much the same except for the litter of well-used cooking and camping gear in this land of tin platters and bottles, delicious dehydrated potatoes, camp chairs, the hiss of the paraffin lamp and all too few books.

Broadcasts from British Honduras (Belize) came through fairly well on our transistor radio and, despite the one-way traffic, created an illusion of contact. We found their homely announcements particularly endearing: 'The Orangewalk Veterans Basketball reserve team will meet for practice in Riverside Hall on Sunday morning' or 'Will Mrs Florence Usher of 1 Monkey Walk please collect baby as Grandmother is leaving today'. How unexpected it was to hear Wimbledon results, Test match scores and world news from London. Each Saturday listeners chose their top ten tunes, the likes of 'Molly', 'As Usual' and 'Twist and Shout', all of which June's sister was listening to back in Yorkshire. And if we wanted John Bull to guard the tent we could listen to loyal Radio Belize playing the British national anthem before closing down; it was encouraging to find that the British are not quite universally reviled.

With the darkness came silence, the prelude to stealthy scrapings and scratchings on the canvas as the land crabs began their foraging. They were quite welcome to the freedom of the tent, but not so the giant centipedes, whose powerful claws and hard chitinous plating scraped particularly loudly and menacingly in the total blackness. Many a nocturnal hunt reduced the tent to a shambles as the speedy centipede flashed into a succession of hiding places before capture. And so finally to canvas, with the dishes stacked ready for the dawn reveille by the mockers.

5

TOWER ISLAND: OUR NEW HOME

JUNE AND BRYAN

'Two bleached skeletons rested side by side on a strip of black Galapagos lava lonely in the Pacific. One domed skull held the nest of a tiny black Darwin's finch. The male habitually alighted on the inviting row of lower teeth, in a mouth prised open as the muscles dried and contracted.'

Despite Bryan's worst imaginings, I knew that we could live adequately on a desert island. We'd just spent three years practising on the Bass Rock. Good friends, we never fought, and three years in a tiny, mostly freezing cold hut had shown that we could cope with most things. We were resourceful, tough and undemanding. We were prepared for monotonous food. As fruit and vegetable freaks, the lack of any fresh food would irk us; nothing edible grows on the smaller islands. Protein would be boring tins with little variety. We'd stowed multivitamins. Though maybe we should have listened to the Guayaquil chandlers, who wanted us to take live chickens, turkeys and a goat.

Having spent our first night on our first desert island hiding in the store tent, with a ragged fishing boat anchored a stone's throw away, we eventually got our camp shipshape. At last, as 1963 ended, it was time to explore the island and its birds.

Tower is low, scrubby, hot and arid, not exactly a rest home or an escapist's paradise. Its six and a half square miles do not seek to delight the intruder with changing moods and landscapes. Most of it is a gently sloping expanse of low trees and scrub, silvery dry and apparently stone dead, their living tissues deeply buried in the hoary limbs. Take away the scrub and the rough, red-brown, ankle-cockling lava and you are left with a crater lake, two or three sandy beaches, an acre or two of green shrub and the crumbly cliffs.

On the southeast horn a magnificent cinder plain stretches into the distance. There is an expanse of clinker on the southeast corner that no product of blast furnace could beat, a sea of sharp-edged lava – buckled, jagged and lying higgledy-piggledy as though millions of slabs had been smashed and bulldozed into heaps. Crossing this toilsome, sulphurous stuff with a load in the stifling midday heat, with nothing but desolation around, one feelingly agreed that Tower well lived up to one of its Spanish names: *Quita Sueño*, nightmare island (literally 'removes sleep'). Return, however, to the bonny white coral beach, backed by the mermaid's lagoon at the head of Darwin Bay and the nightmare relaxes into a pleasant dream.

Our Tower camp sat squarely on this dazzling beach. Coral is relatively rare in the Galapagos, partly because of the cooling influence of the Humboldt; these small colonial coelenterates cannot grow in water colder than about 70F (21°C). Reef-building corals also need shallow water, so that the deep offshore waters of most Galapagos islands are not suitable. The most coral we saw was off the west coast of Tower. It also grew profusely in fairly deep water out in Darwin Bay and chunks of it rolled in with the tides, forming the substantial bank which was our campsite. Each piece had been worn smooth and round, hardly like coral except for the telltale pores in which the living polyps had been housed. Animal skeletons also weathered to just such a whiteness so it took a sharp beachcombing eye to pick out the skulls of tropicbirds, boobies, sea lions and fish that turned up.

From the summit of Tower, looking southwest, it seems as though the whole island has slipped sideways into the sea, plunging the southern rim of the Darwin Bay crater far beneath the surface. From the northern edge of the bay the island gradually rises in a series of terraces to the summit. First come the parallel reefs that menace the approach to the inner bay and at high tide lurk barely beneath the surface, then the rocky shore and then two cliff faces separated by flat-bottomed rift valleys. The faintly conical summit of Tower marks the rim of a second huge crater, this one entirely circled by almost sheer cliffs, terraced with broad and flat ledges, and filled with extremely brackish water. From here the long, narrow peninsula that forms the eastern arm of Darwin Bay curves steadily round towards its opposite partner on the western side.

Both 'horns' are the sites of extensive bird colonies: the eastern one with its several thousand pairs of wedge-rumped and band-rumped storm-petrels, and the western horn with a Nazca booby colony and many great frigatebirds. Swallow-tailed gulls breed in substantial numbers on the eastern horn and lava gulls on the western one. Galapagos shearwaters, red-billed tropicbirds and brown noddies also frequent the cliffs of the eastern horn.

The northern side of the island is difficult to negotiate. Apart from broken ground approaching either horn it is almost cliff-bound. *Opuntia* and *Cereus* cacti, *palo santo* trees and prickly shrubs grow densely right to the cliff edge, forcing frequent detours inland to find a penetrable spot. Along the north cliffs large numbers of Galapagos shearwaters glide and angle, stiff-winged among the swallow-tailed gulls, tropicbirds and noddies. During 1964, the shearwater population of Tower was certainly substantial, at least several thousand, whilst there were over 1,000 noddies, perhaps many more, well spread around the island.

Except for a thin coastal strip, a bare area on each horn of the bay and the inland crater, the whole of Tower is covered with sun-silvered shrub and succulent cacti. The 'rains' fall between January and May, which is also the hottest season – February is about the hottest month. On Tower, one of the driest islands, they are often no more than a few heavy showers with more frequent short periods of mist or drizzle – the *garúa*. Our only really heavy shower quickly turned itself off when June had soaped herself and was standing on the beach ready for the rinse.

But even this small rainfall brings out the leaves. We awoke on 18 February, ten days after the first heavy showers of the year, to find the island misted over with green – nothing more than a hint, but so fresh and lovely. It lasted about three weeks, then all was dead and dry as before. Leafing and flowering were thus extremely compressed, and for this short period the air held a wonderful delicate fragrance which came from tree-like bushes covered with yellow flowers, probably *Cordia*, a member of the borage family. Later, the berries of a tree – I think from the genus *Bursera* – gave out a pungent aroma that was so strong that we could easily smell it on the breath of our tame ground-finch who ate the seeds and then came to us for water. In the rare 'wet' years the island stays green longer and may be verdant as late as July.

But otherwise the only water was that of the ocean rolling up to our very door, from which we could literally toss crumbs into the sea at high tide. Turnstones and wandering tattlers twinkled over the sand in the wake of retreating waves and expertly judged the speed and distance of each pursuer, turning and running deeply into it before it began its backward drag. The tattlers were migrants from Alaska; Arctic tundra to equatorial lava.

Around the time of the Alaska earthquake on 27 March 1964 the extra high tides actually flowed between our tents, fortunately without entering. Behind our camp an idyllic little lagoon filled and emptied with each tide, changing a patch of drab yellow sand into a shining pool. The crystal-clear water entered through yawning cracks along the seaward edge, always leaving, even on the lowest tide, a tiny deep pool in which a few colourful orange-bellied fishlets waged ceaseless territorial war. The lagoon was a delightful swimming pool free from the sharks and manta rays which often wandered into the bay, and infinitely more beautiful than the most exotic manmade structure. More prosaically, it was handy for rinsing clothes, which meant tossing them in, letting two or three tides stir them around and then extracting the surviving socks and shirts from the dark crevices into which they had been carried by the currents.

We never quite knew how to treat the sharks. One learns implicit dread of sharks from every sea tale, but the ones that regularly came close inshore on Tower, occasionally even to the extent of beaching themselves when chasing fish in the shallows, were mainly harmless blacktip and whitetip reef sharks – the latter about four or five feet long, the blacktips perhaps a bit larger.

Despite the many shark stories, the most objective and experienced opinion seems to be that even the species largely responsible for attacking inshore bathers almost always attack by mistake, seeing a sudden movement and going for it. Once they have drawn blood they rarely, if ever, return to the attack, apparently being inhibited by the unfamiliar scent or some other disturbing factor. The literature is full of instances of bleeding victims rescued from the tainted water without further molesting by the shark, thus apparently disproving the popular belief that sharks will attack man if there is blood in the water. It probably depends on whose blood!

This is all very well to know in theory, but it doesn't remove one's apprehensions in fact, or it didn't in our case as we swam out to our rowing boat a few yards offshore. Yet there could hardly be a more shark-blasé population than that of the Galapagos. We witnessed tens of people, including toddlers, bathing at Wreck Bay on San Cristóbal, yet saw sharks only a few score yards further along the coast. We watched fishermen from the *San Marco* diving into the sea after gutting their catch, even though a few minutes earlier the water had been boiling with a dozen blacktips fighting for the fish heads and guts. Lobster fishermen from the Villamil and Floreana swam and dived every day for months on end all round the Galapagos without any shark accident.

Giant manta rays often came into the shallows of the bay and flapped and glided just a few yards from the tent. They are a quite astonishing size; a manta once swam beneath our boat, undulating gently, and its fins stuck out for feet on either side. One afternoon a pod of dolphins, evidently pursuing a shoal of fish, moved regally across the bay in a series of graceful, curving dives one after the other, their great dorsal fins emerging and disappearing in hypnotic rhythm. They fed for several hours, methodically quartering the bay, whilst excited crowds of red-footed boobies winnowed above, probably attracted by the fleeing shoal.

Tower was kind to us. Day after day the sun shone and the waters of Darwin Bay sparkled. When we returned, jaded, from the far ends of the island or across the bay to our modest camp the white coral beach and green tent – even when pinpricks in the distance –

beckoned hospitably. It was never cold, rarely wet and the area was virtually free from gales. Once we were visited by two American couples who were roaming the world on the combined frugality of eight years. Replete on our home-baked bread and lobsters, and sitting by the beach fire in the soft, warm air, they said they wouldn't have exchanged it for any spot in the world. But they were there only for a day.

Research on Tower was a vastly different experience to studying gannets on the Bass Rock. For a start, there was not a trace of the fishy, despairing mud that characterised the Scottish island. Here, our gentler subjects sat tamely within a stone's throw of our tent, two of the species nesting on bushes so we didn't even have to bend. No more slogging up the steep Bass in freezing gales to grapple with their fierce and stinking cousins. Here we wandered out, half clad, in warm stillness. Our protagonists sat calmly on their nests and offered little resistance when we ringed or weighed them. In one session we ringed 34 Nazca boobies merely taking them by hand. About the same size as a gannet but much lighter, they are exceptionally trusting and can often just be put back on their nest even when they have no egg or chick to keep them there. A gannet, and all its neighbours, would have shouted raucously and, whenever we failed immediately to grab the back of its head, inflicted a deep stab wound or bleeding claw scratch.

Without research, life on Tower would have been idyllic for a short time at least. With all tent flaps open back and front, a breeze whistled through, while a film of fascinating wildlife played endlessly and differently back and front. If we got too hot, on Tower we grabbed a cold tinned juice and sank into the warm lagoon; quite different to an icy plunge into a choppy North Sea.

However, Tower Island was no Eden. Much of it was covered by a large *palo santo* forest, which, aside from that glorious January burst of green with perfumed yellow flowers, following derisory rain, quickly reverted to its usual sea of skeletons. The top branches whipped our faces and the mid-level sticks tore endlessly at our clothes and legs. Walking almost anywhere proved a trial, with feet tripping, stubbing or breaking through the endless lava. Large, smooth slabs allowed normal progress. They were rare. The medium slabs cockled on top of each other and threw us every which way. Jagged aero chocolate-bar blocks cut our shoes in no time and caught our legs; after less than two months Bryan was on to his fourth pair of plimsolls and not much later was left merely with boots. Little aero blocks slid or crumbled. But the prize went to stretches of apparently smooth aero that would suddenly cave in like ice. A foot would drop into a hole one or two feet deep, with its jagged edges cracking an ankle as it went down. Our legs and feet quickly resembled maps. We never saw green 'grass'. Maybe one withered clump resembling dead grass occurred about once a mile.

Before our dinghy was delivered in February, we dreaded the frequent lengthy trek to reach a large colony of Nazca boobies. On one occasion we took our usual picnic but by lunchtime it felt so hot on the leafless lava plain that we ate it sitting in a pool. For the remainder of the hot afternoon we toiled marking nests, ringing, weighing and measuring, then trudged back with a terrible thirst and collapsed into the lagoon.

One fine day we decided to complete our tour of the island, searching for other seabird colonies. This involved crossing to the north coast, just a short distance on the map, then along a section that we had not previously covered, thence back round to the sea lion colony and our ringed Nazca boobies. Reaching the coast was hell, with the usual nasty stuff for our feet and the usual other nasty stuff above. No straightforward areas opened up, as on the east of the island, just more nasty stuff extending right to the cliff edge. As usual after these jaunts we went straight to bed before 6pm and drank endlessly.

Another fine day Bryan decided we needed a stab at estimating the number of red-footed boobies on the island. This involved mapping and counting the number of birds in representative 100-yard squares. Our lines, all the odd bits of twine and red plastic cord that we could find and tie together, proved hard to see amongst thick bushes, and meant a lengthy search before we were able to complete the square by finding our starting point. We lowered ambitions, moving to four 50-yard lines instead. We counted boobies in each square then moved the lines to make another. This pretty exercise took six hours.

For the third day we measured out two 100-yard lines, walked along a cliff edge, then completed line four. This connected up remarkably well but squares purely incorporating a cliff would hardly have been representative. Another three days ended in the lagoon and foodless to bed.

Each day we had to check a large area of marked nests, to record when eggs were laid, how long each parent sat keeping the egg warm, how long each chick took to hatch, and most importantly how often parents fed their chick. Avoiding numerous painful scratches from the scrub required wearing trousers; inevitably we returned dripping in sweat.

Bryan clearly loved plotting these delightful tasks. How about checking the number of feeds delivered in 48 hours? Each of us spent two hours on and two hours off. Fortunately he timed that one cleverly. With cloud and a comfortable chair it proved not unpleasant. We noted whenever a parent returned to its nest and fed its chick. Several poor youngsters went over 24 hours without food. It looked as though the Humboldt Current was temporarily veering away from the islands, causing sudden food shortages that resulted in nests and eggs being abandoned and chicks losing weight, before often recovering again.

We knew that nothing edible grew on Tower but we did have hopes of fish so had taken lots of fishing tackle and, fortunately, many spare hooks (as they kept snagging on the stony bottom). Mostly the bait immediately vanished so we failed miserably for months. Finally, towards the end of March, we managed to hook a few fish but they always escaped. By April we cracked it. In the meantime *langosto*, which we first caught in mid-February, filled the gap a little.

Let out of school after our breathless 1963, and despite working hard and amassing endless data, we devised many other kinds of fun on Tower. We made funny squeaks on recorders while painfully playing 'Pease Pudding Hot' and such pathetic fare, which made us laugh. A magazine cutting detailed what physical feats fit 18-year-olds should be able to achieve. Swim half a mile? Did that the previous week. Bryan managed the 80 sit-ups and I coped with 50; no problem. We couldn't test 14 pull-ups; nothing to pull on. We got nowhere near eight-foot-six-inch and six-foot-seven-inch standing long jumps, however much we practised. The running challenge – 600 yards in one-and-a-half and two-and-a-half minutes – hit snags. We had to do it barefoot on loose sand and our 'course' stretched a mere 50 yards. Turning 11 times added a further handicap.

To the left of our beach a long creek ran into the lagoon at high tide. At low tide stretches of sand, pebbles and rocks alternated with deep pools. A large log at the head of the creek provided endless amusement as we tried to ride it downstream, falling off with every wiggle, often by a jagged rock. Paddling against the tide we felt we had done a hard day's work when we reached the lagoon.

We swam most days. At first we carried an oar as defence against sharks, but what good we thought our clumsy thrashing might be against those agents of speed now seems unclear. And we soon learnt to trust the whitetips.

Once our dinghy arrived it provided a great sense of escape, though we made sure to stay well away from the mouth of the bay where a strong current would have swept us north – next stop Alaska. Several times we rowed across to what later became known as 'Prince Philip's steps', to visit the petrel and booby colonies. Both our birthdays happily arrived after the boat and we packed our best picnic for a day on the bay. Fortnum and Mason would have been ashamed but I relaxed rationing temporarily and did my best baking. We opened a precious tin of ham and recklessly ate two slices apiece. However, we couldn't beach the heavy boat, so it rocked romantically offshore, inevitably witnessing June's pathetic attempts to board it. She never managed to get enough push and had to be ignominiously hauled aboard.

June was rarely ill (hailing from sturdy peasant stock, perhaps). Despite Bryan's toughness and determination, he had been dealt a more delicate card. He was driven and careless of his well-being. During 1963 he had pushed himself to the limits and in the Galapagos his immune system rebelled. Our trip to the tortoises on Santa Cruz (*Chapter 3*) began it all. Rather than deflecting the spiny bushes Bryan pushed through impatiently, and his numerous scratches later became infected. He displayed a strange arrogance. Why are these devilish bushes impeding my progress? He reckoned all inanimate objects had a malevolent scheme to thwart him. Even his shoes conspired against him. When he was reduced to boots, June still had two pairs of tennis shoes. Our diaries endlessly recorded: 'sores spreading and painful'.

Any cuts festered. We applied hot dressings and Bryan sat in the tent reading Churchill's *A History of the English-Speaking Peoples* while June carried out the daily nest checks. Seawater exacerbated the sores; many times Bryan needed piggybacking, followed by his heavy equipment, across the creek to our colonies. Penicillin tablets cleared the sores for a while, but they returned. It took many months and an antibiotic injection to clear them for any length of time.

After three weeks on Tower, a tooth started niggling, and Bryan became irritable and easily fatigued. By evening he was always tired, but slept badly, disturbed by rampaging giant centipedes and munching crabs, until the dawn reveille from our too-friendly neighbours, the swallow-tails and mockingbirds. He developed headaches so bad that he couldn't eat, mouth ulcers, cold sores and a queasy stomach. It must have added to Bryan's sense of injustice that his wife remained healthy and consequently good-tempered throughout.

Bryan preferred a bracing breeze now and then. He found midday and photography especially trying, the intensity of light producing a perpetual scowl. Once he commented that he wouldn't mind a week or two in an English spring, then quickly added: 'Bet I'd miss the warmth. I would rather be here than in cold latitudes any day despite the underlying enervating effect.' Even clothes hanging from a cross piece in the tent were damp in the morning.

By February we were getting used to the climate and could spend much longer in the sun without flagging, though we still tired easily. Dark nights brought a selection of insects and after unusual heavy rain we had a tent full of mosquitoes, crabs and sandhoppers. That signalled mosquito nets; another source of irritation. Then horror; one evening we found an earwig, stowed away from the Bass Rock.

On Easter Saturday we plugged a hole in the boat, made two table-tennis bats, put marker pegs on many frigate nests, developed several films, and rescued an abandoned red-footed booby chick. We had already failed to save two starved tropicbirds, despite feeding them with fish which we persuaded frigates to regurgitate. We felt no compunction about stealing these small amounts as they had probably already been stolen from a booby. Although we persisted in trying to rear waifs we never succeeded. Once a wild creature looks ill it is almost always impossible to save it; to survive in the wild an animal needs to be fit.

During 1964, a converted Cornish fishing vessel, *Beagle II*, arrived to take over as workhorse for the Charles Darwin Research Station. We had several trips in her, tasted wonderful soup and less exotic concoctions in her saloon, and remember her with great affection. June usually enjoyed the first course, then had to climb the stairs, defeated by the rolling, the fug and the smell from the loo down below. But after an evening on deck with the ever-hospitable Karl Angermeyer, we often slipped ashore in the blackness of a tropical night.

On a blindingly hot day in July, seven months after our arrival, the *Beagle* took us off Tower. How we sweated, tugging down the heavy boxes and loading them awkwardly into the longboat! And how odd it seemed sailing right out of the mouth of the bay at which we had gazed so often for nearly 200 days, until our camping beach was first a tiny white spot (had we really lived on that for so long?), before being hidden by the curve of the bay. We had been restlessly looking forward to the moment of departure for the previous few weeks, but no sooner had our beach really disappeared than we already felt sad and wondered if we would ever return.

Later the *Beagle* took us to Hood, and off Hood, and back to Tower, and to Daphne and finally put us ashore on Baltra, so it is no wonder that she occupies a favoured niche in our affection; taking us to these wild places, always turning up on time and with the same joking, good-natured crew to help us load our gear and then sailing us back to Santa Cruz. She never failed to make a rendezvous or to time her voyages perfectly. The memorable occasion on which we left Tower at 5pm that July evening yet found ourselves within 25 miles of the island and heading her way at dawn again the next morning shall be as decently shrouded as Karl's comments when he found the wheel lashed and the errant helmsman asleep at his post.

6

HOUSEKEEPING ON TOWER

JUNE

We were poor. Bryan had just spent eight years on a degree and research, living on grants, and I had left my job in the tax office to join him for three of those years working on gannets. Apart from grants we had no money. Our time on the Galapagos would be frugal; bare essentials, make do and mend.

Starting from scratch to organise a year on a desert island would have been taxing whatever. But at the time we were still working on the gannets on the Bass Rock, with Bryan needing to complete his D. Phil. thesis by November. In among all this we somehow had to start planning our expedition. With no internet or mobile phone, ordering equipment and food whilst living on a remote island taxed our ingenuity. There was just Fred, our kindly boatman who posted and delivered our snail mail every few days. We had minimal Spanish and naïvely tried to enquire about sailings to the Galapagos, permissions and the like in English. No wonder we got no replies.

On the Bass we managed well with fresh food delivered by lighthouse ship every fortnight. Food for a year posed a different problem. Maybe if I just multiplied my usual order by 26 it would be a start. That was all very well except that the delicious food that made relief days such a celebration would not keep. Even towards the end of two weeks on the Bass, food became monotonous once we had finished fresh vegetables and fruit. I added vitamin pills to the Galapagos list. On the Bass we used herring gull eggs, preserving some in isinglass. In those days herring gulls were not protected; there were far too many on the Bass, and if you took an egg the female would lay again. We knew there would be no possibility of stealing precious Galapagos eggs. We would need to take the dried equivalent.

Back in the 1960s food in Britain had not yet risen from just about its lowest point. There was no delicious way of drying things such as eggs or vegetables, and tins came in a pretty dire basic range. Plastic was in its early stages (the first plastic shopping bag appeared the year after we left the Galapagos) and we had neither clever bags to keep things airtight nor clever technology to freeze-dry or vacuum-pack. Harrods no doubt had a fine selection of goodies, but we had the tightest of tight budgets. We soon discovered that basics cost much more in Britain and we would have to pay to transport them to South America via three ships. Basics would need to come from Guayaquil, but we realised that with fresh food available only by generosity from the main islands, our fare would be depressingly boring and we would need something to lift our spirits on poor days.

In the end we compromised. Slightly tricky items like dried milk, eggs and vegetables we could take cheaply from Britain. We discovered that Selfridges sold tins of 'vital' luxuries such as butter, bacon, ham, cheese and oats. Bulky items like flour, sugar, rice and most tins we assumed could come from ships' chandlers in Guayaquil. But knowing what items might be available in South America proved tricky; too late we discovered that many desirable ones were not.

Nearly 60 years on, rereading our account of the Galapagos year, I am astonished by our strange foresight. I have a reputation for packing the kitchen sink, but what made me take a sieve to a desert island? I blessed it months later for extracting beetles and maggots from our flour. Knitting needles, wool and a pattern for socks? Yet just extra socks wouldn't have allowed me to reknit Bryan's holey sweater sleeves for lunch with Prince Philip; extra socks would have cost money and I already had patterns and wool. A large selection of needles, different threads, fabrics, rags? Yes. I needed fabric for patching clothes. Rags came in handy for our constant battles with dirty paraffin equipment. And most of the needles broke repairing canvas camp beds and chairs. Fablon? I suppose we realised I wouldn't be able to roll pastry on a splintery box. And when a nightly onslaught of moths had shattered all but the final mantle for our tilley lamp we unearthed a net bag to construct a cage. Surprisingly I had no dustpan and brush. Even that I would have welcomed on the odd occasion when the tent groundsheet became just too indistinguishable from the sandy beach and I swept it out with an old toothbrush.

It would have been a disaster trying to live on either the Bass Rock or the Galapagos as a housewife. With little housework what would one do? Obviously we needed to eat and keep vaguely clean, but, fortunately, working with Bryan filled virtually all my time. Although I had always appreciated wildlife and needed the outdoors, I had no biological training. Luckily, Bryan's research involved mostly observation, practical stuff like weighing and measuring, detailed note taking and writing up the day's findings. I was good at all those. In the evenings Bryan did the analysing, deducing, planning and writing. I typed up the results on our ancient typewriter. Those daily tasks worked equally well for the Bass and the Galapagos.

So we'd had a practice run on the Bass; both working and living for long periods on an island. Several well-tested items went with us, though they were aging. Most importantly came the paraffin fridge, for Bryan's film! And we certainly needed the paraffin oven, and paraffin lights when dusk fell around 6pm. The table and makeshift cupboards from the Bass were too large; we would use the green boxes instead. Chairs, camp beds and sleeping bags would be essential, though I had already patched the beds.

But conditions in the Galapagos would be different in many ways with heat rather than icy gales. Instead of a garden shed, we needed a large strong tent for living and a smaller store tent. So we swapped our 14x8-foot shed for a 12x8-foot ridge tent, made of heavy tropical canvas with a flysheet and veranda. It stood up magnificently to the bleaching and weakening effect of the fierce sun; our store tent of ordinary canvas became so fragile after a few months that even the small Galapagos doves put their feet through the roof. Erecting that main tent proved an almighty struggle. Its large size and heavy canvas meant that as soon as we got one of the heavy wooden poles inserted, it acted as a giant sail in the rising wind and I couldn't hold my side. Bryan later admitted he felt ashamed of his peevishness. Eventually we managed, but it took most of the day, adjusting, levelling the site and fixing the groundsheet.

With no height-constraining beams, after three years Bryan at last could stand upright. Deep pockets lining the side walls quickly filled with string and rings and glue and all my other kitchen-sinkery and from the looped cord above them we hung gun, machete, sword and knife; a fierce outfit. Two of our boxes stood against the back wall, one tipped on its side with its lid removed to form a cupboard and our books arranged on top. The paraffin oven sat on our metal box. Next to that we covered the one huge box with Fablon as an excellent surface for cooking and baking, and a small round table and two chairs stood against the opposite wall. Our canvas beds had to be dismantled every morning. Bliss was a deep veranda, with a box at either side, for tables or seats. When it became too hot we could open four flaps, encouraging a through breeze and revealing salt water back and front. Need a warm loll? Stroll to the lagoon. For something slightly more bracing a few steps took us to the sea.

On our second day on Tower, surveying the mounds of boxes, we couldn't think where to start, but eventually unpacked, lit the fridge and stowed most of our gear. At last, on the third day, 31 December 1963, our third wedding anniversary, the tent looked businesslike.

Neither of our islands had fresh water. We had to take it or make it. Large water containers lined the walls of the store tent but the water soon tasted strange and eventually turned green. Distilled water would be more pleasant for drinking. So, with a tidy tent, we started to make the framework for our solar still. It was rather primitive but perhaps worth describing since people planning to live on a desert island (there must be thousands) may find one useful. We were rather proud of our handiwork; it actually worked, the distilled water was untainted and could have supported us indefinitely on a waterless island. Besides this, there was the spendthrift pleasure of manufacturing real potable water from the Pacific Ocean.

Driftwood aplenty lined the edges of the creek and we soon collected enough for a bit of woodwork; we could have built a hut with what we found along the side of the bay. The base was a rectangular pit in the sand (a tarred wooden box would do) six inches deep, lined with black polythene and filled with seawater. Making the sides of our pit was such a laborious job with a blunt saw. Over the pit we placed an A-frame of driftwood covered with transparent Mylar, gifted by ICI, with its bottom edges bent under to form a trough.

The sun's heat, absorbed by the black polythene, produced water vapour which, condensing on the underside of the roof, should run down into the troughs. The structure sloped slightly, and the water was meant to run into sunken collecting cans.

It stood there, triumphant, until we realised the roof was too slack to allow the water to run. Being the smaller, I was deputed to wriggle into the hot water for final adjustments. Bryan took a photo to prove that he kept a naked woman in a cage, but it seems lost for ever, probably torn by the faulty winding mechanism in his Exacta camera.

The still's first day collected a tenth of a cup of fresh water, the second two and a half pints. Snags lay in getting the apparatus water-vapour tight and persuading the water to run down the roof instead of collecting in droplets and falling back into the pit. Fine striations or perhaps a smear of detergent would probably have helped. Our best day's yield was a gallon, against a feasible yield of 0.09 gallons per square foot of base (a still of several acres, in Mexico, produced 5,000 gallons a day for about 40 years).

A lot depended on the weather, and the performance deteriorated, chiefly from leakage through pinholes caused by small crabs, which meant frequent topping up and so cooling of the system. I wasted a lot of time, propped on my elbows in hot water, trying to repair the holes. Rubber rather than polythene would have made a better job, but cost. Towards the end of our stay on Tower, and with constant attention, the still was producing around four pints each day. As the water in our polythene containers would keep us going, we decided not to keep wasting our time.

Strictly rationing fresh water complicated so many things. All that dried food needed it daily. Bryan's film washing drank large amounts. We drank large amounts. But we had a special container for 'good' water; water that had been used just once for anything not too dirty; mainly Bryan's film washing.

Washing clothes and ourselves in seawater was horrid. Mostly we had to put up with brackish water from the lagoon and seawater soap; a curse on its scummy results. We found it almost impossible to raise a lather and often preferred straight brackish seawater unless coping with paraffin or its sooty offspring. We quickly decided that we much preferred wearing no clothes to washing them in salt water. Those we had to wash got tossed in the lagoon to rinse, then dried on bushes; they decayed quite fast.

Our hair became incredibly sticky so we decided to be rash and use 'good' water. Bryan had to sit dripping shampoo whilst I used the same water, then we both shared more for rinsing. It was such a relief that we decided to do it once a month.

We began with quite a variety of food, and I tried new recipes by the score, but it was hard work. Lunches without our invariable salad were difficult and the dried vegetables a very partial success. They never seemed really tender apart from the onion rings but at last I conquered the dried peas. Soup would have worked but mostly, on Tower, it was too hot. We had lousy meat, the only choice in Guayaquil; spam, luncheon meat, a little tongue and some noxious corned beef hash (I had ordered simple corned beef). We received a case of chitterlings – we couldn't think what they were replacing – that bubbled and stank when we opened the first tin so became the first items we had to throw away.

Fresh fish we loved, and we fared well exchanging them with the visiting fishermen from the *San Marco* for home-baked biscuits, bread, buns and fresh lemonade – or treatment for boils, cuts and leg sores. I strictly rationed the lemons brought from kind friends on Santa Cruz and fortunately had taken the ingredients for a frugal recipe using citric acid that made several bottles of concentrate from five lemons. Mostly we were delighted, but about the large fish head I commented: 'I suppose we are intended to eat it'. Once they sailed back with a stem of bananas for us and caught us two crayfish.

Bryan's first fishing trip ended as did most subsequent ones with both bait and hook taken from the first cast; we lost six precious hooks in no time. Even fishing from our rowing boat, once it arrived in February, at first produced nothing. We watched in frustration as shoals of mackerel-like fish leapt in the bay; we needed speed to catch those. Desperate for fresh fish, we persisted, trying to be creative with our bait. Obvious natural offerings were immediately nibbled to extinction by hundreds of tiny fish. We even tried bits of underpants soaked in anchovy, but the anchovy washed away immediately. We tried wrapping desirable bait in tough fish skin but more swarms of small fish with horizontal stripes and razor teeth tugged it out immediately. Likewise bait tied on with thread. Once we caught small sardines in the lagoon but the sharks quickly gobbled those. Outside the bay there were fish in abundance, but this, Bryan wrote, was 'forsworn territory to us because of the dangerous currents'.

We did catch parrotfish but found their appearance so garish and their flesh so minimal we ate one and no more. A member of the wrasses, Google says their appearance is better than their taste and that they do a vital job on coral reefs so I'm pleased we left them. All the more so because 'they rather disgusted us', Bryan wrote, 'by scavenging for faeces in our sea-washed latrine'.

Eventually, however, we learned to catch giant crayfish or *langosta*. When European settlers first came to the Galapagos,

Bryan wrote, they 'were so common that on Santa Cruz one could pick up any number at low tide simply by paddling'. With snorkel and goggles we searched the rocks and at first found none, but once we identified the sort of deep crevices they preferred and found our search image, often a waving, long, orange antenna, we could find one whenever we wanted. We cooked them in seawater over a beach fire, with fresh bread and cold butter, then danced on the sand to Radio Belize.

I made bread with varying degrees of success, all better than the biscuits we took, but a bit queer. However, one lot eventually tasted very good; a new recipe, so I hoped that perhaps, like the peas, I had at last fixed it. Alas, once the flour really deteriorated, we often tried weird ingenuity to avoid eating any bread. But for the moment, things looked up. Bryan reckoned there was a bread deity.

Nothing edible would grow on either island, though we optimistically took a few seeds, particularly cress. It proved hopeless to try growing anything outside. The odd patches of 'dust' contained no humus and we had virtually no rain. Inside, cress started to grow sparsely on an old blouse and I watered it with tea dregs, but each time it shrivelled before reaching the eating stage.

We had constant problems with our paraffin equipment, which had worked excellently on the Bass. Initially, the fridge, housed in the store tent, caused endless grief and needed constant checking. Either the flame stuttered and the fridge defrosted, or the flame flared and the fridge defrosted. Almost as bad were cooking equipment and lamps that turned temperamental. Eventually we sieved the paraffin twice and the equipment worked better. But the store tent had to remain tightly closed or marauding birds panicked around inside forgetting how they had got in and creating such a draught that the flame flared yet again, and we went iceless yet again. I began to dread needing anything from the store tent.

Predictably we had a lot of tinned fish and a lot of spaghetti, but few of the extra ingredients that are now considered essential to make them delicious, wine being one. Dried herbs began to taste of nothing long before a year had passed. However, I soon discovered that mushrooms and onions sieved out of the mediocre dried soup produced quite reasonable spaghetti sauce and we did have tinned cheese. Another important discovery, though I made it rather late, demonstrated that the 100 tins of revolting corned beef hash became edible if I curried them.

Most days we were jiggered by the time dusk fell so complicated cooking felt beyond me. Having planned a day's expedition, I would cook something the day before and bless the fridge, though several times we were too tired to eat it. All we wanted was a long soak in the lagoon then to bed. After our most exhausting day we drank six pints of juice and seven mugs of tea between us.

I have never been very good at planning menus so our meals were haphazard, though I took care not to have spaghetti every Monday, curry every Tuesday, stew every Wednesday, etc. We needed some anticipation in our lives, though it often became a bit of a cliffhanger when it got to 6.30 and I had given no thought to what might spur us into a happy evening. Many was the day we thought longingly of a tinned chicken or even some proper stew. Luckily we hadn't lost the many tins of fruit and with tinned cream we knew we would appreciate afters.

We were usually hungry and never left any of the often-bizarre food but baking always cheered us up. We had ordered several large tins of biscuits from Elias Mayorga – a simple mid-morning treat, thought I. Although each tin had a different name they uniformly tasted strongly of nothing but ersatz vanilla and were edible only as fridge cake, mixed with lots of butter, cocoa and dried fruit. My crunch and ginger biscuits received the highest votes.

Oh, the nostalgia of baking days. Best in a cold climate, but even in our hot tent, mightily exacerbated by a paraffin oven, the smell of goodies seduced us anew on every occasion. Almost-ready bread maybe provoked the deepest sigh. Hot ginger biscuits came a close second. I didn't lose any weight; too much baking.

Just one month into our stay on Tower, Bryan's diary says: 'Woe is me. Prey to all ills that flesh is heir to. Today adds diarrhoea to my troubles. Whoever portions out life's ills between me and my wife has no sense of equality between the sexes. My lip sores are also painful. If a diary is to record the state of one's mind, the present state of mine is, as Wodehouse says, if not disgruntled, far from gruntled.' Five days later a knock on a rock produced a very bruised knee and two sores on his foot; he was back to limping. Technology did Bryan's humour no favours: 'My Exacta roused me to impotent fury by refusing to rewind and tearing a film into two pieces'. And then the oven needed soldering.

Bryan described Tower as 'an energy-sapping place' but, in addition, it's no surprise that he never felt quite well. Despite a usual nine hours in bed, he slept badly and throughout his life he pushed himself. A typical day would start with checking over 150 nests before breakfast. After breakfast we would weigh Nazca booby chicks and note which parent was keeping guard. Then on to a similar exercise with the red-foots. Two more attendance checks at midday and evening. Maybe some ringing. Photography every day, fishing attempts, exploring the island to find new seabird colonies, equipment maintenance, writing up results, writing papers. And usually the day would be hot, we would be pecked and scratched, and always Bryan would have several irritating ailments. Yet despite afflictions and research he usually managed to find energy and time for things that we both enjoyed.

We have always loved scavenging. Needing pegs for marking booby nests we took time off to collect more driftwood and returned with enough wood to make a rough bookcase. That evening we had a discussion about families. Bryan reckoned the disadvantages far outweighed the advantages and decided that, although it was selfish, he wouldn't want children. I was left to ponder that one while we enjoyed a radio concert conducted by Sir Malcolm Sargent. Not long after, Bryan's diary noted: 'June thinks I cannot have a salary of £2,000 pa five years from now.'

In mid-February we were lying in bed listening to rain drumming on the flysheet; Bryan enjoying it, me apprehensively thinking about sacks of flour getting wet from the walls of the store tent. Several heavy showers followed during the night, and I certainly enjoyed the resultant mist of green over the skeletal *palo santo* trees, and the wonderful fragrance.

After about six weeks I realised we were racing through some foods, though from the start I tried to ration vital things. It seemed we were working on the motto 'eat or drink it before it goes bad, pops, bursts, spills or otherwise eludes one'. Other foods we quickly discovered were too disgusting to eat much of, such as dried egg, dried potatoes and dried vegetables. I tried all ways with the former but it resolutely tasted of cardboard and spoilt any baking. Eventually we took it into the middle of the bay and sank it in small batches in our empty tins. Even there it proved obdurate and floated out of the sunken tins but was quickly eaten by wildlife. We took great care to leave no litter.

Before leaving Britain we heard that Bryan's beloved supervisor from Oxford – Niko Tinbergen – was due to visit the Galapagos with an American expedition. Bryan especially was longing for Niko's humorous, gentle wisdom and stimulating conversations; a chance to discuss our research and get new insights. It was Niko who told Bryan he would make a lousy experimental rat. And Niko who was horrified when Bryan, discounting the tenets of how evolution works, said he could design a better gannet. In high excitement I made the usual lemonade, bread and biscuits. Oh, the disappointment, grief almost, when the expedition arrived with Niko still in Oxford, helping wife Leis with a broken leg that required a bone graft.

An Ecuadorian patrol boat brought out the 12 American scientists and the rest of our stores, but still no sign of the most hoped-for item. It seems that our case of 'luxuries' never came off the *Cristobal Carrier*. We had paid over £20, a huge amount for us then, to make sure we had something a bit special for birthdays or when we needed cheering up. We often thought longingly of the roast chickens, turkey breast or even rather higher-class stew.

The patrol boat had no room to bring us paraffin and our supply was fast dwindling. Towards the end of February we were down to the last pints so started cooking on the beach and writing by candlelight. I was proud of my chocolate pudding baked in a biscuit tin over a fire. And putting dead coral to preheat in the same tin produced bread more successfully than the oven.

We slightly drowned our sorrow over Niko's absence with the fresh food. David Snow had brought oranges, lemons, grapefruit and our first ever squash. He also brought copies of the *Guardian Weekly* and *New Scientist*; we greedily enjoyed catching up on ancient news. We appreciated Radio Belize but it dealt merely in basic headlines for world news and we felt totally out of touch.

A few weeks later the paraffin arrived. As on the Bass, relief days were cause for huge celebration. So many delights in a single package. For starters, our saviours were great entertainers and welcomed us aboard for stimulating conversation, delicious cooking and drinkable alcohol. Our pure alcohol was strictly for preheating our paraffin-based equipment, though the crew of one visiting boat, the *Kismet*, had a daily vote on whether they would eat cold food and drink theirs. I was even more inept at descending into a small boat after one of those evenings. For his second visit David brought a very creative selection of both tinned and bottled food: jam, cucumber pickle, tinned bread, maple syrup and a bottle of rum. Automatically into parsimony, we enjoyed punch each evening for several days and I made rum butter! It's hard to imagine in these overfed times what great pleasure such simple yet novel items contributed to our days.

A few weeks later we enjoyed the best relief ever and ate like kings for some time. As well as the vegetables we had ordered from the shop, three families sent us gifts: 18 eggs, a large box of oranges, lemons, apples, papayas, avocados, two enormous cabbages, beetroot, spring onions, carrots, cucumber and peppers. The Angermeyers grew a lot of their food on a farm up in the fertile highlands of Santa Cruz and were incredibly generous to us. I made marmalade, hotly; naked, standing well back from the splutters, and with all tent flaps open. Salad and fresh fruit cheered us inordinately.

And then, of course, it was back to iron rations as usual. We craved anything to add variety to our diet, including eating the dove that killed itself in the fridge fumes; a minute but tasty morsel!

Although we felt as though we had been on Tower for ever, packing to move to our next island (Hood) came round quite quickly. It proved logistically taxing as we had gone with minimal possessions, most of which we needed till the very last minute. It is telling that many of my thoughts on leaving were about food. I wrote with some feeling: 'Looking forward to fresh food on Santa Cruz. I'm thoroughly sick of this lot.'

7

CAMP FOLLOWERS

BRYAN AND JUNE

Apart from the fur seals and sea lions we were the only mammals on Tower. We felt very much a part of the wildlife and, almost as soon as we arrived, the camp followers moved in. Galapagos mockingbirds, Galapagos doves and Darwin's finches formed an endlessly amusing trio. Poppet, our finch, rarely interfered with either dove or mockingbird, though it was usually master of both. No hunt with binoculars was needed for the doves; they were in our tent as soon as we had put it up. Mockingbirds quickly followed. However, Poppet delighted us most and, unlike the other two, had no downside.

There are three species of Darwin's finch on Tower – the large ground finch, Genovesa ground finch and Genovesa cactus finch. The famous feature of these finches is that starting from common stock they have evolved into 17 distinct species each with their own special features, such as size, shape and strength of beak, and body proportions, which have eventually fitted their owners particularly well for certain diets. The largest, for example, like Poppet and our hawfinch, can crack seeds which other species cannot; and there are two species of insect-eating warbler finch, each with a slender beak. Perhaps most remarkable of all, the woodpecker finch and the mangrove finch have evolved the ability to use twigs or cactus spines as tools, holding them in their bill to probe insects out of cracks. They then drop the instrument and pick up the grub or insect. According to Irenäus Eibl-Eibesfeldt, who studied the woodpecker finch both in the Galapagos and in captivity, they will even choose and shape twigs to their requirements by breaking off a piece and trimming it.

Since the publication of David Lack's famous book *Darwin's Finches*, it has been believed that on islands where the 'specialists' occur the more generalised species nearest to them in bill size and diet would tend to be absent. In competition for food they would be that little bit less successful. This exclusion by competition certainly seemed to work on Tower. There were no finches with a medium-sized bill, but instead two species with very large bills and one with a very small one, specialising in different foods.

These finches make domed nests of fibres, roots and twigs, usually in a cactus or bush. The male seems to do most of the feeding of the young after they have fledged, but perhaps the brood splits up, the female taking half into a different area. The young look rather curious with a strikingly pale, flesh-coloured lower mandible, extremely conspicuous when they beg for food. It may act as a marker, particularly in the rather gloomy places, beneath shrubs and cacti, where these birds feed. The adult pops morsels into the fledgling's mouth with a very deft and pretty action, first making a quick forward bob as though bringing the fragment of food up from its crop.

Poppet, who became delightfully confiding, was a two-year-old male, no bigger than a sparrow but with a huge thick beak, a stumpy little black body and black feet. He wore yellow and blue rings fitted by a previous visiting ornithologist so we knew him for certain.

Poppet learnt amazingly quickly. His best effort, because the most successful, involved gently pecking one of our fingers for a reward. We made sure always to provide the reward. Almonds were his passion, but who would take a sack of almonds to a desert island, so they were rationed, which meant keeping our fingers out of his wily way. I wish I had a film of him leaping up and down on the typewriter as I worked.

Often Poppet visited the tent seven or eight times in a day, beginning around dawn. We'd be still in bed, so he had to squeeze in past one of the socks stuffed into every tent peg gap to keep out giant centipedes. But once inside his jaunty hop would take him bouncing up my body looking for fingers. Unable to reach fingers in a sleeping bag he tried a tentative tweak of a nose. Recognising the spirit of his endeavour I would roll out of bed for an almond. One morning, when heat had driven me out of my sleeping bag, I woke Bryan with my startled yell when the finch bit my sleeping toe; he quickly learnt that toes produced nothing.

Once Poppet realised he'd had his ration, he would fly to the open-sided store cupboard, select a length of spaghetti – his second-favourite food – and methodically work his way down, breaking off small pieces. With his huge beak, he disdained soft bread, enjoying only food that cracked, like hard crusts, flapjack and occasionally thin biscuits or pastry. Prune stones quickly yielded. But all the while he looked for a finger so he could claim more pieces of almond. When thirsty he flew to the water container and pecked it. He would take water only when standing on a spoon, ignoring a dish.

As soon as he had finished he flew swiftly out of the tent and away to a big cactus on the cliff, where he immediately gave his simple though rather attractive territorial song: *too-lu, too-lu*. By coming to our tent he was trespassing in the territory of a coal-black adult male and his behaviour clearly showed his fear.

When we returned to Tower to check our study groups four months after leaving it, a tiny black figure flew down to meet us on the beach, crest feathers raised in obvious excitement. And there were the colour rings to prove that it was our almond-loving friend, delighted to have us back. To our great relief, Station researcher Miguel Castro had a piece of chocolate to reward the friendly little finch – but alas no almonds.

Galapagos doves look quite cuddly, perhaps because of their comforting plumpness. About eight inches long, they are an attractive deep reddish-brown, smartly flecked with cream on their backs, with startling blue rings around the eyes that give them a foolish, staring expression. Charmed by the doves at first, especially by their confiding manner, we quickly sickened; they were so clumsy and unbearably dim. Several of them constantly rummaged in and around our tents, knocking things over. In the store tent they proved a particular menace, and I tried to avoid needing anything from in there. Ten or more would rocket into our faces whenever we entered, creating such a draught that they put out the paraffin fridge.

One day, with boobies to ring some distance from home, we packed a picnic and battened down the hatches. Knowing the doves' passion for our store tent we paid special attention to fully closing its zip and weighed down every edge of canvas. Returning wearily, needing just a huge glass of juice and a loll in the lagoon, we could smell the paraffin fumes from some way off. A mist of fine black flecks prevented us seeing across the tent. Then, as it cleared, we made out a pudgy, rusty shape on the floor. Another reverse Houdini, but this one died. We couldn't fathom how it got in, but its panicky flight around the tent would have made the fridge flame flare yet again. The flaring paraffin produced an oily black soot and fumes which had eventually asphyxiated the dove.

The doves had an amusing habit of sun- and rain-bathing. A sudden shower immediately stimulated all the doves to drop whatever they were doing and keel over, raising one wing vertically so that it caught the rain. The dove's most improbable piece of behaviour, however, was certainly its courtship twist. As human dances became steadily more ludicrous and primitive (or is it merely more realistic?), descending from the sophisticated Viennese waltz beneath the chandeliers of the archducal ballroom to the functional sixties twist in any old place, it was some comfort to see doves making even bigger fools of themselves. Two courting doves seize hold of each other's beak, puff out their chests and violently twist each other's head round as though cranking a car. Their astonished round eyes, brightly encircled with cerulean blue, stare foolishly, and the dance terminates, perhaps to avoid dislocation of their necks, with the partners facing each other breathlessly, before the male returns to his more dove-like flicking and bowing, and the female to her apparently uninterested, but really displacement, feeding.

Even though, breeding aside, Galapagos doves are normally a solitary species, we once had 23 feeding together outside the tent. One could watch individuals take off and fly into the far distance, and we reckoned that we drew these particular camp followers from at least two miles away. They pottered around, pecking industriously in the dove way. At first they tried to dash larger pieces of food into fragments, but eventually acquired the habit of gulping pieces as large as they could swallow, frantically scratching their craw when the food stuck.

Fights over food were common, even when it was littered everywhere around them. One dove would leave its own piece and rush over to challenge another eating exactly the same stuff. Rivals faced each other with head and body tilted forwards whilst making backward movements with the feet – a clear indication of their opposing impulses to attack and flee. All the while they pecked at the ground. This was 'displacement feeding', one of the 'irrelevant' acts often performed by an animal stimulated by conflicting drives. We humans may scratch our head or pull the lobe of an ear when similarly disturbed. Often, the dove's displacement feeding became real feeding, probably because they had put themselves into the right position for feeding, performed the right preliminary actions and then, having spotted a fragment of food, willy-nilly completed the chain of actions and fed properly.

Posturing frequently led to actual attack. Each bird tried to get above its rival and pecked furiously at its crown, plucking out feathers galore. The bird underneath tried to fend off blows by raising a wing and the whole struggle involved tremendous fluttering and scuffling. Soon we had a strange collection of doves, some lacking crown feathers and others with their remaining ones congealed into two or three spiky tufts like a Mohawk American Indian. These tufts fascinated other doves, which pecked away at them until they provoked another fight. Mated pairs tended to forage together and the male would then allow the female to take food from beneath his nose.

Mockingbirds and Galapagos doves were sworn foes on Tower, at least around our camp. Mockers frequently scattered a bunch of feeding doves, dashing up with a fine flourish. However, the attack was mainly bluff, and whenever a dove assumed its high intensity threat posture, fluffed into a huge ball, tail fanned, wings drooped or raised vertically and head lowered, the mocker ran away, though it always gave the impression that it had suddenly remembered something more important and couldn't spare the time to thrash the dove.

The mockingbirds were endlessly amusing. They are thin and agile, like a spare sandy-coloured blackbird, with a long, slightly down-curved bill which they use for a great variety of purposes, and long legs that carry them along at an astonishing speed. The highly cursorial mocker frequently runs rather than flies and covers great stretches at a smart sprint using wings as balancers, like a miniature ostrich. In fact the legs (and beak) of Galapagos mockingbirds are longer than those of sister species resident on the South American mainland, though this is often the case with island representatives of a species and need have no connection with increased running habits.

On Tower, the mockingbirds were of a subspecies of the Galapagos mockingbird that is known solely from that island (nowadays known informally as the Genovesa mockingbird). They were relatively polite, but the mockingbirds that are unique to Hood (a different species, the Española mockingbird), have survived in the extremely harsh environment of this low-lying Galapagos island not by specialisation but by adaptability and incredible sharpness. Any strange object – a shoelace on your foot or anything with a hole in it – is quickly noticed and investigated. Their beaks are ideal for poking into holes and crevices, from which they extract lurking insects. The hole in the top of our can of cooking oil fascinated them and they eagerly queued up to poke their bills into it even though they could never reach the oil; moreover, the same individuals came back day after day to make the same futile attempt before hopping down and running briskly away with a knowing air. Holes and cracks usually mean a point of entry, say into a seabird egg which may be too hard for them to crack. Black spots painted on shells provoked intense attempts to get inside.

We were astonished by the things that mockingbirds would eat and drink. Birds are relatively economical in their water requirements, saving a considerable amount by excreting uric acid instead of dilute urine. Mockers are further adapted for life in arid regions but despite this the Galapagos environment eventually severely taxed their physiological endurance such that they avidly sought all possible forms of liquid.

They gathered enthusiastically around the stinking contents of ancient albatross eggs, probably more than a year old, which we broke open for them and even ate sea lion faeces. They were passionately fond of fruit; swallowed lumps of beetroot; drank vinegar as though it were nectar; and would sell their souls for fat. If we averted our eyes from, much less turned our backs on, the breakfast table, they jumped up and gobbled the butter, laying their slim beaks sideways to get bigger mouthfuls. Often a tug at the hand alerted us to the 40 thieves stealing butter from our bread. This applied only to the mockingbirds on Hood which had evidently acquired a strong taste for fat, perhaps from feeding so much on spilt albatross oil.

They used to gather around an adult albatross feeding its chick and scrape up any oil that fell (albatrosses feed their young by squirting an oily substance direct from their stomach into the chick's mouth). They flocked like bluebottles to the goat meat which we hung from the veranda pole. By pivoting from the hip joint and bracing their neck muscles they dealt hammer blows and managed to tear sizeable fragments from the carcass.

In the most blatant case of opportunism we observed, a mockingbird on Hood noticed a spot of blood on the cloaca of a blue-footed booby, probably pierced whilst excreting an undigested fish bone. The mocker ran beneath the booby's tail and cheekily pecked at the blood on the cloaca rim until it actually lacerated the tissue and pulled off fragments. The booby just stood there, shifting uneasily, wincing with every poke from the mocker and dropping spots of blood on to the excreta-whitened boulders, but never looking down to see what was the matter. This was no isolated incident: the Española mockingbird (but not species on other islands) was subsequently found to habitually 'drink' seabird blood along with scraps of flesh.

The passerine inhabitants of the arid Galapagos islands all eagerly seek liquid, but pride of place must surely go to the Hood mockers which drank a warm and concentrated solution of Dettol; they shook their heads violently after every sip but still returned for more. Birds that will drink warm Dettol must indeed be short of water; their internal parasites must have received a nasty shock.

One prying individual fell head first into a narrow jar of beetroot vinegar, but by bending itself into a U just about managed to get its head out. We rescued a shivering and bedraggled scrap of bird, all skin and bone, which June warmed next to her body. It didn't seem very happy so we put it in the oven; that dried it out nicely and it became a special favourite, tamer than any of the others. It was easy to recognise since its pink feathers long remained stuck together, exposing tracts of pink skin, and it was incapable of flight for some weeks.

On Hood the mockingbirds used to come from at least a mile away, probably much farther, and 30 or 40 pestered us from dawn till dusk. One or two bold individuals, which we could recognise, behaved exactly like mischievous children. When we tried to keep them out of the tent by blocking every conceivable entry, they would squirm and scuffle violently to squeeze through any crack, unshakably convinced that they were missing something. However quiet things seemed, a few moments' inattention inevitably brought trouble from a slyly entered mocker. Their concerted predations, particularly when June was baking, drove a normally placid female into a state of frenzy. Only the bright-eyed mockers dared defy her shouts and gesticulations and, having knocked over the fermenting yeast and scuffled devastatingly through the bowl of flour, finish off by excreting into everything before taking to their heels.

Galapagos mockingbirds show a great deal of variation between islands – as Charles Darwin observed, helping inform his theory of evolution. They are weak fliers and even a few miles of sea forms an effective barrier. The mockers of each island, thus effectively isolated, have become distinct in size, proportions and, probably, in many behaviour traits also. The Tower mockingbirds are the smallest and the Hood ones the largest; we were astonished to see the difference in size between birds from these two islands.

All mockers show intriguing social behaviour. They often feed in groups, ranging over at least a mile or two in a collective territory. At the boundaries group members sometimes combine in display against other groups. They stretch themselves upright then violently flick their drooping wings and jerk their long tails, which sometimes stick up vertically. There is much running to and fro, and harsh, loud calling. Occasionally two birds clash, rolling on their sides and thrusting at the opponent with straightened legs, using their strong feet to grapple, while others run around excitedly.

Within each group there is a peck order similar to that in domestic hens, in which one or two dominant individuals are able to displace lower-order birds from food. Inferior birds approached by a dominant member turn their backs to it and raise their tails vertically, cheeping harshly and repeatedly – appeasement behaviour which is clearly effective in protecting them from attack. If they don't face away they often receive a sharp peck on the head. It greatly amused us to see the way in which a mockingbird would run up from behind, bend round and peer earnestly into the face of another to recognise it before attacking or submitting as appropriate. They have rather striking facial patterns with slight individual differences, and obviously recognise each other by these marks. From behind they occasionally and understandably made a mistake and an inferior bird pecked its superior, who turned, stood stock-still for an instant as though unable to believe its eyes and then tore after the fleeing subordinate which by this time had realised its error and wisely taken to its heels. Once a dominant bird displaced others from food by actually lifting them aside by the scruff of the neck like so many twigs, instead of pecking them in the usual way. It was, in fact, treating them like obstructing inanimate litter and using the appropriate behaviour pattern.

The value of peck orders seems perhaps clearer in mockingbirds than in many species. They live in an extremely harsh habitat; they are small, thin and ferociously active, which means they could not long survive starvation. Much of their food is in the nature of windfalls – anything edible, such as a deserted egg, a dead booby chick, spilt fish or oil. One can easily see the advantages both of the collective territory and the peck order. First, the territory is thoroughly scoured by its highly active group. One bird spots food and begins eating; others come running to investigate and this, in turn, attracts yet others. We could draw mockingbirds to any spot simply by attracting one or two; the others ran madly to follow them, as farmyard hens run to join their feeding fellows or gannets stream to join a fishing flock. Then if there is plenty all the mockers would get some; if not the dominant birds get it all by exercising their peck-order priority. This system obviously means that the stronger birds are constantly in a favourable position, able to benefit from the finds of the weaker members of their group as well as from their own efforts. If anybody dies it is the most expendable members of the community. There is clearly no suggestion of altruism here; the inferior birds are not sacrificing their own interests for the good of the species but are forced to give way to the stronger members.

Conversely there is no kind and considerate treatment from the superior birds. Some anecdotes of birds and other animals helping the unrelated underdog are hard to reconcile with this kind of observation. Yet no two species are organised exactly alike and whilst ailing, wounded or deformed individuals are in some species the butt of persecution, there may be others in which the behaviour patterns associated with parental care are extended to adults that somehow provide the right stimulus. However, it is easy to mistake the meaning of a bird's action and most of us have to contend with a strong tendency to anthropomorphise.

Despite the arid surroundings the mockingbird populations of Tower and Hood were extremely high. Even in the interior we estimated at least a pair for every two acres, which for Tower would give a population of about 1,600 pairs; the large number of insects probably form an important part of their diet. The coastal birds frequently foraged in the littoral zone. They sang mainly in the morning and evening and the Tower mockers sang far more sweetly than those on Hood, superior in tone and phraseology.

Mockingbirds' breeding success must be extremely low in some years. We did not see a single fledgling on Tower; the few nests we found all failed. On Hood, during the whole of our stay, we found only old nests and no young being fed out of the nest. Probably they have no regular breeding season and may miss unfavourable years altogether.

Once we had met the Española mockingbird we realised just how polite the Genovesa mockingbird had been. On Tower we coexisted happily and enjoyed their antics. On Hood we felt invaded, overwhelmed. Or maybe it was June who felt bullied and became so exasperated, sometimes to the point of tears; they were not much interested in Bryan's activities which rarely involved food. By the time we reached Hood our food supplies were dwindling fast. The mockers seemed to believe that what was ours was theirs too. We minded much more sharing our few delicious items with mockingbirds. Tinned bacon had been a huge treat and was rationed accordingly. To have our final piece snatched from the tin by a marauder almost brought tears. We had to laugh as it ran off; a slice of bacon on legs, haring across the lava.

Imagine a quiet morning. For once we have enjoyed breakfast in peace; maybe the mockingbirds are far away quarrelling over a rotten egg. There is little breeze, so we can hear lazy waves and the occasional roar of a patrolling bull sea lion. If we sniff intently we can catch the smell of sea lion dung. They were sleeping round the tent again last night, but after some weeks we are no longer continuously aware of the noxious, fishy stink. The tropical sun has not yet risen fully and the temperature is pleasant though we can sense the coming heat. We have just eaten our last treat – a piece of flapjack to make up for what have become rather miserable breakfasts. So maybe it's a good time to make pastry. The veranda will shade me. I light the paraffin oven and assemble ingredients. After measuring out two tablespoons of our precious water, I begin. No sooner have I got both hands covered in flour and fat than the first exploratory mocker arrives, head cocked inquiringly to one side. After a quiet call it leaps on to the bowl. I shout and it pauses. But others are already on their way, running towards me. From the corner of my eye I notice three drinking thirstily from my meagre pastry water. Others are piling on to the bowl. A vision of midges, but blackbird size, beside Loch Lomond almost makes me giggle. But this is serious and by now I'm leaping up and down, yelling and with my fatty, floury hands windmilling. In the frenzied cloud of flour stirred by myriad wings, with the joy of fat and with safety in numbers the mockingbirds barely notice. I sweep them off the bowl and rush inside to find a towel to clean my hands and cover the pastry. I close the tent flap. The boldest have followed me. More are already squeezing through gaps by the tent pegs. I empty the laundry bag and start stuffing holes. The birds inside are causing mayhem. I open the flap a little and start herding them out. Victory? No. Even now there's a head and shoulders wriggling through an inadequately blocked-off space.

The sun has fully risen and the oven has reached optimal pastry temperature. I was naked already. Sweat is mingling with tears; this pastry will be heavy.

8

GULLS

BRYAN

On Tower, we lived with two extremely rare gulls on our doorstep. They were a great contrast in character. The dusky or lava gull was a typical member of the family in its alert, scavenging, even predatory ways, whilst the highly specialised swallow-tailed or fork-tailed gull showed not the remotest interest in scavenging; it fed nocturnally, often on squid, judging from its regurgitations.

Adult lava gulls are lovely birds, about as big as a black-headed gull, sooty black beneath, grey above with a brilliant white spot behind the eye. The bill, legs and feet are black and the gape is a beautiful flame colour. Their sooty plumage and lurid mouths are eminently appropriate to birds of the black lava, spewed from fiery volcanoes. A number of unrelated birds in the Galapagos have brightly coloured areas around their eyes; the doves have bright blue rings; swallow-tails bright red ones; female great frigates red ones; magnificent frigates blue ones; and some of the boobies have brightly coloured skin on the face. It is very likely that brightly coloured face parts and gapes are often part of the bird's equipment for display and in combination with movements and postures help to make a conspicuous signal. They are not acquired solely in the breeding season.

Young lava gulls are duller and rustier than adults, with brown edges to their feathers and no white spot. They are practically invisible on the dark lava. Black colour may protect the little ground finches, since these are hunted by owls and hawks, but the hawks are themselves black and nobody preys on them. Their colour is probably adaptive in other ways, perhaps connected with the equatorial position of their native islands. Birds and animals in general tend to become smaller and darker towards the Equator, and their beaks, legs, tails, ears, etc tend to become shorter too. Or it may be that their black colour, by making them hard to see against the lava, saves them from at least some persecution by frigates.

Like the mockingbirds, lava gulls were insatiably curious; they also possessed greater lifting power and several movable articles such as socks, brushes, pan scrubbers, string, spoons and cups, mysteriously disappeared. Any unusual activity drew a small crowd of lava gulls; they watched critically as June waded into the lagoon with the week's wash, and ran up with interest when I cleaned a fish. They had an endearing habit of perching on the stem of our rowing boat as we crossed the bay, which swallow-tails would never do, bending low to give the aggressive yodelling 'long call' if another gull flew towards them. Despite their scavenging habits, they were third-rate bolters. A herring gull would have bolted anything within reach before a lava gull could have moved. Eric Parker (in *Oddities of Natural History*, published in 1943) says of a herring gull: 'When the bird was quite small in the down, it one day seized from my hand an entire mutton-chop bone and bolted it before I had time to take it away. The bone was so large in proportion that it greatly distorted the bird.' The chick looked like an animated chop bone.

Lava gulls were rather fastidious and, for gulls, dainty eaters and usually ran down to the sea to wash their food, for the call of the running tide was strong. So was the running tide, and they often lost their morsel in a welter of water and looked rather witless peering round for it. Even when they caught a fish, they seemed to have difficulty dealing with it. One bird snatched a small but lively fish from the sea and ran up the beach with it. He hammered away ineffectually for several minutes, almost lost it three times by washing it when it was still very much alive and eventually after ten minutes and several abortive attempts to swallow it, lost it to a frigate who sailed overhead, saw the fish, swooped, snatched it from beneath the gull's nose and swallowed it competently, finishing off the operation in the usual way by swooping to take a few sips of water in flight. Equally, with crabs and eggs, the lava gull was a bungler. The red crabs that swarm everywhere in the Galapagos are frequently stalked successfully by the yellow-crowned night herons, but the lava gull ran after them too openly and childishly and usually missed. It did a little better with eggs because they couldn't run away, but it cracked them none too expertly and I never saw one drop an egg from the air to break it as herring gulls drop molluscs.

Despite my disparaging remarks, the lava gull continues to exist, though in numbers rather less successfully than most members of the family. In one thing they have done very well; they were until the 1950s, I think, the only gull, perhaps the only seabird, whose nest and eggs had never been discovered. The ivory gull and Ross's gull used to hold that distinction too, but fell before the lava gull, whose solitary nest was difficult to pinpoint in a jumble of cinders and lava in some remote part of an island, usually uninhabited. Also, the lava gull has the distracting habit of making a fuss long before one is anywhere near the nest. They breed on Tower and we once found a young one but never an egg, though several times we drew their full alarm attack.

Lava gulls behave in many ways much like our herring gull, including the well-known 'long call', and the lava gull's alarm call *klee-*

ow was sometimes indistinguishable from the equivalent call in the herring gull. Lava gulls frequently bend their heads down and minutely examine their feet; 'foot looking' behaviour typical of all gulls. The immature birds showed one curious trait that intrigued us. Sometimes they seemed to go mad, jumping into the air and squawking and snatching at invisible objects – perhaps small flies. They reached a pitch of great excitement and frequently stumbled or hopped on one foot.

Somehow the lava gull fits the Galapagos. A settler there said he thought that only escapists or those who could not make their way adequately in the more competitive and high-powered world outside settled in the Galapagos. I believe he was wrong, but maybe the lava gull is a bit low-powered as a gull and ekes out its living in the Galapagos, away from interspecific competition in the most arid parts of the most arid islands. However, to do that is itself no mean feat.

The swallow-tailed gull, endemic to the Galapagos bar a small population on Malpelo, a Pacific island off Colombia, is an integral part of Tower. Its wild alarm calls are often the first greeting as you step ashore on the most outlandish corners of the islands. It is far more colonial in its breeding habits than the lava gull, and adjacent pairs are noisy and tireless in territorial display.

Their most impressive feature is perhaps the huge dark-brown eye surrounded by a scarlet ring and beautifully set off in the black hood of breeding plumage (the hood is lost out of the breeding season). The black beak has a polished grey tip and a large white patch at the base of the upper mandible and a small white spot just where the lower mandible runs into the cheek. Chicks peck at these white patches rather than the grey tip when begging for food. The deep grey mantle, black wing tips with white mirrors, pure white underparts and bright pinky-red feet and legs confer great elegance. The tail is deeply forked and the gull's flight easy and buoyant. Juveniles are strikingly different, with a dark spot around the eye, which consequently appears much enlarged, and a dark diagonal bar stretching across the wings, giving them a distinctive appearance in flight.

Swallow-tails are at home on sand, shingle, rough lava and cliff ledges, though cliffs may be their most typical nesting habitat and perhaps the one in which they breed most successfully. Certainly, the breeding success of thirty-odd pairs around our camp was extremely low; between December 1963 and July 1964, only one juvenile fledged. Like many Galapagos seabirds, it breeds throughout much of the year.

The early stages of the breeding cycle are the most rewarding to follow, for then the gulls are busy establishing their territories and forming pairs. The hours around dawn and before dusk are full of activity and noisy with the thin, aggressive *scree-ee* calls of contiguous pairs. Swallow-tails defend a defined territory. Owners will tolerate neighbours at very close quarters so long as they are on the right side of the boundary but may fly to drive away a more distant bird if it trespasses. As with most gulls, fights are relatively infrequent and inflict no damage. However, the fighting method is interesting. As two males clashed near the top of a small cliff, I clearly saw one bird grip the other's bill and, with a twisting movement, force him off the edge.

After an aggressive encounter, swallow-tails often 'display flight' above their territory, flying buoyantly with slow, floating butterfly wing beats. When swallow-tails land, they shuffle their wings in typical gull manner and utter the faint *scree* and a snore-cum-rattle note, difficult to transcribe. The voice of the swallow-tail is one of its most curious features; it has a bizarre un-gull-like vocabulary, snoring, rattling, screaming and whistling; the swallow-tail is a much less 'typical' gull. The composite effect of a thorough-going swallow-tail medley is quite indescribable.

Common aggressive behaviour against a nearby rival involves a most menacing-looking posture, accompanied by a snoring note. After displacing an opponent, swallow-tails often remain momentarily with their beautiful wings held, tern-like, aloft – a most graceful posture. 'Choking', a signal of site-ownership, and 'foot-looking', which occur in other gulls, then follow. Swallow-tails spend a lot of time nest-building, which helps to strengthen their pair bond. Carrying additions to their neat patch of small pebbles, bones and oddments, they run to the nest in the long-necked position, beak pointing down, calling *kerr-er* or sometimes it sounds more like a high-pitched *ss-coya, ss-coya*.

Courtship feeding in birds is always appealing to watch. The male swallow-tail regurgitates his offering actually on one of the nest sites (he may have two or three within the territory) or walks to the site with the food held in his bill. Often he precedes the feeding by courtship or even copulation away from the site and then 'leads' the female to the site before lowering his head and with choking movements and widely parted mandibles, regurgitating the fish or squid. The female, perhaps recognising some slight intention movements of regurgitation, or feeling hungry enough to beg for food, sometimes upward nods and pecks repeatedly at the base of the male's bill. She does this from the side and in the submissive, hunched posture of the young chick. The food is deposited on the ground for the female to pick up. After feeding, the male may lead the female up to 30 yards away from the feeding spot. This probably reflects the male's initial fluidity with respect to the choice of nest site. Some males even made their pebble-lined scrapes in spots which were submerged twice daily by the tides, though we never found an egg on such a site.

A pair of swallow-tailed gulls were unfortunate enough to hatch their egg just where we pitched our tent on Tower. Despite our terrifying intrusion, they continued to guard the egg during the two days it took the chick to emerge (later we found that incubation takes about 35 days). As soon as it was dry, fluffy and steady on its feet, the adults led it several yards away from the tent, to the edge of the lagoon, where there was unhappily no cover. That night we were startled by a scalp-tingling laugh, a weird, old man's cackle that came from the darkness just outside the tent. The voice belonged to the Galapagos short-eared owl, the only predator known on Tower, and I'm afraid it boded ill for the swallow-tail chick. It disappeared and I suspect it formed the penultimate link in a food chain ending in the owl. It was the first of several chicks to vanish.

The fluffy grey chicks, marked with black, were guarded constantly for several days after hatching, and then they sheltered in a crevice or beneath an overhang. The one surviving juvenile near our camp used to while away the daylight hours in the depths of a shady recess containing the channel through which seawater flowed into our lagoon. Beneath it the gaudy orange-bellied fishlets guarded their territories; above, boobies squawked and screeched in the shrubs and juvenile frigates caterwauled in frenzied supplication each time the adults dropped from the hot sky on buoyant black wings. They were all part of the chick's Galapagos world and it ignored them, interested only in preening and the next squid, fresh from the crop of its elegant parent.

9

THE GREAT FRIGATEBIRD

BRYAN (MOSTLY)

The five closely related species of frigatebirds all occur in tropical and subtropical regions. The great frigatebird is the one found mainly in the Galapagos, though magnificent frigatebirds also breed there. 'Frigates' and boobies are now placed in the same order, Suliformes, based on solid genetic data, but aside from that they do not seem to have much in common. Frigates are entirely and superbly specialised for an aerial life. They have an eight-foot wingspan but weigh about a quarter as much as the waved albatross, of similar size, and less than a third as much as a gannet with a wingspan of slightly under six feet. Even the small male blue-footed booby weighs almost as much.

Frigates have almost twice as much wing area as other seabirds of similar bulk. Their huge wings are deeply cambered, and the enormous forked tail, like an earwig's pincers, is a sensitive rudder and stabiliser. Because they are so light and carry such a spread, frigates fly with leisurely, buoyant wing beats suggesting deep reserves of power, or soar and glide effortlessly. They have been recorded flying at a height of 12,000 feet.

Their plumage is not fully waterproof and they rarely settle on water, though they are certainly capable of rising from the surface even in a flat calm. I have seen frigates splash into calm water in an attempt to seize a sinking fish, then rise from the surface. Their tiny, unwebbed feet, with the vestiges of a fringe between the toes, are useless for walking or swimming but extremely flexible and prehensile – and therefore very useful among the twigs and branches in which frigates usually nest; they can perch with two toes forward and two back or three forward and one back with equal ease.

A great frigatebird's beak is about four inches long and deeply hooked, with a sharp tip. With it, and in full flight, they snatch fish from just below the surface, delicately pick up floating scraps, drink, lift twigs from the ground or tear them from the living bush. That beak, and the exquisite nerve and muscle co-ordination with which it is wielded, is everything to the frigate. Other birds may survive with grossly deformed mandibles, but a frigate works to clearances measurable in thousandths of an inch.

Just how fine is the margin of error we appreciated by seeing a frigate swoop at full speed and, without pausing, bend its head and clean the thinnest smear of spilt fish from a rock surface, making a faint click as the bill tip whipped over the rock. Another was seen to pick up a fragment of food from sand so cleanly that its bill tip left no trace. Still more impressive, a frigate will actually take fish that is being passed from booby parent to offspring, or from frigate to offspring for that matter. Just as the youngster inserts its head into the mouth of its parent, the frigate swoops down and in one movement knocks them apart and takes the fish. When a frigate is itself the victim of such an outrage, it calls hoarsely and lunges at the retreating marauder. One would suspect that frigates must have specially modified neck vertebrae or muscles to enable them to withstand the stress imposed by their method of feeding.

However, on the whole frigates live honest lives, occasionally ranging several hundred miles from land in extensive forays for fish, perhaps mainly flying fish and squid, though also jellyfish, plankton, scraps and whatever else they can catch. Nearly every ocean-voyage account mentions frigatebirds up to 1,000 miles from land. But the image of the frigate as an honest fisherman, snapping up the flying fish as they leap to evade their underwater predators, easily fades before that of the piratical and predatory frigate. It is hard to estimate what proportion of their food comes from other birds; under some circumstances it may be substantial, and it might be more than coincidence that they always nest among large numbers of potential victims.

The skies above Tower were never free from frigates, their distinctive silhouettes poised watchfully above, waiting and waiting. From first light to beyond the brief tropical dusk, the air was likely to rend with the harsh, agonised squawks of red-footed boobies, and a glance would reveal a brown form desperately trying to evade the vengeful black shadow – or shadows, for the frigate often hunted in small bands, probably not in co-operation.

How the boobies fled, flat out, but not nearly fast or agile enough to shake off their persecutors! They came flashing over the beach, the booby glancing fearfully behind, and the pursuing frigates, relaxed even in chase, coming up fast with deep muscular strokes. We cheered the booby on, sorry that he might lose his hard-earned catch, but his only chance was to come in low over the ground or pitch headlong into a tree – there was no time to land elegantly. Sometimes he ended in a tangle of legs and wings and had the devil of a job to extricate himself. Maybe crash-landing in trees was too dangerous to become a routine escape tactic; we saw two or three corpses hanging in forks and it was a fact that, in the last resort, boobies usually regurgitated rather than chance it.

A booby hemmed in by several frigates and stubbornly refusing to throw up was seized by the tail or wing tip and capsized. This usually encouraged him to give in and he then began to regurgitate, pointing his bill downwards to aid the process. The frigates snatched eagerly at the fish as soon as the slimy bolus appeared, catching it in the air or following it down to the sea. I think they must have snapped at the booby's beak; some of our marked red-foots came home with pieces chipped out and I cannot imagine how else this could have happened; certainly not by territorial fighting in these cases. We never saw frigates seriously attack a booby, although, in his 1928 book *Birds of the Ocean,* W.B. Alexander says they may break the wing of their victim. However, frigates certainly manhandled them, and the poor booby was usually left, empty and highly agitated, on the comforting bosom of the sea.

Almost all the piracy that went on around Darwin Bay was carried out by adult males. Frigates will chase each other when one of them visibly carries food, but they will not chase other frigates in order to make them regurgitate. Once the loot had been swallowed, the group separated amicably and each went their own way. It appeared that the frigates had initially no way of telling whether their chosen victim was full or empty – they began the chase on a hit-or-miss basis. However, it was also apparent that after a short chase they knew that certain boobies had fish, for they stuck to them and were always rewarded.

We came to suspect that the frigates might detect a difference in the calls of full and empty boobies. We could ourselves hear that certain boobies called in a wheezing, strangled voice that could have been caused by pressure of food on the windpipe. If the frigates could also associate this noise with fish they could use it as a cue. Probably because they often chose an 'empty' bird, a relatively low proportion (12 per cent) of their chases yielded results and even when they did, only one out of the gang got the fish; the others had worked for nothing. All in all, it did not seem a particularly easy way to live, but no doubt it was a useful supplementary source of food. Also, one should remember that sustained flight needs very little energy expenditure for a frigate. They rarely bothered with anything other than boobies. The swallow-tailed gulls were too agile for them, despite the frigate's reputed ability to fly down any other seabird, and they didn't molest the tropicbirds much.

Frigates seemed to chase indiscriminately. Galapagos shearwaters nested on the northeast coast of Tower, and several times we saw frigates fly down a newly fledged juvenile and repeatedly pick it from the sea and drop it until the shearwater was dead. These victims were never swallowed, probably because they were too large. But even a warbler flying from bush to bush sometimes released chasing behaviour in frigates – a ludicrous sight – and they would swoop on to a ball tossed high into the air. This instantaneous reaction to a falling object must be vital to a species whose existence depends on catching flying fish or dropped food.

The frigate's feeding methods are clearly highly specialised and not likely to be acquired in a day. In December 1963 there were scores of free-flying juvenile frigates on Tower, probably from eggs laid in March of that year; they were still being regularly fed by their parents. In July 1964 some of those same juveniles were still receiving food from their parents. This astonishingly long post-fledging feeding period – six months or perhaps considerably more – means that a complete breeding cycle takes considerably more than a year, since incubation requires 55 days, rearing young to the free-flying stage takes about six months, and then about a month for the period of display and nest-building prior to egg laying. Altogether 15 to 18 months are probably required for the complete cycle.

On 5 January, eight days after we arrived on Tower, the first frigate display enlivened the scene; the fashion spread almost overnight and by February, displaying males, ardently vying for females, dominated the island. Even though I filmed the whole performance so could check the details, it nevertheless seems unreal – because it is so bizarre. The display is built around the male frigate's enormous scarlet throat sac or gular pouch, just as the peacock's centres around its tail.

No real bird should possess a sac like the frigate's. It is creative licence gone mad. Outside the nuptial period, the bird's black plumage is relieved only by its glossy, elongated scapular feathers, which form a fancy cape, and the shrivelled pink strip of gular skin running down on to the throat. But for three or four weeks at the beginning of each breeding season this innocuous pink strip turns scarlet and can be grossly distended, blown up like a balloon, until the frigate fades into insignificance behind the glory of his fantastic pouch. Naturally he is not saddled, or chinned, with this ornament for longer than he chooses; he can blow it up and deflate it at will. The pouch is connected to the bird's air-sac system, and inflation, which takes 20–30 minutes, is accomplished without visible effort. The walls of the sac are covered with a network of conspicuous capillaries and when fully extended it feels soft and warm to the touch; a useless fact which we felt compelled to discover, and he, so impeded, powerless to prevent!

The scarlet sac is couched between the frigate's huge black wings, which in display are fully spread. In this position the male stations himself on a perch and waits, bill resting on top of his sac or pointing upwards as he scans the sky. He is looking for a female and as soon as one flies over, even at a height of 100 feet or so, he unleashes his full display. The naturalist William Beebe, writing in 1924, eloquently describes the display thus:

'Then another emotion obsessed him; he bent his head back until it sank between his shoulders, the red balloon projecting straight upward, and the long angular wings spread flat over the surrounding bushes. The entire body rolled from side to side, as if in agony, while the apparently dying bird gave vent to a remarkably sweet series of notes, as liquid as the distant cry of a loon, as resonant as that of an owl.'

Although the males of different frigate species are in some cases extremely similar, the females all have distinctive patterns of black belly and white breast. Furthermore, the juveniles have completely different patterns from the females, being dark on the throat and upper breast and white on the belly. A female magnificent frigate flying over a group of great frigate males will not elicit their display, but let a female great frigate appear and they respond immediately.

Swivelling on his perch so that he is oriented towards her, the male turns the undersides of his great wings upwards and trembles them violently, making their silvery surfaces flash in the brilliant sunlight. He throws back his head and turns it from side to side, revealing the full size of his sac, and utters a high, falsetto warble. Sac, wings or warble; any single one would draw attention; in combination they must hit the female like flak. A displaying male attracts others, so nuclei of a score or more flower exotically on the bright green shrub or among the sun-silvered branches of the *palo santo* trees. When they all throw back their heads, tremble their wings and warble in concert the effect is best left to the imagination. The whole display is one of the most spectacular sights of the animal kingdom.

The female descends, attracted by this display, and sends the males into a frenzy of warbling and head waving, often interspersed with a fine-drawn rattle exactly like a fisherman's reel. All their attention is concentrated on the female and even though they may cluster so closely that they are in actual contact, they do not jab or threaten each other. They are in strict competition, but in this instance, it is purely sexual and not hostile; they are not on territories that they will defend. The female chooses one of the males, though it is impossible to say what guides her choice. One may see her descend as though to land near one displaying male, then rise again and fly off to some other part of the colony. Or she may actually land and perch opposite the male, almost literally embraced by his outspread wings. The successful male keeps his wings out – indeed it is such an effort to furl them that he may sit for hours like that – and continues waving his head from side to side and warbling, but he also frequently utters the fine rattle. At this stage he has no nest, for the simple reasons that he may move his display site elsewhere if another nucleus springs up and he has been unsuccessful, and that no nest material would survive more than a few minutes if left unguarded as he has not even a territory at this stage.

The female seems mesmerised by the male's display and stands opposite, looking exceedingly vacant. Eventually she too begins to waggle her head and call in a hoarse counterpart of the male's falsetto. So the pair stand, reaching down to the twigs, passing their heads over and around the other's and calling intermittently for hours. If this happens, the female has attached herself to this male and the initial part of pair formation is over. But she may stand for a few minutes, stolid and unmoved, then open her great wings and beat away, rejecting the male for at least that occasion.

[June adds] We had a mere six months with Galapagos frigatebirds, whilst they require significantly longer than that to complete one breeding effort. Their breeding strategy differs markedly from most other birds; we had never come across anything like it! Bryan's struggles to make sense of it, in the dark, echo his tendency, which so horrified Niko Tinbergen, to regard the efforts of evolution as sometimes falling short: 'I could design a better gannet'. He reckoned frigates should have a more efficient regime. Nearly 50 years later, however, Professor Dave Anderson of Wake Forest University (USA) shared some helpful comments that clarify or illuminate some of what we observed and what Bryan tentatively concluded.

In the gannet, Bryan noted, the nest is a fixture and the meeting place for the pair each season. In frigates, males that had bred before had only a slight tendency, if any at all, to stick to their previous site. Dave considered this observation 'well-supported by available evidence'. One reason for frigatebirds to forget the old nest site, he said, 'is that it will have fallen apart by other birds stealing twigs and its flimsiness in the first place. Another is that males generally desert their family before the nestling is independent, leaving mom holding the bag. He will try to pair again then, but of course she is otherwise occupied. Frigatebirds usually change mates, and sites, between nesting attempts.'

Bryan also suggested that male frigatebirds were more likely to be attracted by other displaying males in the general area. Experienced females would probably return to the area in which they had bred, and maybe around the same time. But with males moving to different display groups, the chances of changed pairings were vastly more likely. In response to the peculiar problems of feeding their young, frigates have evolved a regime in which a permanent attachment to site and mate doesn't much happen. Indeed, the effects of the long cycle, complicated by variations in individuals, especially in response to failed breeding, will inevitably make it difficult for pairs to stay together for the next breeding attempt. So the male's habit of displaying anew each year and being ready to accept any female is to be expected.

Apparently the nest site is of little importance until frigates have paired – hence the remarkable tolerance of other males, and even of bodily contact, during display, and the movement from one display site to another. The important thing is to obtain a mate that particular season. Since collective display would almost certainly succeed more than a solo performance, an unsuccessful male leaves a group in which display is waning to join a newer one. Thus frigate nests tended to occur in clusters, where displaying males have performed, but not necessarily where those of previous seasons have been.

Once the pair has really formed, nest-building gets under way. Frigates build flattish platforms of twigs, sometimes substantial but often rather flimsy, depending on the supply. The female does not contribute nest material until the egg has been laid and even then she brings relatively little, though she does most of the actual building from material brought by the male. Before egg-laying, sometimes for as long as ten days, the pair sit together on the nest, the male occasionally leaving to gather nest material and returning for bouts of head-waggling. They make a pleasing picture, the male with his high metallic sheen, the scapulars positively iridescent, and the female matronly respectable in her more sober black, lightened by the white breast. They look gentle though the impression is misleading and due mainly to the effect of the dark eye; they cannot seem gentle to the unfortunate frigate chicks which adults occasionally peck to death.

We found frigatebirds less prone to attack a human intruder than are boobies and we were rarely bitten. Their beaks have no great ripping power, although the hooked tip can impart a respectable cut in a peevish, snapping sort of way. They find it such a trouble to take off that they usually prefer to sit tight so, with a cautious approach, one can feel for an egg beneath the sitting birds without suffering so much as a scratch.

The first egg of 1964 was laid on 1 February and the last around 24 June. Frigates lay a single large white egg and the female usually hands over to the male relatively soon after laying, though even her first incubation spell may last for eight days. Since she usually spends about six to eight days more or less continuously on the nest prior to laying, a first incubation stint of that length means that she probably went at least 14 to 16 days without food or water; 14 to 16 baking days. No wonder she looks listless and drooping at the end. It must be a great relief to lift her wings and float off into the familiar spaciousness of sky and sea after the cramping confines of a small twig platform.

The average incubation stint lasts about ten days and since the egg takes 55 days to hatch this means that male and female take three stints each; only five or six occasions on which nest relief need occur. This may sound an odd kind of emphasis but it became clear that nest relief was a significant hazard to the egg and anything that reduced the number of times the pair changed over thereby reduced the risk. Moreover, frigates probably need a substantial time to find food and the most economical way of ordering things is to take a long spell off duty and feed as heavily as possible. This, in turn, probably enables them to build up reserves of fat upon which they can then exist during the equally long spell of fasting. Even so, frigates lose up to a fifth of their weight with each incubation spell.

With egg-laying fairly under way, it became obvious that something was sadly amiss; nest after nest lost its egg. Soon eggs littered the ground or lodged in bushes, fresh and some broken by mockingbirds. Predation had not caused the problem. Nest relief might have. Frigates, with extremely short legs, have to take off by raising their wings, beating them with mounting vigour, and gradually lifting into the air. This tends to sway the flimsy twigs cradling the shallow nest, and the egg can easily roll out.

A more important cause of egg loss was interference by other frigates. We never discovered why there were such destructive goings-on within our Tower colony in 1964. Of 315 eggs, 205 were lost before hatching and in many cases a third party was clearly involved. We were never lucky enough to see the entire sequence of events. On one visit the nest was intact, with owner incubating peacefully, and sometimes only an hour or two later, the egg was beneath the nest, which was occupied either by a male with full display sac, a female, or a pair – the male with inflated sac.

The 'explanation' was far from obvious. Everything depended on the identity of the bird(s). Unfortunately, the males were neither recognisable by natural features or by rings; their legs were too small to take the size we had, and we short-sightedly omitted to take plastic wing tags. Various measures, more optimistic than informed, failed to mark the birds for long. One was a code of sticking plaster bill-adornments, which made the frigates look like stretcher cases. Another was marking females with dye on their white breasts.

Circumstantial evidence was surely enough to show that in many cases these males were intruders. Ordinarily, males would be at sea feeding, never at the nest between incubation spells. Secondly, who was the female, either alone or with the intruder? Probably females alone at the nest soon after egg loss were the rightful ones, recently returned. Some with intruder males were known, from absence of dye, to be newcomers and the conclusion must be that they had quickly joined the intruder displaying on the site. In two instances, the rightful female was actually sitting nearby. Where egg loss occurred almost at the end of a female incubation spell, the male could have returned and the pair recommenced courtship; pairs will replace a lost egg in one to three weeks, the male regaining his sac and displaying again before the new egg appears.

Allowing for such cases, there was still a great deal of intrusion causing heavy loss of eggs. Small chicks often went the same way, evicted by the intruder who had displaced their parents or, in some cases, evicted after the parents had stopped guarding them. Altogether 45 per cent of the 110 chicks that were lucky enough to hatch were killed before they were six weeks old. The reasons remain obscure; there were both spare males and females, and certainly plenty of nest sites. There seems no good reason why such birds should not have paired up and nested in the usual way without upsetting the affairs of established pairs and drastically reducing the breeding success of the colony.

When invited to comment on these observations, Dave Anderson suggested that: 'Undoubtedly the incubating parent resisted the intruder as long as possible, but the facts suggest that intruders often succeeded. Of course, small solo chicks had little defence against an intruder.

'How can we understand the intruder's motivation?' Dave continued. 'Let's take the male intruder's point of view: nests are a chore to assemble, and it is basically a male's job, and look, here's a complete nest and a female that already likes the site. Taking over the nest would save time and effort. If the territorial behaviour and pair bond is that much weaker than in most seabirds, for reasons given earlier, it follows that territorial invasion and the disruption of the pair bond will be correspondingly easier. Some males may have more ability to intrude successfully, and hold their gains than others do.' Explaining such things is never watertight, of course. 'More detailed behavioural work on individually marked birds with known recent histories,' Dave concluded, 'would do much to clarify this peculiar failure to protect the eggs and chicks better.'

Back to Tower... The frigate chicks lucky enough to hatch were unimaginably ugly. Even a newly hatched booby was beautiful by comparison. Apart from their sickly colour, they had heavy down-bent bills, and enormously thick eyebrow ridges. Apparently reluctantly, they sprouted white down and began to look more tolerable, especially when the precocious scapular and interscapular feathers grew, giving them neat black shoulder capes. We concluded that they protected the young against the weather. However, we went a little further. Perhaps black is specially useful in absorbing heat from the sun and so warming the chicks after the shivery Galapagos nights!

Frigate chicks have a very old-mannish look as they squat, hunched up, on their guano-whitened platform. When approached, they open their livid blue beaks to the widest extent and, mandibles trembling with the stress, produce the most piteous caterwauling, snapping and lunging among the squeals, so forcefully that they almost tumble from the nest.

The measurements that we took suggested that the chicks' weight rose slowly from 61–85g at one week old to 632g at eight weeks. They are fed by regurgitation, inserting their heads into the parent's gullet. Fully feathered juveniles, as big as adults and capable fliers, squat by the hour on their favourite perch, scanning the hot sky for their parents. They cock one eye upwards, rather than looking binocularly as gannets and boobies. Hunger often compels them to intervene when a luckier juvenile is enjoying a feed, but they are soon pecked off. Unlike the adult males, who will try to snatch food being passed from frigate to offspring, the juveniles do not attempt such advanced piracy.

In April and May, the frigate colony looked far from healthy; besides the many nests with eggs lying outside there was a growing number of dead youngsters. Some had fallen from their nests and been unable to climb back, though they had crawled pathetically far along the ground beneath the canopy. Many had fallen prey to the Galapagos short-eared owl. Their parents had stopped guarding them, so at the very tender age of about five weeks, still clothed in down but for their little black capes, the chicks were left to cope with whatever marauder chanced along. The owls chanced along quite regularly, and hardly a night passed without another frigate victim.

Considering that simply by extending the guard stage for another three or four weeks, the frigates could have given their offspring a chance to grow big enough to defend themselves, it seemed crazily inefficient behaviour, explicable only on the supposition that the parents were experiencing such difficulty feeding their young that they could not afford to have one adult as nursemaid any longer; both were needed for hunting. Maybe in better years the guard stage is extended. By November, when we returned to Tower, the juveniles with their characteristic rusty-coloured heads and white bellies were squatting stoically on or near the same perches that had held juveniles when we first arrived in December the previous year. We are sure that the scarcity of the frigate's food supply in the Galapagos has had many effects on its breeding biology.

One of the most famous characteristics of the birds in the Galapagos is that they are so trusting of humans. This young red-footed booby (the same one that perched so confidently on June's hand) was equally happy on her head.

ABOVE We spent seven months living in this tent in idyllic surroundings on Tower (Genovesa) Island. The tropical canvas easily lasted our year. By contrast, we abandoned the store tent, of ordinary canvas, when we moved to Hood. Sunlight, together with bird claws and droppings, had destroyed it.

LEFT We brought this starving red-footed booby chick into our camp in an effort to save it, but we always failed in these efforts.

BELOW A typical wash day – our clothes soon rotted after washing with seawater soap and drying in hot sun.

ABOVE Poppet, a large ground finch, became the favourite 'camp follower' and the only one with a name. He discovered a love for almonds and learned to peck a finger to get his treat. At dawn when we were in our sleeping bags with no fingers available he would gently peck a nose.

BELOW Although desperate for liquid, Poppet deigned to drink only from a spoon.

On her first voyage as research vessel for the Charles Darwin Research Station, the *Beagle II* transported us from Tower to our next island, Hood (Española), and brought welcome company in friends Karl Angermeyer, Julian Fitter and Richard Foster. On board, Karl proved an excellent barber.

TOP Our campsite on Hood was less pleasant than our first one. No lagoon, no Poppet for a gentle awakening, and the only place to set up camp was bang in the middle of sea lion territory; in this photo, the tent is visible above the beach. Rampaging bulls kept us awake most nights, or they snored noisily close to our heads.

BELOW Unlike their fathers, young sea lions like this one were a delight.

ABOVE The Hood species of mockingbird were altogether less polite than their cousins on Tower – they drove us mad with their efforts to steal our food.

BELOW Why wear clothes if you don't need to? By now they were falling apart anyway.

Catching albatrosses in order to weigh, measure and ring them could be hazardous unless you got there first and grabbed them by the bill or the back of the head.

Fortunately we had a few days' warning of the visit of the Duke of Edinburgh. Showing the royal visitor round Hood, having lunch on board the *Britannia*, and meeting the Prince several times when back in Scotland, was a surreal ending to an extraordinary year. Prince Philip's warmly expressed foreword to *Galapagos: Islands of Birds* caught the attention of the tabloid newspaper *The People*.

10

PREDATORS AND SCAVENGERS

BRYAN

It seems rather remarkable that the Galapagos should be as free from predators as they are, and particularly that, except for the endemic Galapagos hawk, nothing resembling the scavengers of Central and South America should be present. The main predator on Tower Island, the Galapagos short-eared owl, has already forced its predatory habits on our attention. Occurring on all continents bar Australia and Antarctica, this owl has one of the most widespread distributions of any bird in the world – but the subspecies present in the Galapagos occurs solely on the archipelago. The owl has small ear tufts, a heart-shaped face and a wild yellow eye, encircled with black. Male and female look alike though the female is larger. Like other island forms, the owl is darker and smaller than mainland ones. Overall it is a warm brown above with variably sized flecks of pale orange, which match the pale orange feathered legs, often held in a rather appealing knock-kneed stance. The underwings are contrastingly pale.

This owl is widespread on the archipelago, occurring on practically all the main islands – a measure of its ability to live on a variety of prey. Unlike the common barn owl, of which an endemic subspecies occurs rather rarely on a small number of Galapagos islands, it is largely a bird-eater. Even on islands such as Santa Cruz and Champion (now Floreana), where there are rats and mice, these formed only about 30 per cent of the prey taken by short-eared owls. The rest were mostly birds, and usually the species most common on the island in question – ground finches on Santa Cruz and petrels on Tower. Scattered over the lava on Tower, in shady recesses, there are many sinister owl 'parlours' containing the remains of scores of petrels, probably the main diet of several pairs. We saw more owls in that area than anywhere else and estimated that if each owl ate one petrel per day at least 3,000 petrels a year would fall prey to them. The short-eared owl will also eat insects, baby marine iguanas and bats, and it is a scavenger, feeding on carcasses, particularly goats.

Like our own subspecies, the Galapagos short-eared owl hunts partly by day, but mainly rests quietly in dark holes or roosts in trees. In 1905 more than 20 were recorded in one day on Tower, preying extensively on giant centipedes, a habit which made them welcome visitors to our camp. The centipedes didn't disappear, but the swallow-tailed gull chicks did. The owl population of Tower was certainly high, which may be linked with the enormous number of petrels, in particular, and with the absence of all other predators that might compete. The owl often tackles birds considerably larger than itself, striking with its talons at the back of the victim's head and neck. One killed a whimbrel (a large shorebird) and was quite unable to carry it away. Many frigate chicks, abandoned too young by parents unable to find sufficient food, fell prey to the owl. Several red-footed booby chicks were taken and even Hood's blue-footed boobies fell victim (though mainly to hawks) when food shortage forced both parents to fish. Even when the chick is almost fully feathered, it is still not completely safe; six of our chicks were killed when about 12 weeks old, in a sudden burst of depredations, though perhaps the hawk was responsible. It seemed surprising that a large booby chick, with a formidable bill, should be unable to defend itself, but probably it was caught unawares.

The Galapagos hawk, a most beautiful raptor of the near-cosmopolitan buzzard family, is very like the common buzzard that will be familiar to European readers. It has for me that subtle quality (perhaps the adult's blackness) that makes it far more of a special Galapagos bird than the owl. Tower surprisingly lacks Galapagos hawks, which are, in fact, absent from several islands to which its powers of flight could easily take it. Hood held two pairs on Punta Suarez. For a while one pair seemed about to build on a lava outcrop near the tent and may have been deterred by us. The pair often swept in together, screaming and calling wildly, shooting their legs forwards to clasp the knobbly black lava with ochre talons. There they shuffled their powerful wings and settled into a hunched posture, black lumps against the sky as though carved out of the lava. We could almost always find a pair near the tip of the point, sitting on top of a bush or rock, watching the sea lions sporting in the shallows.

The Galapagos hawk is not common in the archipelago and had decreased in the 30 years before our arrival. Fast-forward half a century and it is classified as globally threatened – with fewer than 500 adults thought to remain. It takes quite a wide variety of food, and among birds the remains of young penguins, albatrosses, frigates, blue-footed boobies and shearwaters have been found at its nest or seen taken. It is reputed to prey extensively on marine and land iguanas, which, if true, makes its absence from Tower all the more mysterious since there the marine iguanas are a particularly small and convenient size and incredibly numerous. In fact I would suspect that only very small lizards would be available to hawks;

medium or large specimens would be too strong and well-armoured. Darwin recorded that the hawks were important predators of newly hatched tortoises, as well as the small Galapagos landbirds (doves, finches and mockingbirds).

Small birds form a large part of the hawk's diet and the mockers, at least on Hood, have evolved a dramatic response. If a hawk sails over when a group of mockingbirds is feeding, one member, presumably the one that first spots the hawk, gives a short, loud chirp and they all vanish like magic beneath the nearest bush. We saw this several times and never knew the signal to fail in its effect. Recently, it has been discovered that iguanas respond to mockingbird warnings. The hawk is also a scavenger, eating carrion and probably sea lion placentas. Goat entrails that we left on the rocks soon attracted their attention and Miguel Castro found the remains of a kid which he thought had been attacked by the hawks.

The Galapagos hawk lays up to three eggs, usually one or two, in a substantial nest of twigs, the cup lined with finer material and with fresh greenery added, as in our buzzard. One at Punta Suarez in August 1964 was built on top of a commanding crag but trees are also used. The season is ill-defined; although eggs seem to be laid mainly in the first half of the year there are records of eggs for practically every month. The incubating female on Punta Suarez slipped off her egg long before we reached the nest. The only danger lay in the nosy-parker mockers, which arrived within less than a minute and would certainly have taken a stab at the egg but for our intervention. With difficulty we managed to keep them away whilst ourselves retreating far enough to encourage the hawk's return. Despite successful efforts on this occasion the egg later disappeared.

It seems surprising that the scavengers of Central and South America should be absent. Presumably too few individuals of such species ever strayed there to become established. This general lack of predators must have contributed to the tameness of Galapagos species, just as the lack of human persecution on the hawks had until the last 30 years or so made it unnecessary for them to fear man.

Not all scavengers are carnivores, of course. Fortunately for the vegetation there were no goats on Tower and one hopes there never will be, but in 1964 they were everywhere on Hood (and it took until 1978 to eliminate them all). More than on other, mainly larger islands where they have been introduced – Santa Cruz, Barrington (now Santa Fe), San Cristóbal, etc – usually to provide fishermen with a source of meat, goats have played havoc with Hood's vegetation. Their tracks criss-crossed the island and it was almost impossible to examine a square yard of ground without finding a dropping. It is miraculous that they could exist at all in this lava desert. They are phenomenal vegetable scavengers, eating cactus and the thick, fleshy leaves of *Cryptocarpus* shrubs when they can get them, but also turning to a lichen, as dry as tinder, seaweed or tough corrugated bark which, one imagines, contains about as much nourishment as steel shavings. Elsewhere we have seen goats persistently eat cardboard. We often saw them drink seawater and they also licked the stones and twigs wetted by the fine Galapagos mists.

On the whole Hood's goats seemed in good condition, though some were painfully emaciated and obviously diseased. One weary female, doubtless riddled with parasites, collapsed whilst feeding, rolled on her side twitching convulsively, then lay still. Her puzzled little kid ran jerkily away from and back to her, clearly showing its conflicting feelings of fear and attachment. Eventually she climbed shakily to her feet but died within a few days. The kid tried to join a slightly older one, but the nanny gave it short shrift and it never found a foster mother.

Most of the goats were dun brown, variously marked with white, though there were some rich chestnuts, strawberry roans, yellows and handsome blacks. They were genuinely wild and, like deer, the Hood ones went about in tightly knit groups, usually comprising a female with one, two or even three generations of young, probably her own. Sometimes two or three nannies led a congregation of younger beasts. Youngsters often split off or were driven away from the family units and moved about together. The old billies had separate groups, always the same individuals together like old men in their exclusive park-bench groupings, and never showed any hostility to each other.

Galapagos is rightly famed for its reptiles. A recent scene of baby iguanas fleeing land predators is engraved on the memory of anyone who watched, mesmerised, the 'racer-snake sequence' in David Attenborough's *Planet Earth II*. Here the fleeing babies headed for cliffs rather than the sea, to accomplish their escape. Racers are the only snakes in the archipelago, and recent research suggests that ten native species – all endemic – now occur, all having presumably evolved from a single common ancestor. Well, they were thought to be the only snakes until the discovery of an Ecuadorean milk snake, accidentally run over, which could be the portent of another invasive species. Most of the unquestionably native racer species occur on just a few islands, or even just one. We saw the Española racer, found only on Hood and on adjacent islets. Populations of racers have been greatly reduced by introduced mammals.

Another reptile is one of the islands' most efficient marine scavengers: the Galapagos 'dragon' or marine iguana. These lizards have turned back the evolutionary clock and returned to an amphibious life. Thus there are now aquatic as well as arboreal, burrowing, aerial (gliding) and terrestrial lizards. The age of the greatest flowering of reptiles, though, ended more than a hundred million years ago; now there are only the remnants of this order, which sprang from primitive amphibians during the Carboniferous period and dominated the middle or Mesozoic era with such a profusion of fantastic forms. That said, as long as giant tortoises, turtles and iguanas remain in the Galapagos, the reptiles will not lack notable examples. The literature may have been unkind to iguanas – from James Colnett's perception that they had 'the most hideous appearance imaginable' to Darwin's 'hideous-looking creature of a dirty black colour, stupid and sluggish in its movements' – but we found them amusing and by no means unattractive.

Marine iguanas are corpulent lizards with exceedingly tough, sagging hides and immensely powerful five-fingered feet equipped with sharp curved claws capable of clinging to a slab of greasy marble. At least they easily grasp the similarly slippery, wave-scoured, slime-covered surfaces of the intertidal zone, where they feed on glutinous algae, or to the seabed where they browse on sargassum or others of the 300 seaweeds found in the Galapagos. The largest specimens, from Santa Cruz or San Cristóbal, may reach a length of four feet from nose to tail tip and weigh, according to Beebe, 20 pounds. Tower iguanas are a coal-black pygmy race, never more than 18 inches long and usually less. Hood's iguanas are much more colourful, brightly decorated with red and green patches.

It is not known when the now distinctive Galapagos marine iguanas (closely related to the iguanas of mainland South America) reached the islands, but they are obviously strong candidates for an early assisted passage from the mainland, capable of clinging powerfully to flotsam and doubtless able to swim from the continent if lucky enough to escape predators. It would help that they can survive long periods of starvation: a specimen taken by Beebe endured 100 days' complete starvation without weakening. It would similarly help that they could withstand prolonged submersion. A member of Darwin's *HMS Beagle* crew submerged one for an hour, after which it was still lively. A member of the 1964 Galapagos International Scientific Project frightened one that was in mid-water, returning to the surface after feeding on the bottom. It returned to the bottom and stayed there a further half hour.

When the iguanas arrived they would have needed neither land vegetation nor any other forms of land-based life, so they would have stood an excellent chance of survival. At any rate they and their relatives, the land iguanas and tortoises, have successfully filled the large niche occupied elsewhere in the world by mammalian herbivores. That is, they had filled it until man introduced donkeys, goats, pigs and cattle.

On Tower we could rarely entice the marine iguanas into the camp area, though their natural feeding grounds were only a few yards away. Occasionally we came across them as much as a quarter of a mile inland and wondered if they were beginning to appropriate the niche of the Galapagos land iguana, which does not occur on Tower. We also found them many feet up in trees. Mainly, though, the marine iguanas stick to their sea rocks, retreating a few yards beyond high tide to sunbathe and rest on the dry lava. The little black beasts crouch low on the slimy boulders, applying their blunt muzzles closely to the minute growth and cropping to right or left, or laying their heads sideways like a dog with a bone, the better to graze with their sharp tricuspid teeth. Their sturdy limbs move in the dogged crawl typical of the primitive land-walking animal before the further evolution and improved joint mechanism of the pentadactyl limb allowed the mammalian way of locomotion. The waves break and foam around them, scouring the boulders and their industrious black gnomes, but the gnomes are still there when the water sucks back. Like the red crabs in whose company they so often feed, they can resist enormous suction pressures. Unlike the crabs they are none the worse if a heavy wave does dislodge them, for they wear their skeletons under their tough, scaly hides, nicely packed around with resilient tissues that are difficult to break. One often sees a swimming iguana absorb a thunderous hammering on the stormy southwest coast of Hood, hurled violently against the rocks in the foaming water, but unruffled at the end of it.

On the other hand, and despite its willingness to enter water of its own accord, the iguana has a well-known dread of remaining in water when forcibly immersed. It will always return straight to land, time after time. I imagine dozens of people have confirmed Darwin's account of this, as we did. Nor will iguanas enter water as an escape reaction when disturbed on land. They persist in hiding in crevices or running over the cliff edge and part way down the face. Darwin's interpretation was that iguanas had an innate fright reaction to sharks and reacted to any form of fear by the appropriate 'shark' reaction, namely flight to land. This implies that iguanas have a single type of fright reaction and indeed it seems that they do not fear much else, even if they do fear sharks.

Iguanas on Hood completely ignored the Galapagos hawks, even though they have been recorded among the hawk's prey. Certainly the iguanas have no tendency to use their armoury of weapons. Beebe remarks that they would do great damage to any bird of prey with their powerful clawed feet, but in fact they never try to bite, scratch, butt or use their dorsal spines when handled. Any scratches they inflict are quite incidental. Their potential defences surely suggest that land predators, at any rate, do not bother iguanas. This, incidentally, would make the small Tower iguanas even more suitable as potential prey for hawks, if they ever got there.

In his 1960 book *Galapagos*, Irenäus Eibl-Eibesfeldt provides an entertaining account of the iguana's behaviour on land. He describes their interesting method of finding their way to customary resting places by smell, licking the ground and then testing the result by applying their tongue to an olfactory organ in the roof of the mouth. Aggressive iguanas have a vigorous nodding display and – to cope with its high-salt diet – snort spurts of water from their nostrils to expel the sodium, potassium and chloride they have ingested. Then there is the highly formalised territorial 'jousting' behaviour, in which rivals push against each other with their formidably spiked heads, but do not bite. The victor also responds to the submission of his opponent by suspending his attack and allowing the loser to escape.

In March 1964 we found a spot on the northwest coast of Tower honeycombed with the burrows of egg-laying iguanas. Spurts of sand emerged from the openings as the iguanas excavated with their forelimbs and kicked out the debris with their hindlimbs. We tripped and stumbled as we repeatedly broke through the crust; the whole of one small sandy area was undermined. Iguanas lay two or three eggs which they cover with sand and leave to hatch. Like all reptiles they leave their young to fend for themselves from the very beginning.

Predators, we have concluded, are a negligible factor in iguana lives. So is starvation (the El Niño of 1982–3 being an exception; see *Chapter 2*). They must die of disease or senility! I imagined this scene:

> 'One day, in the full heat of the Galapagos sun, with the black lava at a temperature of about 140F (60°C), the ancient lizard, as black and craggy as the rock, clambers lingeringly on to his favourite slab. Nodding ever more slowly, he directs the last derisive vapour puffs from his nostrils. Then, with his smug lizard's smile unchanging, he returns to the womb of the island that spawned him.'

Many Galapagos creatures, doubtless 'encouraged', if that is the right word, by the harshness of their environment, have taken to extraordinary feeding habits. I have already mentioned the mockingbirds eating faeces, the finches and mockers 'drinking' blood, and the amazing tool-using finches that probe out insects by using appropriately shaped twigs or spines.

Life is hard there, and many empty or near-empty niches – though these are often unprepossessing – have encouraged inhabitants to experiment. We could add to the list the crabs that pick scales (or ticks) from the marine iguanas plus the amusing crab-eating antics of the Galapagos yellow warbler. On Tower these colourful little warblers, with crimson crown feathers, often stalked the tiny fiddler crabs that formed a dense colony in the sand of the creek, inland from the open bay. As the fiddlers emerged cautiously from their burrows after the departing tide had laid a new supply of detritus at their doors, the warbler dashed and fluttered here and there, snapping feverishly at the crabs, which withdrew in a twinkling. With persistence it would catch several, which it dismembered by dashing against the ground before swallowing some fragments. Another case of grist to the mill in the harsh and demanding Galapagos environment.

11

INTRUDERS

BRYAN AND JUNE

On the Bass Rock we had no time for intruders, in both senses of the phrase. They arrived by the boatload and, with gannets covering much of the Rock and the lighthouse level off limits, they had nowhere to go apart from the single path rising steeply up and over to the foghorn then across the grassy slope to the gannets. We had to leave whatever we were doing and race them to our colonies to prevent disaster. By extreme contrast to our stealthy manoeuvring among the gannets, eager photographers created mayhem in their need for an eye-catching close-up. Surprisingly none lost an eye; I suppose the camera protected them. But on flat ground, with hefty gannets denied time to psyche themselves up for a safe take-off, such brazen intrusion had the adults scrambling in all directions, kicking out eggs and small young with their desperate feet and flailing wings. We were sickened by the resulting devastation.

Numerous yacht names on the cliffs showed Tower as a favoured destination in the Pacific. Those visitors, too, arrived by the boatload but usually in single figures, stayed a while maintaining their boats, but spent little time ashore. The wildlife more or less ignored them.

Even the remotest uninhabited Galapagos island rarely passes a year unvisited, and about three months was our longest spell without glimpse of a vessel of any sort. This chapter provides an honest record of our visitors who, though welcome indeed once the ice was broken, initially induced the oddest mixture of excitement, apprehension and a real desire to flee. On the few occasions when a strange boat appeared in the mouth of the bay we almost willed it to pass across and out of sight. When the dot indeed became steadily larger our hearts began to beat uncomfortably hard and the nature of the arrival was discussed in feigned calm. The final manoeuvres before the boat anchored and somebody came ashore were hard to bear. Ought we to carry on as normal, which might mean leaving an empty camp and giving the impression of unfriendliness? Yet to hang around often wasted hours, while no doubt the visitors dubiously considered the unexpected phenomenon of a camp on an island charted as uninhabited.

In the beginning I dreaded visitors. They might be dangerous or unpleasant, and we were vulnerable. In fact they were almost always delightful, with fascinating yarns and invitations onboard with more interesting food. In turn we invited them for barbecues on the beach or showed them our colonies, so we have pleasant memories of those interludes. The visitors would have been more than welcome had we needed rescuing.

Living on desert islands is a serious matter; accidents usually involve other people in the end, and there is no excuse for irresponsible behaviour or lack of proper planning. We took reasonable care and were luckily accident-free, but it might have been otherwise. Two young German biologists could well have lost their lives in the Galapagos just before we arrived. They were camping on Wenman Island (now Wolf) which, like Tower, is waterless and extremely inhospitable; a peculiarly oppressive and dead-looking island. One night heavy rain started a landslide which swept away their precarious camp, burying food, equipment and notebooks in rocks and mud. They managed to save their drinking water and a few oddments of food and equipment, though conditions in the black of night were difficult in the extreme. They transferred the remains to a sheltered ledge, almost a cave, which sea lions used as a resting place; it was heavily fouled with excreta and pools of urine. Then they had to face a wait of over two weeks before Miguel Castro came to collect them. Their food situation was grim. They caught lobsters and, with great difficulty, a few fish, but the heavy seas frequently dashed them against sharp rocks. To make matters worse an exceptionally heavy sea swamped their ledge, washing more things away. One of them had to cling to the rocks to avoid a similar fate. If they had been forced to survive three months before rescue instead of two or three weeks their position would have been desperate.

So our first job was to plan an escape route and a place to store our movables in the event of a sea swamping our precariously low beach.

I did occasionally remember the do-it-yourself instructions hastily scribbled by a doctor friend before we left Britain, especially the one headed *Appendicitis*: 'Try, in this order, Fasting, Penicillin, Prayer. If these fail stick a knife into the tenderest spot as far as it will go.' We had briefly debated 'do-it-yourself' versus 'call-on-the-other'; a horrifying thought locating Bryan's correct spot and plunging in the knife. Which knife? Or could I trust him with my tenderest spot? But appendicitis seemed remote. We scorned the tactics suggested by Hans Haas to his expedition members, have your appendix removed, or Dr Friedrich Ritter, the ill-fated Berlin dentist who settled and died in the Galapagos and had all his teeth replaced by a steel plate. We were young and healthy and cavalier.

Only nine days after we had set up camp on Tower a rakish black yacht sailed into Darwin Bay. The crew buzzed ashore in an outboard-powered dinghy, their swarthy, bearded faces obviously Spanish, Italian, Turkish or perhaps Greek. Bryan waited in the surf, mentally rehearsing greetings in Spanish ('Hello, who are you? I am etc'), a difficult job since he was only at lesson three in his pocket grammar guide. But from an orifice somewhere amidst the visitors' hairs an unmistakably cockney voice hailed us. The yacht was under the charter of Francis Mazière and his Tahitian wife, on their way to look at the archaeology of Easter Island, with a three-man crew held together by the inevitable Englishman. Madame Mazière, a nurse, helped Bryan from persistent sores by painfully injecting his posterior with streptomycin. But the relief was not permanent; the sores continued breaking out. Indeed, a constant run of minor ailments, peaking on Hood, required the patience – or endurance – of Job. As a former preacher Bryan often quoted Job, who was repeatedly afflicted by sores, and apologised for being tetchy.

The yacht tried to buy fish from the *San Marco*, the small fishing boat from San Cristóbal, which was still in the area, but the fishermen seemed to have no sense of proportion and asked a ludicrously high price, or failing that, a few pints of rum (certainly an optimistic request). Eventually they exchanged 20 large fish, about a hundredweight, for an old jacket, which the captain wore with great elegance.

The *San Marco* caught an astonishing quantity of fish. Each morning in the grey light before dawn, when the lava looked its most desolate, they worked the shallow waters at the edge of the bay, netting small fish to bait their lines. Soon after sunrise they started up the engine and chugged out to the open sea off the island's southwest coast where they fished steadily till noon. Occasionally, when working on that side, we saw their tiny boat tossing up and down against the lonely waste of sea and sky. Then they returned to the bay and, ignoring the swell, anchored hardly a spit from the cliffs and beach, to gut and salt their catch before spreading the fish on the beach to dry. Finally, they trekked at least two miles over toilsome lava to collect driftwood; back they stumbled with awkward, heavy loads for the brazier which burned on a cradle at the stern of the boat and cooked their food – poor fare too. Just before dark they finished their working day of 12–14 hours. Seven men lived for three weeks straight on that boat, hardly 20 feet long. One developed sunstroke, another became infected with boils, and a third fell, deeply gashing both legs on the razor-edged lava. It seemed a gruelling existence under harsh conditions for little reward and inspired us with great respect for the strength and endurance of the islanders.

Every day blacktip sharks swarmed around the boat and soon began to wait for its arrival, their dorsal fins restlessly cutting the green water. The smaller whitetip reef sharks seemed not to compete with them, though there were plenty around. As each fish head was thrown overboard the blacktips went mad in a maelstrom of swirling wafts. Occasionally, for fun, the fishermen hooked one and attached the line to a glass buoy against which the fish struggled savagely. Eventually they beached it and it lay motionless, its streamlined blue-black body gleaming with a dull metallic sheen, its head menacing – a weapon. Every line of a shark is powerful and graceful; the blunt, smooth slope of the forehead inclines upwards to the torpedo-shaped body equipped with small wings, the forward-set pectoral fins, and a powerfully propulsive, unequally fluked tail. From the clifftop we could often see their distorted outlines wavering in the glassy water as they contoured the seabed in the shallows, gliding slowly and gracefully. But to see their true power one had to watch them feeding, chasing their prey in spurts of unbelievable speed, beaching themselves with the savagery of their rushes. The fishermen delivered the *coup de grâce* by severing the shark's head, releasing rivers of blood that stained the sea for many yards around. Sometimes a dorsal fin would be used to sole their shoes or a jawbone removed as a trophy. The heavy body moved sluggishly for weeks afterwards as the fringe of each high tide washed the rotting form that had once moved so irresistibly.

We watched the death struggles of the shark during the casual and pointless kill, and – not for the first time – it struck us that even kindly people easily become inured to seeing animals suffer, and to killing them if they do it often enough. Probably this is a useful psychological defence mechanism and seems not necessarily to imply the danger of equivalent callousness in other spheres, though there may be some risk. Extreme illustrations of this divided approach are people like Charles St John, the Scottish naturalist who slaughtered birds of prey in the 19th century. Quite sincerely, it seems, he lamented the shooting of eagles, whilst in the same breath describing with the greatest gusto and detail just how he lured one down, shot it and then dispatched its mate which was returning again and again to its stricken partner, calling it to rise. Then he went on to shoot Britain's last ospreys, even as they sat on the nest.

An instance from Beebe shows how irrational and emotional we can be towards animals. 'Desiring a specimen but not wishing to injure the skin, I backed away and at a considerable distance fired at it with fine shot in the third barrel of my gun. The bird turned a complete somersault, landed on the ground on its feet, lowered its head and ran full speed towards me and brought up exactly between my legs. I picked it up without resistance, placed it in a large basket and took it off to the yacht where it readily took fish, preened itself and made no attempt to escape. Today, seven months later, it is living in good health at the New York Zoological Park.' Beebe fired at the hawk to kill it, yet when it actually delivered itself into his hands, he protected it. Had it run away, probably he would have chased it and finished off the job.

After three weeks the fishermen loaded the *San Marco* with 15 boatloads of fish, dried on the coral beach in the fierce sun with flies swarming over them and at night the centipedes gnawing them. Tying up a bit of ragged canvas that served as sail on board and awning ashore, they set out on the 100-mile trip home. We believe they used no navigational instruments, despite the dangerously strong and variable currents. By report, this same captain of the *San Marco* once broke down on the way to another island with a boatload of women and children. After drifting for part of a day and a night they were incredibly lucky to be picked up by a liner heading for New Zealand; the ship's crew even repaired his engine and took him to his destination. Ships are rare in these waters. The *San Marco* could easily have drifted for weeks, and those on board had no provisions, water, oars or sail. Under such circumstances sailors can be curiously fatalistic. We heard at first-hand an account of another breakdown to which the islanders on board reacted solely by making matchstick crosses and tossing them overboard, whilst the Europeans got on with the job of rowing and trying, successfully in the end, to repair the engine.

In January we were invaded by 12 American marine biologists who zigzagged into Darwin Bay draped all over an Ecuadorian patrol boat whose steering gear was damaged. They were some of the 60 scientists who had arrived on Santa Cruz for the Galapagos International Scientific Project, marking the official opening of the Charles Darwin Research Station by carrying out a short but varied investigation of Galapagos fauna and flora. An hour later a motley assortment of tarpaulins and bivouacs sprang up alongside our tent; new and elaborate camping equipment lay everywhere and our peace was cheerfully shattered. Three busy days later they pulled out with their collection of marine life and our outgoing mail, leaving us a crate of outdated tinned emergency water, some dried egg, half a tin of cooking oil and three 'sea rations'.

Their medical doctor, Martin, had lived in Samoa, investigating a species of anemone that is apparently used as a narcotic. When eaten it first anaesthetises and then if enough is taken kills painlessly; most natural poisons, such as snake venom, are harmless when swallowed and need to get directly into the bloodstream to take effect. No doubt the Samoans were practising anaesthesia and maybe even euthanasia whilst we were still in the dark ages.

The *Floreana* and the *Vilamil*, lobster boats from Guayaquil – some 600 miles away – often stayed in the Galapagos a month or more, moving around the islands. The thorny and exquisitely beautiful Galapagos 'lobsters' are very large marine crayfish and lack the large claws typical of our lobsters. They are very reluctant to enter creels and are simply caught by hand; the Ecuadorians dive and extract them from their crevices and holes on the rocky bottom. Over 30 men live aboard the lobster boats, diving in small groups which each receive a tiny commission on their catch. They buzz around the coasts and reefs in small dinghies powered by outboard motors; one man cruises in small circles while his two friends dive repeatedly, often coming up with a lobster in each gloved hand. It must be exhausting work diving for hours each day.

The *langostas* are stored in a refrigerator on board and eventually taken to the mainland hotels and shops. Some find their way to North

America, where the poor Galapagos crayfish, like Scottish grouse, endure the final ignominy of nourishing overfed businessmen in an overfed land. Surely the lobsters preferred to end up in an old bucket over a driftwood fire on the beach. An American in the Galapagos recently had the bizarre and certainly unbiological idea of breeding a strain of lobsters that could regenerate their entire abdomen, which he would sell whilst his obliging crustaceans got on with the job of growing another: an extreme case of the relationship between the red crab and the great blue heron, in which, according to Beebe, the heron snaps off and eats a leg or two but the crab scrambles away to grow new ones. The unco-operative lobsters quickly died because, as Edgar Potts (manager of the Charles Darwin Research Station) suggested, they didn't know whether the entrepreneur was cutting off their heads or their tails.

These spiny lobsters became a vital source of revenue for the Galapagos, but continued massive overfishing caused great concern and, by 2001, spurred the establishment of 'no-take zones'. Eleven years on, research showed these had made little difference. With the involvement of the WWF, locals managed the fishery, instituted better monitoring and sold live or frozen whole lobsters at a higher price (rather than simply tails via middle men). Conservation measures protected females with eggs, created both nursery areas and a closed season, set catch limits and encouraged fishing by hand. By 2020, the combination of initiatives led to a solid recovery in the spiny lobster population.

Back in 1964, a trio from the *Vilamil* spotted our tent and came to investigate. Some dubious characters from Guayaquil serve as casuals with these boats but we were charmed by the courtesy of our visitors as they drank coffee and politely ate our vile vanilla-flavoured *galletas*. Conversation was limited but, as usual with our Ecuadorian visitors, worked round to a topic which, judging from their covert glances, evidently bothered them. Yes, we were married – and for three years. But no, we didn't have any children. They always persevered: 'Why no children?' The explanation was too involved for our Spanish, so June answered, perhaps a trifle ambiguously and certainly to further mystification: 'muy difícil' (very difficult).

It soon became automatic to glance frequently towards the mouth of the bay, so we always spotted and scrutinised our visitors through binoculars long before they reached the head. How many people on board? Men or women? Did they look English (bearded, ragged and dressed in bits of canvas no longer good enough for the boat)? Yachtsmen who call in at places like Tower are sure to be interesting characters. The 20-foot yacht *Popeyduck* (the old Cornish name for a puffin) sailed into Darwin Bay on 17 March with its English owner and builder, Bill Procter. At the age of 55 he was sailing single-handedly round the world following a severe illness and premature retirement from a Civil Service desk job that could hardly have been worse training for the physical hardship of such a voyage.

Bill built his yacht in two years in the garage at home, to blueprints drawn by Laurent Giles & Partners. It looked beautiful; light and graceful, yet strong. The interior was planned to use every inch of space, and there was an automatic rudder so that one could leave the yacht on course and go to sleep. That must be the eeriest thing on a solitary voyage – to lie in the pitch darkness alone, listening to the gurgle and swish of the water as your little boat cuts along, trusting that no unsuspected hazard is looming nearer and nearer. Imagine the panic when (as Procter did) you suddenly become aware of the roar of breaking water; amid the blackness how can you tell where it comes from?

Bill spent three days with us, helping to catch and ring Nazca boobies. He showed the keenest curiosity about wildlife and panted, as he pursued the fleeing boobies in the fierce heat and caught them with his bare hands regardless of snapping beaks, that this sort of thing was exactly what he had dreamed of doing when he first conceived the idea of emulating Joshua Slocum by circumnavigating the globe (Slocum was the first person to do so single-handedly). We swapped a few trifles of food, passed on one or two paperbacks and off he went, a tiny figure dwindling to a speck as his little boat sailed out of Darwin Bay. Ten months later he wrote from Fiji, full of praise for the charming South Sea Islands. His creed was: 'If you really want to go before you die, you will.' Bill did indeed die on his voyage – when the *Popeyduck* was shipwrecked in unknown circumstances in the South Pacific in 1966.

The American yacht *Kismet* brought to Tower two American couples who featured briefly in *Chapter 5*. The women lavished infinite care on their boat, almost beyond reason. One remarked, perhaps unoriginally, that there was something about the womblike interior of the boat (with, no doubt, the slopping of the sea as amniotic fluid) that aroused strong maternal feelings. They spent the day after arriving in Darwin Bay on hands and knees filling in minute holes in the deck, or up the mast renewing stays and retrieving the remnants of their pennant which frigates, attracted by its fluttering, had ripped to shreds. Boobies, frigates and tropicbirds could come and go; there was work to be done. The saloon stove gleamed brightly and every piece of equipment had its once-over.

We admit to rather liking the free and easy *Lucent*, where any locker might yield a few marine specimens among the debris and one had to open a can to know what was inside, or the *Beagle* with its cat, marmoset and crabs.

The *Lucent* had left us on Tower in December 1963, due to return in March or April with more paraffin and water. The weeks flew past so quickly that it seemed no time before she slipped back into Darwin Bay. Edgar Potts came ashore with a basket of fruit, vegetables and eggs from the Angermeyer and Potts households; typical of the kindness one receives from these hospitable people. Edgar and his kind could do anything from mending a watch and restoring Bryan's failing old Exacta camera (without which much more film would have been torn or spoiled by wayward light) to building a house.

These days such people are the true inheritors of the earth; wherever they go they can animate sullen machines and have an unerring mastery of three-dimensional objects and topology; they know what goes where and how. Their comments are always practical and heavily jocular: 'How many fish have you caught? Not many?' And our saviour would point out that the hooks needed sharpening, that the angle of the barb was wrong, that we had probably used the wrong bait and fished in the wrong spots. 'Let me demonstrate,' said he.

During that morning, whilst parties of graceful tropicbirds flew round the *Lucent* screaming in their courtship display, frigates soared above and inquisitive, deeply interested lava gulls watched from the rails, Edgar fished, and caught one pathetically small blowfish or puffer. It puffed itself out on the deck and lay there, totally inedible. One can make an unusual and effective lamp from a blown-up puffer with a bulb inside, but we had no electricity.

Back at the camp under the veranda we cheerfully made without fish for lunch whilst the *Lucent*'s crew helped dispose of the six bottles of pilsner that they had kindly brought for Bryan. We floated a 50-gallon drum of paraffin ashore and then they left – and we tasted for a second time that peculiarly forsaken feeling as the last link with people slowly parts. What may not happen before another boat sails into the bay?

At midday on 21 May 1964 a tall-masted ketch under full sail swept into the bay, probably the first to do so for over half a century. She was *Beagle II* on her first visit to an outlying island; we were the first visiting workers to have the privilege of welcoming her. She was manned by most of the crew that had sailed her from England – Roger Jamieson, Richard Foster and Julian Fitter – with the prospective skipper, Karl Angermeyer, on board and David Snow trying out his Station's new acquisition on her maiden scientific trip.

Roger had been commissioned by the Station to find, fit out and deliver a vessel suitable for visiting scientists to work and live on, in addition to carrying out conservation patrols between the islands; the Gulbenkian Foundation was to donate most of the cost. He found the ship's hull rotting at Falmouth after a harbour accident and with the help of strong and willing natives from the south of England (including Richard and Julian), who hammered, sawed, caulked and painted for the price of several pints, eventually transformed her into the *Beagle* then sailed her from England to the Galapagos. She seemed a romantic boat, beautifully shaped and – with her high poop deck, giant bowsprit and great spar-rigged masts – magically appropriate to the wonderful Galapagos landscape with its anchor sites of wild bays and coasts. The red-footed boobies approved, for she was full of comfortable perches so they flocked in droves, winnowing above, striving to find footholds and quarrelling over the best perches. Before she anchored in Darwin Bay she was festooned with the descendants of boobies that doubtless perched on Darwin's *HMS Beagle* in 1835.

We had been sick in the *Beagle*, and the loo stank a bit, and she creaked and groaned as I imagine any old and well-weathered ship does, but these were trifles. The bunks were good, the food was ample and the crew were grand. The bronzed, bearded faces in the lamplight, smoking vile mixtures, grouped round the table, looked fine and friendly to us after months alone and there was always Karl, strumming his guitar and singing German songs to the sea lions (more appreciative than we) or trying to call Edgar Potts over the ship's radio.

Despite new high-powered radio transmitters, with aerials specially designed for rough work, the *Beagle II* rarely managed to establish two-way communication with the base on Santa Cruz – at least from Tower, 70 miles away, though a little more successfully from Hood. Perhaps it was especially difficult because of interference from the higher islands. Whatever the reason, Karl's nightly call became an amusing ritual.

'Dis is de *Beagle* calling Charlie D, Charlie D, Charlie D; *Beagle* calling Charlie D – do you hear me Edgar, over.' Pause.

'*Beagle* calling Charlie D, you faint Edgar, you faint away. I hear nuthin Edgar, nuthin; you are dead man, dead, dead, dead; try again – over.' Pause.

'Dis is de *Beagle* calling Charlie D, Charlie D, Charlie D, no good Edgar, I tell you no good. Will try again in de morning, try again in de morning – so good night from de *Beagle*, over and out.' Click.

Karl would turn towards us, grin and show his fine gold fillings (everybody had gold fillings in the Galapagos). 'Don't know what de hell's wrong with dat set. Edgar must be on de wrong channel.'

Back on Santa Cruz, Edgar would mop a perspiring brow (he always perspired) and stick pins in a wax model of Karl.

12

THREE BOOBIES

JUNE

Our year in the Galapagos – and this book – would never have happened without boobies and gannets. They offered so many delights, and so many insights into the lives of birds, that Bryan dedicated four chapters to them in the original book. Here I have sought to distil their wonder – and what they reveal about the way creatures tick – into a single chapter.

Our main characters are boobies in the Galapagos and gannets on the Bass Rock, both in the 1960s. Elsewhere and now, with climate change, they live different lives. Our task was to ferret out the many ways in which the three Galapagos boobies differed from their gannet cousin. As already hinted back in *Chapter 1*, we expected that nesting on warmer Pacific islands rather than in the icy North Sea would produce rather different animals.

Differing climates have had a huge impact on this family. Summer and winter extremes for the gannet, with long summer days, contrast with a year's relatively consistent tropical weather and just 12 hours of daylight for the boobies. Cold water year-round is better for fish, which helps the gannet, whilst the boobies are bedevilled by a range of sea temperatures and unreliable currents with poorer fishing.

The cast

Chapter 1 included the briefest of pen portraits of our actors, which now deserve a better introduction. Although gannets and boobies look different, being in the same family with a similar way of life means they have much in common. All have streamlined bodies, with narrow wings and webbed feet, which makes them well suited to fishing, diving and swimming underwater, frequently far from their colonies. Many have brightly coloured faces and feet, and striking signals. Although differing slightly in size and shape, as befits their owners' different prey and hunting tactics, their dagger-shaped bills are similar.

Many readers will have seen a **gannet**, Europe's largest seabird. Sober, sleek, mostly white with black trimmings, but a striking yellow head, piercing cold blue eye and fine blue lines on its dark legs and feet. Teenagers, contrastingly, are completely dark. Gannets nest tightly packed, on ledges or spilling on to flatter ground, on small islands with cliffs, within reach of reliable food.

The three boobies share out their Galapagos feeding area, have different food and different nesting places. Add to this living in the tropics, where creatures often weigh less, and may be smaller and darker, it becomes clearer why boobies look and behave differently to gannets.

The **Nazca booby**, first hived off as a distinct species in 2002, is the eastern Pacific version of the masked booby. Heavier than the other two Galapagos boobies, the Nazca looks quite ponderous and more serious. Its appearance is quite like a gannet, with a white body, black wing feathers and sober grey legs and feet. However, adults go a bit tropical on the face. A stout pinky-orange beak sets off the dazzling white plumage, and a striking black face mask surrounds a piercing orange-yellow iris, in contrast to the gannet's cold blue. And its teenager is mostly white below and dark brown above. Quite unlike the gannet, male and female Nazcas sound quite different to one another. Females and teenagers have a raucous, trumpeting voice, but the male a piping whistle – particularly evocative when several birds, outposted on boulders, pipe in the mist.

After spending so long with hefty gannets, we were amazed to find a cousin nesting on trees or bushes. Unsurprisingly, given their choice of residence, these **red-footed boobies** are lightweight creatures. Nesting aloft, they rarely need to walk, and when they do, shuffle awkwardly on very short legs, but they can spring from bushes in sprightly fashion, and are agile enough to catch flying fish.

Red-foots have brightly coloured faces. A blue beak runs into the surrounding red skin, whilst a bright blue-green ring encircles the large brown eye. A neat black velvet patch under the chin adds a weightier touch. And, of course, they are named after their tomato-coloured feet.

Confusingly, the red-foot has two colour versions, brown and white; so different that they look like different species. Even more confusingly they have a number of in-betweeners; different mixes of brown and white. The commonest on Tower (about 20:1), is almost entirely brown. In other parts of the world, the white one – more like a small gannet, with its black wing feathers and a yellow tinge to its head – is much more common. Once they have fully lost their chick down, teenagers of all varieties are easy to recognise by their dark feathers, black skin around the beak, blackish feet and a polished black bill.

Red-foots are noisy birds, with harsh, brassy notes. Male and female voices differ much less than in other boobies with the male merely sounding higher pitched, sometimes nasal, and more metallic than the female's gruff version.

The **blue-footed booby** must surely be the reason why this group of birds got their name, derived from the Spanish for fool. You could imagine that the looks and behaviour of this booby were specially designed to entertain. The blue-foot stands upright, a sparse bird with a lean look, snaky neck and a cocked tail. It moves a bit like a shag, running and walking rather than waddling.

At first glance the blue-foot looks a bit drab, with burnt brown back and wings. It begins to lighten up with pale patches on its neck and rump, but beneath is pure white with a neat little darker patch on each thigh. The head and neck are striking. The spiky look, like a variegated chrysanthemum, is due to its combination of older feathers (frayed and split) and newer ones (whole and wedge-shaped). Both have a dark base and paler outer edges. They don't lie in a smooth sheet, as in most birds, but stick out separately, like wet fur. Young blue-foots haven't yet acquired this chrysanthemum head. They rather resemble teenage Nazcas, but the blue-foot has a sharp division between a brown upper breast and a white belly. Like the Nazca, male blue-foots whistle whilst females and youngsters shout raucously.

The blue-foot's formidable, rather slender spear of a bill is darkish blue and the keen-looking eye bright yellow (particularly in the male, which has a pinprick of a black pupil compared to the female). Most impressively, the blue-foot has gone mad on the foot front, with adults' limbs of a quite ludicrous hue ranging from pale turquoise to deep ultramarine. The blue-foots' astonishing behaviour doesn't waste such an asset – but more of that later. Younger adults have paler feet and males often slightly lighter blue than females. Apparently colour can vary with fitness; a bit off colour maybe.

Time for lunch?

Across the whole gannet and booby family, the fishing strategy ties in with the size and shape of their body. Their fishing conditions depend on where they live and hence on the sea temperature and typical weather.

The male **gannet**, needing insulation against icy winters, and strength and weight to dive deeply in pursuit of muscular fish such as mackerel, weighs more than 3,000 grams (considerably heavier than the female). Starting at a great height helps it dive deeply for hefty fish. It can also manage a slanting dive for small stuff or even paddle for sand eels (useful food for small chicks). Cold water contains lots of varied food, which means that gannets can produce a teenager ready to leave home within five months, before dire winter weather sets in. Parents are usually able to fatten up and return for another go the following year. The youngsters leave and are left to cope with winter weather alone; many die.

The tropics lack grim winters, so exactly when boobies nest largely depends on food, and a red-foot may be around the colony for well over a year. Despite sharing out the feeding areas and the kinds and sizes of fish they choose, boobies are all affected by unexpected lean periods such as around El Niño or when the complicated currents move and fish often become scarce. Many chicks die on the nest in difficult times.

In contrast to gannets, male boobies weigh considerably less than their mates, with a male red-foot just nine-tenths of his female. The very light male blue-foot weighs only two-thirds as much as his female. The **red-foot** seems to have been dealt the areas with warmer water and struggles virtually the whole time. The little male can weigh under 1,000 grams, a third the weight of a male gannet. Light and agile, with proportionately longer wings than the others, it can fly vast distances to catch its main prey; surface-feeding fish, squid or flying fish. But with distant and erratic food, it can only hope to supply a single chick – and frequently fails in even that. Some red-foots cannot manage to breed every year and go 15 months between laying.

The **Nazca booby** is almost as large as a gannet, but living in the tropics means no need for insulating fat and it weighs only two-thirds as much. Fishing in both cold and warmer water allows a more regular breeding regime, although with lean periods. In the 1960s it could feed sufficiently just 5–25 miles from the colony, then tracking in the 1980s found it needed to venture further to find food, averaging 30–50 miles away, and by this century the distance travelled had increased to 150–400 miles offshore.

The Nazca booby usually plunge-dives from below 40 feet but occasionally as high as 330 feet. As the heaviest booby, it can dive deeper than its cousins to catch larger fish, usually sardines, but also flying fish, squid and anchovies in lean periods such as El Niño, when sardines are less available. Like the gannet, the Nazca usually nests once each year, though at different times on different islands, and never manages more than one chick.

The **blue-foot** seems to have struck the best deal, with the cold Humboldt Current. It also nests with its closest relative, the Peruvian booby, in mixed colonies mid-Humboldt, off Peru. Blue-foots make full use of their good fortune but suffer correspondingly when the currents shift. They often nest once every eight or nine months, and throughout the year. In the Galapagos, the pair often manage to raise more youngsters than the other species, occasionally as many as three. Blue-foots fish singly, in pairs and in flocks, sometimes with a signal co-ordinating diving. Agile and adaptable, they can dive from a considerable height, though more usually plunge from 30–100 feet up to catch sardines, anchovies, flying fish and sometimes squid and offal.

Male and female blue-footed boobies show a greater difference in their measurements than any other members of the family. The agile, adaptable male blue-foot clocks in at 1,200 grams, with his female half as heavy again. Having the longest tails relative to their weight and (in the female) the longest spear of a beak, they make for superbly equipped fishers. Being larger, the female fishes further offshore for larger fish, whilst the smaller male can make speedy fishing trips in shallower water closer to home. Bryan watched one apparently power-dive into rocks, but actually into a small finger of the sea just two feet deep. Prof. Dave Anderson found that mostly non-breeders fish very close inshore.

Watching their travails, I frequently felt sympathy for 'poor boobies'; it is hard not to empathise when their colonies are littered with broken eggs and dead chicks. Dead young gannets are rarely seen, but they have to struggle to become independent with no help from their parents and without even flying or fishing practice. Layers of fat pin them to the often-turbulent sea during gales, which is when many die. Yet all four species are still around by finding different solutions to their different problems.

For example, plumage colour may connect to feeding strategy or safety. Some youngsters and the brown version of the red-footed booby aside, all four species – like most birds that dive from a height – have striking white bellies, which make it harder for fish to notice a plunge-diving attack from above. The odd ones out use dark plumage seemingly to specialise in fishing at dusk or night on surface prey, and for food that does not require deep diving. The young gannet, meanwhile, needs to be completely dark to avoid the attention of aggressive adult males, particularly on narrow cliff ledges. It develops a white belly only once safely out at sea.

Being white above – as in the gannet, Nazca booby and pale red-foot – often attracts others to fishing flocks far out at sea. Those that are dark above seem to feed closer inshore or at night. The red-foot often fishes at night, and we recorded many blue-foots returning to their nest up to six hours after dark and feeding their young at night. White gannets don't land in the colony in darkness but sometimes fish at dusk, and near boats with floodlights. Similarly, Nazcas do not fish at night and rarely land in the colony after dark.

Settling down

All members of the family can live a long time, with one gannet nearly 40. Old-timers often return to the same site and mate, though booby pairs often split up. Most return roughly to where they were born. However, virtually all birds have pioneers; exploring new areas and maybe nesting there. New gannetries start, and a Nazca nested 20 miles away from where it was ringed as a chick. Although blue-foots didn't nest there, we saw at least one almost every day on Tower, more than 100 miles from their colony on Hood.

If you could somehow simultaneously watch a live feed of the colonies of these four relatives, first of all you would be surprised by how different they look. **Gannets** packed tightly on islands and cliffs, **red-foots** on bushes, **blue-foots** wandering about their quite large, flat patch, and **Nazcas** more stolid on slopes. Then you would probably think, particularly about the gannet and blue-foot gatherings, 'what on earth does all this seeming chaos mean?' So much raucous shouting and whistling, often non stop from dawn. Endless comings and goings, stirring up threats, jabbings, biting or fighting, and a flurry of bizarre semaphore – which makes it a wonder that any of them manage to find time to rear youngsters at all. But if you watched for long enough, you would see that it is only *apparent* mayhem. Watching for even longer, you might begin to understand their languages. By the end of our time in the Galapagos we had been watching for four years and knew more or less what they were about.

Like us, these birds have to find somewhere to live, entice a mate, learn to co-operate, get along with neighbours, build a nest, and eventually rear a family, which also means providing enough food, and, because they can't talk it over, having signals to prevent family or neighbourly mayhem. That requires a lot of communicating, with yells and signals, because they all nest in groups and are somewhat quarrelsome.

There must have been various reasons why seabirds chose to nest like this. Firstly, it makes sense to be as near your marine food as possible. In the past, large mammals would have been a threat, so cliffs and islands were the safest spots. And, also in the past, the once-numerous seabirds would soon have been fighting for space on an often short supply of suitable places. Dense colonies, the only solution, would then lead to competition.

Choosing the right spot

An early, important task is to find and keep a nesting space; once they have secured a spot, even non-aggressive boobies defend it with vigour. How you find a patch varies a lot depending on how tightly packed you need to be.

Squashed together, **gannets** need to be very aggressive and prepared to fight to keep their patch, requiring the most and clearest signals to avoid mayhem. Boobies have more space, usually in less dangerous places, so don't need to be fierce; they rarely fight and need fewer signals.

The **red-foot**, with a reasonably large patch, differs most keenly from the gannet. Stuck aloft on bushes, it takes more effort to get about and mates spend more time apart than any of the others. Red-foots are less aggressive, and several signals used by the other boobies are either missing or more a token.

The **Nazca** – the heaviest, most aggressive booby – prefers a cliff, slope or boulder to help take-off, but happily waddles about on flattish, quite large territories. Weight and space have inevitably affected it; for instance, it has fewer antics in the air than its two agile cousins but wanders about its patch signalling.

Nests of the more versatile **blue-foot** are often widely spaced; on Hood, birds were sometimes unable to see their nearest neighbours. The blue-foot's agility allows it to nest easily on flat ground, even deep inside the crater on Daphne Island, but also tightly packed on ledges or flat ground on the Peruvian guano islands. It often nests between boulders used for displaying. Although the least aggressive of the lot, a large territory, lean agility and ludicrous feet allow it a range of bizarre signals, involving aerial acrobatics and parading about – almost goose-stepping – while flaunting those remarkable webs.

Hanging on to their patch

So what are the key messages that males need to convey during the breeding season? First up: 'this is now my patch'; 'do not trespass'.

Hot on the heels of those they need: 'I want to move', 'there is no need to attack me' and 'I am available and a worthy mate'. Once a female agrees with him and has been welcomed, both need to keep saying to each other: 'you are my mate'. And they need to repeat this to others: for she might leave, or be driven off if he changes his mind, or other suitors might muscle in. They also have to keep saying 'this is our patch' for rivals are forever trying to steal desirable spots.

Getting and keeping a site proves the most harrowing for a **gannet**. Large and heavy, facing great competition, within pecking distance of hostile neighbours, the experienced male arrives, probably in February, to reclaim his old site – usually, after winter storms, a circle of bare mud – sometimes by fighting. He repeatedly flies around, lands and, by 'bowing', signals 'this is my territory'.

Having reclaimed his tiny patch, he has no space for the flying-around or walking signals used by his agile, widely spaced relatives. He needs more signals than them, especially as he continues aggressively in most situations. For instance, he bites his mate on the back of her head every time he lands from February to October, thousands of times a year; an awful lot of biting. The female, expecting it, turns her beak away and avoids looking threatening. Constant battles between mates and neighbours would create mayhem. Gannets need a large tool bag of signals.

An 'inexperienced' gannet trying to find his first site flies around his chosen bit of colony, usually on the edges as the rest is full. He keeps landing, loudly shouting 'this is my patch', and usually has to fight for it. Once he has a chance to stand unmolested he really goes about trying to convince that it is his. And 'bowing' is a spectacular way of doing it. He begins with opened wings, shaking his head, and calling loudly. He then simultaneously leans forward, lifts his tail and sweeps his head down, before lifting his head back up and pressing down his tail. Very early in the season he often actually bites the ground aggressively when his head goes down; the head shaking dislodges lumps of mud but he continues the shaking, even with a clean beak, as part of the display. After repeating the ritual maybe five times in quick succession, the final flourish involves tucking his bill hard into his chest for a few seconds before relaxing. Any possible hint of intrusion will set him off. Fights regularly break out over prime spots. Should this young male chance to fly off for food a rival would surely take over, and usually they fight for the bare patch of mud. Blood-bespattered losers, often with damaged eyes, stand forlornly on the extreme margins, head in wings, recovering.

On Hood, **Nazcas** began arriving in September, but quietly. Most just slept or spent their time preening or waterproofing their feathers from the oil gland at the base of their tail. Then, on 25 September, Bryan spotted a male advertising to a female, signalling a new breeding season as surely as a cuckoo signals spring. Males began to take an interest in nest material, picking up and dropping small pebbles, stationed themselves on boulders and displayed aggressively to other males.

Soon they started performing 'this is my territory'. It began with the male briskly shaking folded wings, hesitating with wings half spread, before crouching and springing into the air. After a wide circuit, he flew in whistling loudly and landed on his patch with wings aloft in a steep 'V' and tremoring gently. Once landed, he swiftly touched the ground with his bill then swung his head in a wide arc from side to side, simultaneously nodding rapidly up and down. This 'yes–no head shaking' is to Nazca boobies what bowing is to gannets.

The **blue-foot**'s version of this head shaking involves only the 'yes' element – vigorous nodding up and down, without swinging from side to side. The male makes a territorial virtue of his agility. Even on flat ground, he springs neatly off the mark, frequently taking off, circling and landing again. In a showy, acrobatic, vertical salute, his spread feet lift upwards to flash blue against his white belly. Just as it seems he will fall flat on his back, he lands neatly. Each circuit-and-landing proclaims 'this is my territory'. The heavier Nazca doesn't attempt such virtuoso aerial saluting.

The male **red-foot**, meanwhile, comes rushing in, shouting, not on to his nest but nearby. With wings tightly wrapped around his lean body, neck really stretched forward and swinging from side to side, he grips twigs and shakes them (the gannet bites the ground or nest, whilst the Nazca and blue-foot merely touch it). This is the red-foots' aggressive display, threatening rivals and saying – you guessed it – 'this is my patch'.

Once a red-foot male finds a site, he defends it with extreme vigour. Fearsomely screeching, with plumage bristling, he lunges at any intruder with wildly waving wings. He then keeps circling, landing and shouting to proclaim his ownership and attract a mate.

Pointing up and pairing up

All four species use a display called 'sky-pointing' where they lift their bill to the sky, stretching their neck, then peer forwards either side of the bill. The wings stay closed yet raised upwards and stiffened in a busk, while the feet are slowly lifted up and down. But here I hit a snag. This striking display signals one thing for boobies but something very different in gannets. For **boobies** it means 'I am available and will make a good mate'. Yet to a **gannet** it means, exceptionally clearly, 'I want to go'. For a gannet, leaving the nest unguarded means pilfered nest material and attacks on egg or chick. So departing the nest is risky and needs partner consent. If both mates want to leave, they each keep pointing skywards until one backs down, freeing the other to go.

In boobies, and with a whistle (or a grating call in the red-foot), it is mostly the male that sky-points to attract a partner, and with such a different meaning: 'come be my mate'. When a booby wants to go, its signal, completely missing in gannets, takes the bill upwards, backwards and sideways ('bill up, face away'). In both leaving and soliciting, the spear of a potentially threatening bill is lifted well out of the way.

By mid-October, Hood's **Nazca** males really get going. If a female flies over or lands anywhere near a male, he becomes alert, stretches his neck, points his bill skywards, lifts his wings slightly and whistles. Here we have a happy performance that immediately clicks with us. He really is whistling to a female.

Blue-foots are great advertisers, and any bird of the opposite sex flying over sets them off. A male suddenly throws up his head, swivels his wings and whistles. Or he may turn with comical goose-step, and repeatedly and passionately advertise to a nearby female. At first sight this manoeuvre looks impossible. You blink and watch again; his wings looked broken, twisted out of all relationship to his body. With neck stretched, bill pointing skywards and tail cocked, he has somehow managed to swivel his wings so that their upper surface is presented towards the object of desire. Yet his incredible effort, accompanied by a most beseeching whistle, often leaves the female entirely unmoved.

Although the **red-foot** dispenses with many of the signals used by the other species, its way of attracting a mate makes a striking exception; it is obvious and both sexes use it. The male begins by staring at a likely contender as though willing her to look at him. Then up goes his bill on extended neck, up go his tail and wing tips, and out comes a grating call. Next comes slight reaching as if he might bite the female or suddenly attack her. Indeed, when she responds he often does jab her fiercely. Ruffling her head and neck feathers, she trembles (they did this when alarmed by us). Keeping her bill well out of the way, she turns her head aside as though flinching. The male may aim a savage jab at her and though she pulls away, she often jabs him back. The male then sets about shaking twigs.

Eventually the female will usually sky-point in return. The pair then stand quite close, and repeatedly, and with utmost solemnity, perform the display alternately or together: stretch and groan, stretch and groan. This can last for an hour. Every few minutes the male looks restless and rapidly flicks his wings open and closed. Eventually he gives them a brisk shake, hops to a take-off point while pressing bill to chest, springs into the air, circles a few times, feinting to land with each circuit, then sweeps in calling before waving his head to emphasise that 'this is my patch'. The pair get back to stretching and groaning. All this lot replaces the ecstatic meeting ceremony of the gannet (see later). The female red-foot will quite often do it too, but, unlike the show-off blue-foot, they never salute in the air.

Gannets, with sky-pointing booked as a signal for 'I want to leave', cannot, like the boobies, use it to say 'this is my patch'. Instead they use bowing to repel intruders. A young gannet, trying to breed for the first time, and after precariously booking a patch, soon tries for a mate. He automatically regards anybody near his nest as an intruder and begins by bowing. As that is doomed to failure (as it tells potential mates to go away) he eventually discards the aggressive parts of that signal, restricting himself to shaking his head and reaching towards any young female 'prospecting' for a partner by wandering about the colony fringes or finding a higher spot to scan around. Sleek and long-necked, her peering stands out, unlike the male's efforts, which look like half-hearted, non-aggressive bowing with closed wings and no shouting.

Should the female approach, they briefly touch bills, then she turns her head and the male fiercely grips it. She expects it and, as I keep saying, it happens every time they meet (she eventually ends up spotty headed). Despite her best efforts she is often driven away. But if she prevails, they start to perform a meeting ceremony.

Leaving without mayhem

Given its packed colonies, the **gannet** needs the clearest signals. At the beginning and end of their months at the colony, gannets talk loudly all day. Neighbours recognise each other, but still make their feelings plain about any possible intrusion. Movement without an explanation will provoke a severe reprimand; probably an indignant jab with a spear-bill and gannets use sky-pointing to signal that they want to move.

Boobies do things differently. When it needs to leave, the **red-foot** has it easy. On bushes, well away from neighbours, a red-foot can't parade; a wing flick seems to be all it needs to signal that it's off. With nobody near they don't even need to be discreet with their bill. When a **Nazca** wants to move, mostly away from its nest, it merely gives the 'bill up, face away' signal; an exaggerated form of turning away but leaving it free to respond to a jab. It will then rattle its wings and take off.

The extrovert **blue-foot** starts to signal take-off by 'parading': waddling around with cocked tail and fully spread gaudy webs raised high with extreme and ridiculous deliberation. Next he briskly rattles his wings, giving them a brief and violent shake whilst loosely folded. For his next trick he gives the 'bill up, face away' signal, turns away, and starts goose-stepping to ensure others have seen his feet. If he sees no objections, he walks or runs to a boulder, hiding his threatening bill by pressing it hard to his chest. With an agile spring he is airborne and flies swiftly away, often for just a couple of circuits before dashing back in, landing with yet another flourish of his impressive feet and whistling 'this is my patch'.

Maintaining marital harmony – and home

Once they have a mate, couples need to keep making sure that they both keep the pair bond strong and repel interlopers. The male **gannet** keeps on jabbing and biting his mate; the female is still an 'intruder'. Remaining aggressive to keep his patch in such a competitive life is more important for the gannet than being pleasant to his mate. She deflects his aggression by pushing up against him and makes sure her beak stays well out of harm's way; mild aggression may even help the pair bond. She will fight for their site, guard it when her man needs to feed, repel intruders and fiercely fight rivals for her partner's affections.

In order to help deal with the male's aggression and his mate's fear, **gannets** have an elaborate and ecstatic greeting ceremony that continues throughout the whole breeding season. The male gannet lands like a thunderbolt, fiercely grips the back of the female's neck, then releases her and – breast to breast, wings outspread – they immediately begin fencing bills, often for five minutes at full pitch, shouting loudly throughout. It's bowing for two, without the pretend nest-biting bit. Both call raucously on landing and bow at any possible threat to ward off intruders. But sometimes things can go wrong. We once saw a gannet with its beak caught in netting. Whenever it tried to greet its mate it seemed to have an aggressively open bill so was attacked.

Being less aggressive, boobies have no need of a complicated meeting ceremony. **Red-foots** have what looks like the hostile jabbing of rival males. Mates then take care not to point their beaks at each other, and one, usually the female, hops off to one of their perches. To keep their mate and patch, red-foots mainly use sky-pointing.

The peaceable **blue-foot**, similarly, has no complex greeting but, of course, has an impressive repertoire that serves the same purpose of dealing with their aggression and fear. Each time the male returns to the site, he flies in swiftly, flings up his feet, lands neatly, runs towards his mate repeatedly tucking in his bill, nods then jabs at her. The pair touch bills, he throws up his head, swivels his open wings and whistles, walks off goose-stepping with his bill up and facing away to signal 'I'm off', and with a rattle of wings, jumps into the air, circles and returns. Occasionally the male shakes his head aggressively, up and down, at his mate. He still carries on soliciting long after he has a female, but now she does it too, either to a passing male or to her mate. Then they solicit together. Standing opposite each other, one throws up its head, bill to the sky, throws up its tail, then swivels its wide-open wings till they look broken, and their top surface faces their mate. Sometimes the other goes into a mirror image or they may take it in turns. His piping and her gruff voice mingle throughout. Amid this signalling, the male flies off on circuits, landing with his acrobatic signalling salute. 'This is my patch,' he says, 'but I also want a mate.' Once the pair are settled the female may go circling too, either alone or with her mate. She also salutes but less often and less dramatically.

Nazcas do none of the blue-foot's mutual soliciting, nor do they attempt it in the air, though they make their presence known by calling whilst flying and give a sober salute as they land. Partners continue to greet each other with hostile-looking jabbing, particularly males towards females. The latter look ruffled and apprehensive but angrily shout and quack in short quick bursts, rising to a sharp yell whenever the pair jab at each other. Males whistle indignantly, even in the air. They touch beaks then, mouth slightly open, fling their heads at each other, clashing beaks. Next, they turn away and pointedly stand parallel, as though to avoid looking at each other. Any movement produces a jab and another bout of 'sparring'. This may continue for many hours and the sound carries for miles.

Staying good friends

To further help the pair to bond, the gannet, blue-foot and Nazca frequently and delicately touch the tip of their partner's bill. All spend much time delicately and simultaneously preening the other. Red-foots do neither of these, as that would mean pointing bills at each other.

Maintaining their nest together also makes the pairing stronger and protects their patch. As a vital bonus, in **gannets**, a good nest protects the chick from wet mud. The male **blue-foot** parades to and fro, collecting fragments to add, daintily, to the pathetic circle of bits that pretend to be a nest. The pair bend their heads together and busily 'build' the fragment.

Nazcas also spend much time parading and collecting nest material. A nest can contain over 2,000 items; 2,000 opportunities for the female to receive each offered piece, share 'building' it and build up their relationship. **Red-foot** pairs interact closely only for a short time before egg laying, collectively building their often large nest and displaying. Otherwise they usually sit well apart.

Dealing with the neighbours

Nazca booby pairs, the most aggressive-looking of the Galapagos trio, fight more with neighbours to maintain their patch, engaging in hostile jabbing or 'yes–no head shaking' to proclaim 'this is the boundary of my territory'. Although real fighting is not part of **blue-foot** behaviour, pairs interact a lot with neighbours, with what passes for aggressive displays mainly being used against rivals and intruders. When neighbouring pairs meet, they face each other, 'yes head shaking' violently, over the invisible fence dividing their territories. Occasionally they forcefully beat their wings and jab with speed and vigour. These exchanges can go on for hours, with a chorus of outraged whistles and grunts, plus many a brave stab. Our own walks through the blue-foot colony stirred up some aggression, with much noise, nodding and goose-stepping. Neighbours are rarely a problem for the **red-foot**, given their widely spaced nests.

Leave me alone

To ward off frequent jabbing, the whole family use a 'pelican posture'. This involves, like a pelican, tucking the bill deep into their chest. Moving about with a sharp weapon sticking out looks intimidating, so concealing it indicates pacific intent. The red-foot's pelican posture also includes arching its neck.

Homebuilding

Having found their patch, convinced rivals that it really is theirs, found a partner and started learning how to co-operate, boobies now need a nest. Where and how this family lives also affects what sort of a nest they need and how to go about building it.

For the **gannet**, site and nest are critical. Squashed together, in a wet climate, they build sometimes huge nests of seaweed and grass. They can be seen in mainland fields gathering beakfuls of grass, or flying in to the Bass Rock trailing lengths of seaweed. Often bizarre plastic objects appear; false teeth or, horribly, chunks of discarded fishing net which can tether birds until they die. Rain even as late as August has them all flying off for nest material to raise their chicks above the mud.

Boobies do not usually have to cope with mud! But building a nest together plays a big part in helping partners to get on. Apart from the rare Abbott's booby, which breeds high in the tops of jungle trees only on Christmas Island, the **red-footed booby** is unique in using trees or bushes. Its nest may be large with twiggy greenery, but some were so small that the egg or chick fell through or off. **Nazcas** breed on dry, sandy ground, with a minimalist nest of thousands of small twigs or pebbles. The **blue-foot** similarly ends up with a bare circle surrounded by thousands of fragments of sticks and pebbles arranged by the pair as part of courtship.

Along comes a family

Once they have an egg, gannets or boobies do not shuffle it into a brood patch amongst their feathers as, say, albatrosses do. Instead, they overlap their warm feet over the top of it. If they lose their egg, they can lay another within quite a short time.

All their eggs take around six weeks to hatch, but the distance each parent travels for food obviously affects how long its partner must sit for each stint to keep it warm. The **blue-foot** often gets away with a mere 17 hours, **Nazca** around 28, **gannets** spend around 30, whilst the poor **red-foot** might be on duty for 60 hours.

Yet again, feeding conditions dictate how many eggs each species lays and how many chicks they can rear. The **gannet** goes for one massive chick that is hopefully able to survive northern winter gales, though many die at sea. The **red-foot** has no hope for more than one and loses offspring at all stages. The **Nazca** lays two eggs, but unless the insurance policy is needed and the first one somehow dies when very young, the first chick always ousts its nest mate, lunging and worrying away, though it can hardly control its own wobbly head. That chick is likely to finish in better condition than if the parents tried to rear two with unpredictable food. Our efforts to produce two evenly sized chicks by removing the one with the upper hand till the lighter caught up always failed. One was eventually kicked out during the night and died, though later researchers managed to help some pairs to raise two. A similar attempt with several gannet pairs had produced two healthy youngsters. The **blue-foot** occasionally manages to rear three chicks, though when food gets short the youngest dies and if food is really short the elder turfs out its sibling.

Coping with baby

Rearing offspring is no easy business. Tyro **gannets** breeding for the first time sometimes have very small nests and, when the chick hatches, don't manage to manoeuvre it on to the top of their webbed feet. The chick dies, trampled into mud.

More adept individuals of this family gently prod the scrap of chick – helpless, blind and naked – into position. The mind boggles at how **blue-foots** manage to do so with three chicks. Mealtimes initially involve the parent digesting its catch then regurgitating it so that tiny chicks may 'drink' it from the parent's beak. Sometimes the parent's head bends over so far that its beak lies on the ground and chicks feed from the trough. When they no longer risk drowning the chick in fishy fluid, parents drop first sloppy food, then appropriately sized lumps, into a chick's yawning gape. As soon as chicks can control their heads, they insert their bill into that of the parent. Older chicks can reach down into the parent's throat for huge feeds.

When food is scarce, desperate booby parents may have no option but to abandon chicks, focusing their energies on catching enough fish to stay alive themselves (when chicks were starving, parents were loafing about at the colony). Given that many chicks die anyway, it makes more sense for parents to prioritise surviving to breed another year; something we couldn't imagine in the gannet during our time. However, climate change could affect that and recently there have been signs that conditions are becoming more challenging.

Isn't it beautiful?

With no mud to make nesting perilous, however, most tiny booby chicks survive, and to be frank, all are incredibly ugly. Helpless, wobbly headed and naked, their skin shows through the sparse down, which grows at a slow rate. Newly hatched **blue-foot** chicks have bluish skin and are guarded for their first few weeks. If the parents become desperate for food, both may go fishing, which risks chicks falling victim to a Galapagos hawk. Six of ours did so.

A young **Nazca** seems ugly for longer. Even as it acquires proper down it is less attractive than the red-foot, with its sparser down showing bare pink skin around its face. The flat, receding, barely covered forehead gives the chick a brutal, unintelligent look. Its parents brood it until the chick can better adjust its own temperature.

Red-foot chicks start off weighing as little as a mouse, grow at a snail's pace and in spurts. If the food supply is sufficient, parents keep the chicks warm for around five weeks, by which time they become covered with thick woolly fluff, impishly sharp-eyed, and with a polished black beak.

With its parents often struggling to find enough food, red-foot chicks are soon mostly left alone in tropical heat, trying to keep cool and sleeping. Unguarded, some were killed by frigatebirds or short-eared owls (there are no hawks on Tower). The single chick, some distance from any other, spends much time with head dangling over the nest and stumpy posterior raised to the air to lose heat from the bare skin. Other booby chicks mainly stand, to lose heat from their legs and feet. In contrast, **gannet** chicks usually lie flat, sticking out a leg if the weather turns unusually warm. All chicks pant when hot.

When feathers begin to grow, chicks lose their charm and resemble ragbags, with down still clinging to their feathers. Red-foots often look sadly pinched, standing with guano-whitened webs on the wreckage of the nest. Once they start flying regularly their plumage becomes glossy.

Feeding the monsters

We were fascinated to know how wide variations in food supply affected the number of times the chicks were fed and how they prospered. To check this, we weighed some chicks every second day, then every three hours for two weeks, and finally, watched them constantly for 48 hours to note every time a parent arrived, and count the number of feeds each chick was given.

Until they were around two-thirds grown, **red-foot** chicks, with parents flying long distances to fish in warmer seas, received roughly half a pound of food less than once a day, often in the evening. Inevitably, they grew the most slowly and many starved. **Nazca** chicks, whose parents often fished nearer to their island in cooler water, averaged one and a half feeds each day. They often reached a reasonable weight. **Blue-foots**, usually able to nip back and forth with fish, could return with a full crop within half an hour and feed their chicks almost twice a day. With a bit of luck, the youngsters, even with two on the nest, could end up weighing more than their parents. **Gannet** chicks received frequent, hefty feeds, laid down impressive fat and ended up dwarfing their lean parents.

An older, well-fed gannet chick, needing to avoid falling off its nest, begs sedately for food. Young half-starved boobies look demented – seemingly about to murder their parents with frantic begging, wings flailing, and a flurry of jabs at the parent's beak, sometimes even violently rattling it. In no species is this more apparent than the red-footed booby. The red-foot parent lands away from the nest, prompting the often exceptionally hungry chick to bob and feint, violently flailing its wings and uttering a subdued but impassioned calling. Once the reluctant parent hops on to the nest, the chick, too eager to control its movements, thrusts its head into the parent's throat, and with a violent pumping that threatens to lacerate, transfers the contents to its own mouth. By continued frenzied pestering it usually persuades the adult to open up another two or three times, though may not always find food. The harassed, ruffled parent, eyes darting, escapes to one of its perches. After a short rest, it again flies way out into the Pacific to try to locate yet more food. Even after several hundred miles of effort, the catch may remain poor; if so, the chick will continue to lose weight and maybe starve.

Stranger danger

In addition to surviving starvation, chicks also need to avoid aggression from adults. As mentioned many times, **gannets** need to be aggressive to any intruders and severely attack any youngster that, in an emergency, has been left alone or fallen off its nest, despite it always submitting by hiding its beak. Youngsters never try to defend their parents' patch; a severe hiding by an aggressive adult would be too dangerous, especially on a cliff ledge. As the teenager's dark first feathers are the complete opposite of the adult's white, young gannets on their nest with their parent can never be mistaken for an intruder.

Nazca chicks also need to hide their beaks. Not only do non-breeding adults frequently attack youngsters but breeding males become more aggressive again as the chick nears fledging.

As we have seen, **red-foots**, nesting well apart, rarely need to be aggressive so chicks do not need to hide their beak. However, male **Nazcas** whose breeding efforts had failed sometimes attacked or tried to mate with the red-foot chick. If he tried that with a Nazca chick it would hide its beak but the red-foot, not used to being attacked, retaliated – a bad move, for this released an all-out hammering that sometimes ended up in the red-foot being killed.

A **blue-foot** chick, from an early age, helps to defend its patch, but on the rare occasions when it is attacked will hide its beak. If displaced, it just wanders back home and, later, parents join their young well away from their patch. Across the whole family, parent and chick recognise the other's voice.

Teenage angst

Once they are almost ready to fly, booby youngsters start to mirror the behaviour of their parents. The young **gannet** never does this; it wouldn't dare make itself obvious and have to face a threatening adult, which means that, before they fly, they virtually never practise territorial or sexual behaviour.

Young **blue-foots**, even when still downy, look ridiculous advertising to overflying adults, calling and rotating their stumpy wings. We saw a fluffy chick displace a mockingbird by using an aggressive signal. From about six weeks old, they defend their parents' site from intruders, jabbing and using threatening head shaking, just like adults.

The down-clad **red-foot** similarly defends its site and attacks invading youngsters. It is agile, moving about its territory even when young. Fledged birds signal 'this is my territory' when landing and join dense clubs where youngsters quarrel and use adult signals.

As soon as the young **Nazca** starts flying off to explore, it also begins behaving like an adult. It kept surprising us to see the drab brown youngster, until so lately a helpless, downy beggar of food and appeaser of adults, soar into its parents' territory, shouting loudly in a typically aggressive way, then follow it up with a perfect 'this is my territory' display. Nor does the juvenile now hesitate to attack a marauding adult, which it can easily put to flight.

Leaving home... eventually

A 13-week-old **gannet**, sitting on a nest usually high up on an island, can take days to psyche itself up to launch into its first flight. Some die on rocks below. Those that make it to the sea are too fat to lift off again to return to be fed. But that fat store will keep it going as it learns how to take off, to fly and to fish. It is a perilous time for young gannets, many dying while seeking independence – while their parents, ignorant of their youngster's fate, continue zealously defending their nest site.

By contrast, the young, lightweight boobies have been practising leaping about, madly flapping their wings as they test the air. Their first flights are very modest affairs, but they have weeks to keep practising and trying out fishing while being 'subsidised' by their parents.

In the Galapagos, the juvenile **red-foots** took their first proper flight when about 19 weeks old, compared with 14–15 weeks elsewhere. This means that they were completely dependent on their parents for over a month longer than in places with more reliable food. That first flight, however, was not a home-leaving trip; the youngsters returned for a daily feed for another 15 weeks or more, meaning they could have been fed by their parents for 35 weeks (almost three times longer than the gannet) – and, in one case, 46 weeks.

Nazca chicks generally first flew when around 16 weeks, but poor feeding could delay this by three weeks. Even once proficient fliers, they kept coming back for food for another 50–60 days. After this long subsidy, the juveniles suddenly disappear for two or three years of wandering. Prof. Dave Anderson recalls keeping track of presence at the nest of ringed parents and offspring. 'Parents slacked off their attendance and provisioning at some point, and after four to five days of being ignored Junior would leave for good,' he said. 'And the very next morning the parents showed up at their site! Apparently they were surveilling the site from afar, waiting for Junior to leave.'

Blue-foot chicks can fly at around 14 weeks, when they usually weigh more than their parents, yet parents continue to feed them for 30 days or more. Finally leaving home when around 20 weeks old, the blue-foot wanders for two or three years, often turning up well away from where blue-foots usually fish, sometimes in groups.

Empty nesters

With the next generation on the wing, learning about the world and preparing to become parents themselves, what of the adults? Gannets continue aggressively defending their sites for some time, fattening up to survive another freezing, stormy winter in northern waters. Booby parents, meanwhile, look haggard and bedraggled at the end of the long, long season. Once their young have left, they also spend time at sea recuperating in preparation for their next effort to produce offspring.

And so the wheel turns...

13

HOOD ISLAND

JUNE

We reached Hood Island on an unusually quiet day in July 1964 and, with help from the speedy crew, had five loads ashore from the *Beagle II* in under two hours. Instead of our playful rowing boat, which we had desperately wanted to take but had reluctantly abandoned after warnings about rough seas, we more prosaically had taken 105 gallons of water, 35 of paraffin, 50lb potatoes, a stem of bananas, plus oranges, papaya and avocado.

Several suitable campsites had all long been booked by sea lions; the large boulders polished shiny by their constant shuffling. With no other acceptable spots available, we had to choose one of them, a semi-cleared area at the edge of thorns just above the high-water mark, and make do. Bryan described our first impressions:

'The place stank of sea lions; droppings lay in whitening piles or revoltingly fresh. Like those of all carnivores, sea lion faeces contain the noxious skatole and indole which are responsible for the repellent odour, quite unlike the (to me) innocuous ones of herbivores. We shovelled the muck away and pitched the tent, now bleached and whitened by the excreta from the red-footed boobies of Tower, though alas, there were none in the colder waters around Hood. The camping place was ideal after we had gathered up the tin cans (left by hash-eaters anonymous) decorating the topmost spikes of the shrubs. The reassuring old *Beagle* rolled gently at anchor and the camp was so quickly organised that

Miguel Castro and I had time for a quick trip to the bird colonies on Punta Suarez before dark. A thin July drizzle wetted and darkened the red boulders and there was not much activity among the albatrosses, though there were several groups sitting quietly among the shrubs. The white [Nazca] booby colony was practically deserted, the stones sprinkled with the sun-dried corpses of the many starved juveniles. Blue-foots, fortunately, were more active and in evidence, and heartened us no end. Early next morning, the *Beagle* slipped away with a farewell toot on her lung-powered horn and left us to the sea lions.'

We should never have pitched our tent in a sea lion colony. Most nights they shuffled up to bed by our tent, then quarrelled. When the bulls decided to fight around the tent, a sleepy, angry figure would emerge and fail to make even the slightest impact on hides like polished cement. We constantly feared the tent would be ripped when the bulls tangled with guy ropes.

Again, our campsite looked out on to a bay, much smaller than on Tower, and with reefs, a much rougher sea, and coarse sand instead of Tower's coral beach. We had no enticing lagoon behind this camp; just grey scrub and cacti, which stretched away to the centre of the island, in places totally impenetrable, but thinning out towards the southern tip.

Hood Island seemed a different world. BirdLife International has declared Hood an Important Bird and Biodiversity Area for its many interesting species, especially its colony of waved albatross, which otherwise breeds only on La Plata, an island closer to mainland Ecuador. With them and the blue-footed booby, we had two new and unusual subjects, plus other endemic Hood species to discover. And the terrain pleased us mightily. After all the stumbling on the jagged, sharp Tower lava, here, on this ancient island, we had large smooth boulders; it was such a relief not to be constantly watching our feet.

More importantly, the heat of Tower had been replaced by something often more like Scotland. The Humboldt Current veers to the west long before it reaches Tower but keeps Hood cold. Mornings would often bring rain or the *garúa* (drizzle), which cut out the sun's heat and produced dull, grey weather. Both air and sea temperatures often showed a gloomy 67F (19°C) compared with days up to 87F (30°C) on Tower. On Hood we went long periods without sun – and any sunny spells often arrived around midday, rendering them hopeless for photography so endlessly frustrating for Bryan. In a mid-August letter home, I wrote about an exception: 'a pleasant day, like a summer morning in the UK'. And about a sunny day in September I unwittingly remarked: 'I'm glad we nest on the south side, the cold is bad enough there. This is the Galapagos weather we had heard about, and Tower was a pleasant surprise.'

Hood, one of the oldest Galapagos islands at around four million years, is also the most southerly, some 137 miles from Darwin, the northernmost. Accounts of its size seem to range between 23 and 40 square miles! It rises to nearly 700 feet at the highest point. Two areas in particular attract visitors. The long and beautiful white sandy beach of Gardner Bay stretches for more than a mile along the northeast, with sea lions, good walking and fine swimming. Our coarser beach in the south was one of a series favoured by sea lions, and three separate colonies occurred all within the 300 yards between us and Punta Suarez, with the largest colony at the end.

Punta Suarez, a low peninsula of lava, projects into a frequently rough complex of currents dominated by the cold Antarctic waters of the Humboldt. Although within one degree of latitude from the Equator, the chilly water – sometimes only 65F (18°C) – made us gasp. But, unlike on Tower, we had no worries about high tides infiltrating our camp. The broiling seas occurred on the opposite side of our peninsula. Round the southerly point, waves broke savagely on the cliff side, creating a churning sea of foam. Marine iguanas trying to come ashore had to flatten themselves and cling to the high rocks with each huge wave but were usually sucked back several times before making a battered landing. A gigantic blowhole channelled surging waves into mighty columns as much as 100 feet high and their muffled explosion boomed across to our side of the island. From it a mist of salt spray would sweep across the hinterland, killing every blade of vegetation, encrusting boulders with salt and leaving salt pans in hollows. Looking across the waste of smooth reddish boulders into the setting sun conveyed an overwhelming impression of desolation and the feeling that we were intruders. The whole southern peninsula consisted of a litter of boulders, to the east divided by lines and patches of thorny scrub.

From the tip of Punta Suarez the ground rose steadily along the north coast for about two miles with a passable route along the clifftops. Large numbers of tropicbirds and shearwaters nested in the high and pitted cliffs. Beyond them the previously sparse, spiny, lichen-covered shrubs extended right to the cliff edge. Until the scrub became just too dense, breeding waved albatross pairs were scattered thinly all along this section of clifftop. Soon the vegetation became penetrable only with extreme difficulty. The albatrosses did not try, and after spending ages covering half a mile we too abandoned the attempt.

About a mile inland and three or four miles further north, a high, rocky outcrop gives fine views down to the south point, up to the north coast and across the 40 miles of sea beyond to the island of San Cristóbal. Galapagos hawks nested on the outcrop. Along our side of the peninsula, firm boulders allowed a pleasant walk to the next point northwards. On one walk, two Española racer snakes, with their pale yellow zigzag stripes along each side, curled beside our route, and thousands of very small lava lizards scuttled in all directions. Back then it was impossible to push any further through to the beach of Gardner Bay. A trail now connects the two areas.

Bryan described how we got to know Hood and the pleasures afforded by familiarity:

'There were no tracks to our bird colonies, but we soon found our feet wandering precisely the same way each day, threading automatically across the stony flats, through scrub and over heaps of lava. Here was a slab that always cockled; there a complete goat's skeleton, every bone in situ; in this bush a half-finished finches' nest, maybe it belonged to the Darwin's finch I saw carried off in the yellow talons of a hawk. These and similar landmarks were our milestones. Like wild animals we had our home range mapped and used the easiest routes. In its way such familiarity, especially when extended to animals, is as satisfying as more dramatic experiences, though less spectacular and harder to communicate.'

Our beach sat in a bay that curved out to a reef. One warmer, calmer morning we swam out to try fishing, as usual unsuccessfully. The old bull sea lion followed but seemed to have accepted us as part of his harem. Sensing a shape beside us, we felt a frisson as a large turtle swept past. We had to take care to avoid stepping on a beautiful green carpet. Not a carpet at all but thousands of bright green sea urchins, similar to ours at home but smaller, resembling a forest floor of slightly open beech masts. Despite the fierce surf, the underwater world of the littoral zone was staggeringly prolific for huge stretches of this coast. In a few square yards tens of thousands of sea creatures – sponges, molluscs, algae, crabs, seaweeds, cowries and so many more – painted an intricate pattern of yellows, greens, whites, purples, reds.

Several of the birds we had got to love, or swear at, on Tower were there to meet us on Hood. The dopey doves quickly moved in, blinking their staring blue-rimmed eyes, flying dementedly around and being always in the way. But what was this? A bigger and better mockingbird with a longer, more curved beak and, we quickly discovered, an omnivorous, carnivorous appetite, and a total disregard for good manners. It was a different species, the Española mockingbird. They seemed ubiquitous, poking their longer noses into everything. Their numbers, fearlessness and passion for fat or anything liquid, drove us into a frenzy. Meals and their preparation became a constant trial, like a jam-sandwich picnic, with wasps.

Hood has many ground finches but nothing equivalent to our coal-black Poppet from Tower. Swallow-tailed gulls nested there, though not by our camp, their reveille duties taken over by the night-long cacophony of sea lions. And we saw many Galapagos hawks, sadly recording their depredations, especially on booby chicks. Short-eared owls also took a fair share.

Compared to the marine iguanas on Tower – which are small, solemn and black – the subspecies present on Hood is much larger and gaudier. Outside the breeding season they sport red mottling, but in full courtship flow they add large areas of green to the mix, becoming the 'Christmas iguana'.

There is also a lava lizard that occurs only on Hood (the Española lava lizard) and a unique form of giant tortoise (although there are different views on whether it is a separate species or subspecies). The latter almost became extinct; its eggs and young providing food for various predators, the adults being easily shipped by whalers, and their habitat reduced to spiny scrub by introduced goats. From an initial estimated population of 2,400 individuals, the 14 remaining tortoises were shipped off for a most successful breeding programme in the 1960s. Once reintroduced, they began breeding again on Hood in 1990, with 860 now thought present. Following the elimination of goats in 1978, the centre of Hood became virtually impenetrable. It is hoped that the reintroduction of tortoises will eventually control the vegetation and restore the large cactus forests destroyed by the goats.

Unlike our time on Tower, we didn't have a typical day and felt ourselves tossed about by the whims of a weather god. His malign and unpredictable influence caused havoc with our subjects, too. For much of the time, most of them seemed to be doing very little; lethargy reigned. Bryan ascribed our apparent laziness to the euphoria of suddenly having a selection of new reading matter, but things were pretty quiet at this time of year.

We had been on Hood for over two weeks before we saw 15 Nazca boobies at their colony one evening. At the end of September and through October they started to tune up, and eventually we recorded some displays; their new breeding season was about to begin. It seems that on Hood they lay their eggs between November and February, rather than August to November as on Tower, and usually breed about once a year.

Several waved albatrosses sporadically attended the colony to feed their fat chicks, normally sunk hunched under a bush. Although often absent, some days a few younger albatrosses gathered in groups; ringing 14, we began recording and filming their displays. In mid-August their breeding area was almost deserted and any birds that did appear were very inactive. Towards the end of the month groups were arriving, often dividing into pairs, with some displaying a little before leaving again. We ringed a further few. Albatrosses are extremely strong and, as in ringing any large bird, the trick is to always use one hand to hold them firmly by the bill or the back of the head. Once I fluffed this and found my hand held firmly in an albatross grip. Not a bleeding incident, as with the serrated gannet vice, but impossible to extricate myself with just one remaining hand. Yells for help were met with: 'Just wait till I get some photos.' And, of course, that particular film happened to be torn by the faulty winding mechanism.

It wasn't until late September that any albatrosses resumed their desultory display. So although we were able to film and record their display and ring quite a number, the albatrosses attending the colony were either feeding young or were young adults maybe having a practice before returning the following year. Apparently all albatrosses leave Hood in late December or early January, the newly fledged youngsters dispersing out to sea for up to six years. Breeding adults return around March to begin a new breeding season, and some younger adults return to choose partners and territories, perfect their dancing and perhaps breed for the first time.

Ringing enabled us to follow individual life stories, which was most rewarding, as Bryan explained:

'It is fascinating to know individual animals, as people prove by their strong emotional identification with the animal *dramatis personnae* in Tarka the otter, Elsa the lioness, Goldie the eagle and many others. Every naturalist is rewarded for living a while in one spot by getting to know his neighbours. We could hardly keep pace with ours. Besides our colour-ringed boobies and albatrosses, our dyed frigates, tame finches, mockingbirds and doves and battle-scarred bull sea lions, we had a nodding acquaintance with individual snakes, lizards, owls, flycatchers, iguanas and goats.'

Early in our stay, only the blue-footed boobies demanded much of our time, with groups at different stages of their breeding cycle, up to nine-week-old chicks. The first chore was to mark our birds and their nests. Still lacking paint, we improvised markers with strips of different materials, hence the obscure references in our field notebooks to 'red pyjama', 'June's pants' and 'old sock'. Soon scores of nests, and even empty sites in case they later acquired tenants, appeared on our large map. We easily caught a few parents by hand to colour-ring them, then tramped up and down the whole peninsula counting nests. Some 282 were occupied, of which 230 had eggs or young. Finally, we selected our 'victims' for regular weighing, prepared clean attendance sheets which would soon be tattered, smeared and covered in hieroglyphics, and began the old routine all over again.

Such a rush of activity proved premature. Towards the end of August there were broken eggs, starving chicks and corpses everywhere. Fishing conditions had deteriorated again. However, two weeks into September, after mists for several days, the remaining chicks put on weight; we found new eggs; and doves, hawks and ground finches started building. Then, towards the end of the month, came more high tides and very rough seas, and the chicks were back to losing weight. Almost no nests still had twins; a clear demonstration of the effectiveness of having young hatched around five days apart. In good times, two chicks and, very occasionally, three would survive. In bad times, the elder, more importunate chick would be given more of the scarce food and the younger one would starve to death.

Come 1 November, just three days remained before our departure from Hood. Under wholly cloudy skies, we morosely performed a final grand round of duties: weighing, measuring and noting nest contents. Bryan was desperate to finish filming the boobies, but the day remained obdurately dull. It seemed that we would leave not with a bang but a whimper.

Yet the bang did arrive, with two days of glorious weather, Bryan's final filming, and the Royal Yacht *Britannia* (see *Chapter 16*). Even the albatrosses started displaying again.

14

THE WAVED ALBATROSS

BRYAN

Albatrosses are both clownish and magnificent, goony birds and royal. In their element, windswept oceans, they are peerless. On their breeding grounds they dance and display with incredibly droll antics, their regal dignity shattered in one bout of a 'bill-clappering', head-swaying, donkey-braying ritual. Albatrosses are notably oceanic, ranging vast distances, especially out of the breeding season. They are associated mainly with stormy Antarctic seas; the black-browed and wandering albatrosses breed in the rigorous fastnesses of South Georgia and the royal, sooty, grey-headed, Buller's and others range the cold southern oceans. But the black-footed and Laysan albatrosses, the 'goony' birds, nest on the tropical Pacific atolls of Midway and Laysan, and the waved albatross breeds nowhere in the world except Hood, that speck of time-smoothed Galapagos lava, and – for a few pairs – La Plata Island, 650 miles away, off the Ecuadorian mainland.

Like the rest of their order (an evolutionary grouping including fulmars, storm-petrels and shearwaters), albatrosses are 'tubenoses'. All albatrosses have a hooked upper beak covered with horny plates, and the nostrils open from short tubes, one on each side of the middle plate. They have relatively long, slender legs, with feet webbed between three toes instead of between all four as in boobies. Their food is digested to produce the oil on which the young are fed.

Waved albatrosses are a bit larger than a farmyard goose, with imposing chests covered in fine wavy lines. Their eight pounds are gracefully borne on a majestic eight-foot wingspread. They walk easily on long, rather thin legs, placing their large pale grey feet with rolling dignity, rather, one imagines, as Dr Samuel Johnson rolled his majestic frame. Their huge bills, about six inches long and very deep, with a respectable hook on the end, are a shiny yellow; grossly artificial like that of a bathtub duck. The deep brown eyes, with prominent eye ridges and a rather flattened forehead, give them a peculiar facial expression, at once stupid and severe. But no bird with large brown eyes is devoid of dignity; indeed, one illogically tends to expect more intelligence from brown-eyed birds. Hens, with their pale yellow eyes, look as silly as they are, whilst the limpid brown eyes of the tawny owl contrast with the mad yellow light in the irises of the short-eared owl; it is the tawny that symbolises wisdom.

The southeast Pacific is albatrosses' to roam. We first saw them between the Guayas gulf and the Galapagos, some 200 miles east of the islands, but they range vast distances from Hood. Albatrosses probably range further during the breeding season than any other bird, and waved albatrosses have been seen in Japanese waters. They have the long, narrow wings of the far, fast flier and glider as in our own fulmar. They revel in wind and are helpless without it. In ocean areas covered by dependable wind systems, vast crossings are no energy problem to an albatross. In flight their feet project slightly beyond their tail and doubtless add a few welcome inches of surface area with which to combat unruly currents.

Before landing on Hood, waved albatrosses often gather in large rafts half a mile or more offshore – a habit common to several, though by no means all, oceanic birds that nest in colonies. Landing and taking off is difficult for an albatross on Hood. Natural runways, used literally as such, are thickly strewn with boulders large and small, and stubbled with scrubby, spiny bushes. Albatrosses cannot brake very effectively because they have the high stalling speed that goes with long, narrow wings with a high aspect ratio, so they hit the ground quite fast instead of floating gently down like a gull. Perhaps because of the boulders, they try to stop suddenly instead of landing at a run and often fall flat on their faces. Leg and foot injuries are common results of bad landings and we found two birds that had killed themselves, obviously when landing. Accidents of this kind are probably one of the main hazards for these long-lived birds (a waved albatross was known to be 40 years old and a Laysan albatross 70); large predatory fish may be another. They are capable of recovering from extensive bone injuries, and skeletons (of another species) have been found that had repaired massive damage to the sternum. Waved albatrosses were not the only ones to come croppers; when chasing them we fell too and were far from confident of our ability to repair broken bones.

When taking off along their runways they run fast, with wings outspread and feet pattering lightly and loosely over the ground, gradually working up speed until airborne. Or they may collide violently with a boulder, coming to a jarring halt before limping off with their ludicrous nautical roll. At other times they plod dourly to the cliff edge – a wearisome business calling for frequent rests. They rise from a sitting position in two stages, first on to the tarsi, which rest flat against the ground, and then on to their large flat feet.

Like most long-lived seabirds, waved albatrosses do not breed until they are several years old. Five years old is usual; the youngest breeder was three, while others have been older than six. Birds returning to the colony for the first time since leaving as a youngster begin practising their 'dance'. All species of albatross have an extremely complicated courtship ritual, which they practise long before they breed.

The waved albatross dance intrigued us, and we spent many hectic hours watching and recording it. It was easy to find displaying birds: they gathered in groups in clearings amid the scrub, with their courtship audible from easily half a mile away thanks to its prolonged howls, derisive *ha-ha-ha* call and loud bill-clappering like a football rattle. We devised a shorthand sign for each movement and I dictated the sequence of events, scoring them with a stopwatch while June scribbled frantically. It would have been far more sensible to have taken a tape recorder. We used a column each for male, female, and pair, to record the exact relationship in time between each bird's actions. Anybody overhearing us might well have wondered at the monologue: 'Fifty seconds, male *ha-ha-ha*; female clappers; male skypoint and moo; fifty-two seconds, pair bill-circling' and so on.

When we arrived on Hood in July, egg-laying was over and there were already some month-old chicks hiding under the dry scrub while their parents were away at sea. Being on Hood for just three months towards the end of the albatross breeding season made our research difficult. I tried to work out their breeding regime from our records of 32 ringed birds but had insufficient information.

Nevertheless, there was some spirited display among birds without egg or chick, particularly in the early morning and late afternoon; during the day they mainly rested quietly beneath the bushes. By marking them with coloured rings we discovered that these footloose birds returned to the same area each time they came to the island but wandered quite extensively and danced with several different partners, even if they stuck mainly to one for the duration of their 'shore leave'. Some of these dancing birds, all of which were obviously without egg or chick, were young adults, three years old. We knew this because they were ringed in 1961, on Punta Suarez – in other words, they had returned to the precise area in which they were born, as do most seabirds. This isn't always the case, however. Interestingly, in the 1960s, a bird recorded breeding on Punta Suarez was found dancing at the opposite end of the island the following year. More recently, a group of presumably young birds has been recorded on Tower, with an egg (that did not hatch) laid there in 2006. Most seabirds have 'pioneers' who go off exploring.

The dance, or 'ecstatic ritual', is one of the most extraordinary displays imaginable. When several pairs display simultaneously the air is full of weird noises – whoops, grunts, rattles and clunks and mad laughter. Highly entertaining, but also exhibiting complex ritualised behaviour, the dancing partners co-operate with great precision. They face each other so that, leaning forward, their bills meet from about halfway down then rapidly slide over the top of the other's, in a half circle and back again. The bills mainly remain in contact, but often jump apart, before meeting again, making a wooden, clattering noise.

Dancing 'excites' the birds and oil on the nostrils, applied from the preen gland at the base of the tail, lubricates the bills, which become glossy and slippery. Whatever other movements intervene, the partners return to bill-circling. One bird, usually the male, frequently breaks off and snaps bolt upright, staring fixedly ahead with the peculiar expression imparted by the flattened head and conspicuous 'eyebrows'. The other may follow suit or else keep on bill-circling in mid-air, too slow to react. After a forward bow, they return to circling with sustained vigour. Then, suddenly, one arches its neck and, holding its head motionless, fixedly touches a particular spot on its flank.

While weighing adults, I examined this spot closely but found no obvious difference. Beneath the thick, quilt-like contour feathers there was a large discrete patch of feathers with loose, downy structure. Perhaps it was particularly sensitive to touch and reinforces the display with a pleasurable stimulus, or has some other connection with the movement, but it seems an area worth closer study. Allying a display movement to a feature invisible both to the displaying bird and its dancing partner seems an unusual phenomenon, worth adding to the movements directing attention to local colour or external structures. Why or how the specialised patch of feathers evolved is another question.

Even as its head sweeps down to touch its flank, the partner, still in the forward, low, bill-circling position, clappers its mandibles together so rapidly that they are just a blur, whereupon the side-touching bird stretches its neck, throws its bill vertically upwards and utters a loud, prolonged and high-pitched call: *whoo-ooo*. Following a swift bow, it is back to bill-circling. In another part of this esoteric and athletic display one or both birds suddenly click into an upright position, necks fully stretched, and silently open their bills to reveal the widest possible gape, as though advertising Bird's custard powder. Then they snap the bill closed with a loud resonant 'clunk', which owes its quality partly to the sounding chamber formed by the mouth (one cannot produce the noise with a dead beak and skull) and return to the circling.

After some time one bird turns away and with the most ridiculous walk imaginable – a grotesque caricature of a movement in which, with the bill tucked into the chest, the head sways right over and down at each step – leads the other, also walking in the same exaggerated fashion, to some particular spot. After several minutes, perhaps even half an hour, the display ends for the time being with one bird assuming a squatting position, head down, neck retracted and bill pointing between its feet, while bobbing jerkily up and down and uttering a repeated low note. This 'forward bobbing' is actually a special display indicating ownership of a site; it is unfailingly performed, for instance, when a bird settles down after returning to its egg or small chick. As we shall see, it also plays an important part in the chick's life.

A well-practised pair performs together very smartly, whereas birds new to each other seem indecisive and do not synchronise correctly. If things go awry the male will sometimes break off in an apparent tantrum and even briefly attack his partner or redirect his frustration by attacking a nearby male. Rival males stretch to their full height and with beaks gaping widely, run at each other, calling (*ha-ha-ha*) and occasionally biting. Although these skirmishes seldom develop into a real fight, at least one male was seen to die after a prolonged battle.

Display strengthens the bond between pair members and ensures their compatibility perhaps by encouraging the disruption of pairs that do not function well together. Compatibility between pair members of extremely long-lived birds like albatrosses can be of decisive importance in breeding. Albatrosses may expect to live at least 20 years, probably very much more, and it will be well worthwhile acquiring a compatible mate and sticking to it; most seabirds keep the same partner for several years or for life.

The single large egg of the waved albatross, weighing nearly half a pound, is laid on the bare ground, mainly in April and May.

There is not even a pretence at nest building, either real or symbolic. Sometimes, indeed, the female lays the egg in a crack between boulders and then cannot incubate it and is apparently too dull-witted to roll it out with her beak. The egg is incubated for around two months against a single large brood patch, into which it fits snugly. Because of this, albatrosses cannot incubate a donated extra egg, unlike boobies, which incubate their eggs underfoot and can manage to stretch their webs a bit further to deal with an extra egg. Albatrosses settle on their egg by lowering their breast and then giving a gigantic hitch upwards and forwards. They make the same awkward movement when hoisting their bulk on to a tiny chick, much to its discomfort.

Initially, albatross chicks are most delightful objects, thickly covered with chocolate-brown, beige or a beautiful silvery-grey down, and with their eyes open when they hatch, so they look attractive from the start. They cheep musically and constantly, and each time the parent lowers itself to brood, it utters soft disyllabic calls; each call covers a considerable range in tone, giving room for variation between individuals. Poor albatross chicks; they have five and a half boring, uncomfortable and undignified months ahead before they can take to their wonderful wings and become ocean wanderers; they have first to become little more than gigantic bags of oil. The parents brood their chick for the first two weeks or so and then leave it unguarded, returning only to feed it, though for a short period they brood it after each feed.

Soon the chick hobbles and wobbles away from its nest and finds a hiding place under the bushes. It often favours one resting place for weeks, excavating a snug hollow into which the convex curve of its bulging stomach fits comfortably. Albatrosses nest in scattered groups, so there is often a handful of chicks dotted about a patch of scrub, into and under which they burrow, probably to find shade.

I quickly began to wonder how the parents located their chick; obviously not by wandering around peering under every bush and calling their offspring by name. Luckily I saw what happened. An albatross swept in from the sea and began walking towards a chick nursery a good many yards away. I immediately dashed to the area by a roundabout route (to avoid scaring the bird), then hid behind a bush. The adult came along, stopping every few yards to assume the 'forward-bobbing' position and repeatedly utter the low disyllabic note. This call electrified one of the chicks hidden in the bushes; it stumbled to its feet and moved towards the adult. When still out of sight of its parent it gave the plaintive chick version of the call.

Just as the baby sea lion homes on to its mother by calling, so the albatross chick and its parent found each other by moving towards the right voice, and the two made contact about five feet from the site. This immediately suggested one good reason why adult and chick call so frequently in the first hours after hatching; this is when they learn each other's voice. It also explained why that particular call was used; it was capable of considerable individual variation. Even I could detect individual differences in the two-syllable combination so there would be little chance of the chick mistaking its parent's voice.

Lying hidden beneath the scrub I could also watch the entire feeding operation from extremely close quarters. Tubenoses feed their young on oil manufactured by a part of the stomach and mixed with more recent stomach contents such as fish, pieces of squid and crustaceans. The whole lot is then poured from the opening of the oesophagus at the back of the adult's mouth. A great advantage of this system is that the adult can continue feeding for days at sea until it has manufactured large quantities of oil and then fly vast distances back to the colony. By contrast, a booby or frigate has to hasten back once its crop is full. Far from making food for their young from it, they can give them only the raw material and cannot even significantly hold up digestion. Accordingly, the fishing range and duration of boobies and frigates is limited by this factor quite apart from anything else. If they take too long there will be nothing left for their offspring.

When the parent first returns, the albatross is usually willing to feed the chick unasked but the chick helps matters along by nibbling gently near the base of the parent's mandibles, a way of begging very different from the frenzied lunging of the hungry young booby. The chick's nibbling is highly stimulating, and the parent lowers its head and foreparts, without actually squatting, and opens its bill. The chick usually inserts its beak from the side, the adult depressing the lower mandible extensively and also lowering the tongue to reveal the pink, slightly swollen tissue surrounding the top of the food pipe. The chick places its bill above the swollen epiglottis and strokes by moving its lower mandible up and down. The chick continues the nibbling movements directed to the adult's bill but now with its beak sideways against the inside of the parent's throat. It has gained entry and works the adult up to regurgitating. A thin stream of stomach contents squirts into the chick's mouth from the side of its parent's beak. Much to the disappointment of the attendant mockingbirds, very little is spilt. Sometimes chicks take liquid from the trough of the adult's lower mandible. At intervals the adult closes its bill and swallows convulsively, clunking its great mandibles together. A chick may wheedle as many as 12 feeds though the last ones involve much effort by the parent, which makes a deep snuffling, almost a grunting, and pumps violently as it forces the food up. Its supply exhausted, the adult moves away and rests, champing noisily and head shaking so vigorously that the mandibles rattle like false teeth in a tumbler.

The chick swells visibly as the oil hoses into its stomach. In one bout of feeding, lasting a few minutes only, an albatross chick can take about 2,000 grams of oil; over four pounds of concentrated food at a sitting. For the first almost six months of its life the chick is hardly more than a great, oil-filled skin, covered in matted brown down. It is now grotesque, with the fascination of the truly ugly. After hitting the oil hard, its bulging stomach protrudes in a majestic curve, and it waddles slowly and heavily, with its tarsi flat against the ground; it is far too heavy and unbalanced to stand on its feet. Its head and neck feathers become oily and stick together in spikes, revealing large patches of corpse-like bluish skin and the rather ugly external opening of the ear.

But its eyes redeem it; full, liquid, dark brown eyes invite one to project an air of patient suffering on to this obese, obtruding belly and these prolonged indignities. Oil dribbles from its bill and it constantly gapes and swallows as though exhausted by its gargantuan feast. Even the mockingbirds that run round scraping up the spills were heavily oil stained. We called them the mechanics and could always recognise the oily mockers from the albatross area when they came scavenging around our camp.

Between feeds the oil bags just sit in the shade, but nevertheless lose weight very rapidly. In the 24 hours after a feed a young albatross may lose as much as 1,100 grams (more than two pounds) though the longer it goes without food the more slowly it loses weight. The chick may be fed on several successive days (seven was our highest figure) but it may, on the other hand, go just as long unfed. Youngish chicks, on average, get a feed about once every two or three days. This regime gives the parents the opportunity, on occasion, to remain at sea for between one and two weeks or alternatively, if food is available near at hand, to return daily. Once they are older, chicks have to wait much longer.

No albatross chicks starved during our stay on Hood. There was nothing to suggest that the parents encounter the bad patches common to the frigates and some boobies. However, occasionally mass desertion of eggs occurs and parents are recorded rolling the eggs, which often crack. Both behaviours are yet to be fully explained. Both El Niño and, it has been suggested, mosquitoes, exacerbated by climate change, can lead to loss or desertion. In some years, such as 2015, virtually no young are raised. Since a female lays only a single egg each year, the species is exceptionally vulnerable. And since albatrosses are usually faithful to their breeding areas, some colonies have been lost as vegetation has regrown and taken over the bare rocks following the removal of introduced goats. It is hoped that the reintroduction of tortoises will eventually control the vegetation.

The period between hatching and flying is around five and a half months. Once juveniles are ready, they start flapping their wings a lot, jump up and down a bit, then make their way to the cliff edge and eventually psyche themselves up to launch themselves off. They do not return to be fed by their parents. The young albatross, magically transformed from the ugly duckling, heads out into the Pacific.

In all we ringed 100 chicks. Subsequently, Prof. Mike Harris, who started checking the albatrosses at Punta Suarez the year after we were there, retrapped 70 of these during the period 1969–72.

This showed that the bulk of the chicks from our year survived to return to breed. He also found 17 of the 21 older birds that we had marked. Survival of albatrosses of all ages from one year to the next was obviously very high during our time. Recent research, however, has shown that survival has declined (more of which later).

One of my field notebooks is heavily stained with yellow oil. Its dirty, smelly pages are limp, and the pencilled figures look impressively ancient. It holds the albatross weight records for those unfortunate young which regularly suffered our intrusion, and the oil signifies their detestation of this interference. I don't know who disliked the job most. As soon as we appeared they rose from their dusty scrapes among the boulders, in which they had been squatting impassively, and stumbled and lurched off to the bushes, falling over their stomach and feet. The unfed ones were light and could even sprint; the others were easy prey. When we put out a hand towards them they adopted the submissive beak-hiding posture that they show to an attacking adult. The idea was to snatch their bill and keep it firmly closed, not only because we wanted their true weight but because their oil stank like rotten turnips. Poor birds, but at least they were not harmed; it is a miserable attitude that regards higher animals simply as specimens for collecting or for scientific investigation, regardless of the suffering caused them.

It's easy enough to weigh a small bird: pop it into a breathable pouch, where the dark and confinement stop its struggles, then hang the pouch on a spring balance. Simple. Small albatross chicks went the same way with no problems. It was the indignant oil bags that presented difficulties. And remember we had to hold their bills firmly or their last feed sprayed over both of us, our equipment and records. A sling was the only answer, for eventually it held their kicking feet and pinioned the flailing wings. But getting to that stage left us both hot, scratched and bad-tempered, especially if we had first to chase the lighter ones. Imagine weighing an adult, though somehow it felt easier to hold them under one arm, thus restraining the wings whilst grappling with the feet. Unlike the slashing gannet, most were actually stoical and submitted with dignity.

It was difficult to understand why the Hood albatrosses nested where they did. They generally avoided the cliff edge even though it was easy to land and take off there, because the young were so clumsy that they often fell and would have toppled over the cliff at the slightest excuse (I saw one do it). The youngsters' total lack of elementary caution was astounding; they also seemed unable to distinguish between spatially dangerous and spatially practicable manoeuvres. Ignoring their girth they hurried themselves down inclines with the dignity of a runaway barrel or jammed their portly bulk between boulders with equal disregard for consequences. I was in no doubt whatsoever that waved albatrosses were basically adapted for flat-ground nesting and it was of great interest to find that the young, when in the nest scrape or in a resting place, even showed the backward-kicking movements by which the black-footed albatross chick, for example, prevents itself from being buried alive in blown sand. Nowadays the waved albatross no longer needs such behaviour but it has apparently survived as a relic from its ancestry and no doubt is still slightly functional in preparing a more comfortable scrape.

But why did the waved albatross nest many hundreds of yards from the cliff edge, among dense spiny shrub that meant picking a tortuous, obstacle-strewn route to their nest, when there were lovely open spaces, fringed with the necessary scrub for shelter and yet empty of albatrosses? The factors responsible for the precise choice of habitat in birds are far less understood than might be expected.

In the past, although the population of the waved albatross fluctuated according to the vagaries of El Niño, it seemed to hold its own. Whilst its population was far from large – indeed, at a level that would be perilously near to extinction for some species – the waved albatross was in no danger. The population was thought stable during the 20th century, with 17,000 pairs in 1994. The removal of goats and subsequent increase in vegetation has made it extremely difficult to count the inland albatrosses, so a realistic assessment of the present whole population has not been possible. However, recent work has shown that the numbers at Punta Suarez and Punta Cevallos are declining. Now considered Critically Endangered by the IUCN, waved albatrosses are unable to produce enough young to compensate for the higher rate at which birds are dying.

The huge increase in local fishing along the Peruvian coast and industrial long-line fishing are the major causes of mortality. Apparently by-catch in local waters takes more males, further reducing the number of breeding pairs, and there has been a recent increase in harvesting for food and feathers. During the breeding season, waved albatrosses fish extensively within the Galapagos Marine Reserve, where long-line fishing is prohibited. But albatrosses spend a third of their time on high seas where no country has jurisdiction. It needs international co-operation to ensure their survival. Several organisations are attempting to encourage fishermen to reduce their threat to waved albatrosses by incorporating bird-scaring devices and underwater line-launching so that the bait is out of sight and reach of the birds. Fortunately, research continues and strenuous efforts are being made to ensure that this unique bird does not become extinct.

15

SEA LIONS AND FUR SEALS

BRYAN

With fish swarming in the seas around the islands, which themselves offer miles of rocky shore and fine beaches, the Galapagos provide wonderful breeding grounds for Galapagos sea lions. Following genetic analysis, this is now considered an archipelago exclusive distinct from the Californian sea lion, those highly intelligent eared seals that are the source of captive sea lions.

Sea lions will breed among jumbled boulders, on the rocky platforms at the base of sea-worn cliffs or on any kind of sandy beach. We first met them on South Plaza. The bulls filled the air with bellowing as they patrolled the coast where the females and pups lay. In the evening, several females played around and under the boat with marvellous grace in the clear green depths; with a lazy sweep of a foreflipper they turn, accelerate or decelerate. They sensitively control each sinuous twist of their supple bodies, banking, turning, rolling or shooting straight down with a decisive burst of power.

They love play and often seek out the biggest rollers. As the breaker rears before dissolving into a welter of foam, the sea lions are swept up in a wall of water and hang embedded, cavorting gaily before crashing down with the broken wave. They often played around as we swam, shooting round and under us and leaping clear of the water. Small ones were fine, but the bulls are another matter. Even on land, we fled the first time a huge bull launched itself into a ponderous but ground-devouring charge, urging itself on with lolloping, head-rolling bounds. We soon realised that they would sheer away at the last moment, but when half a ton of bone and muscle bears down with a fearsome grunting, the instinct for self-preservation suddenly takes charge. Even uphill, a bull sea lion can gallop at ungainly speed and downhill, for a few yards, you have to be pretty nippy to keep ahead. In the water, of course, he moves like a torpedo.

On Hood the beach in front of our tent was sea lion territory with a bull in constant attendance. It was nerve-racking to fetch a bucketful of seawater in the dark for that rock dimly discernible at the water's edge might suddenly rise and charge. It wasn't much better even in daylight. I can still see June standing naked in the shallows, rinsing clothes and saying 'shoo shoo' ever more apprehensively as the bull urged its bulk balefully through the water, then backing hurriedly, and retreating pell-mell as it gathered for the final rush. In fact, we never met one that pressed home its attack if you so much as flipped a handful of sand or water in its face; they always made off with an eye-rolling backward look and much roaring.

We were intruders from the start. Our camp on Punta Suarez was pitched just where scores of sea lions were accustomed to sleep. The procedure was always the same. After a day of constant noise from the tireless bull patrolling his stretch of beach, darkness fell and a short period of silence followed. Then the procession began. Just beyond the feeble range of our paraffin light, we would hear snuffles, snorts and dull thuds like somebody dragging a sack of potatoes. If we were lucky, it would be a female or a partly grown youngster arriving; not too bad. Inevitably, sooner or later came a short bellow and much more impressive crashing and slithering. This was a bull who had slipped past the beach master in the darkness and gained the sanctuary of the bushes and sandy clearings near our camp.

Camp? It wasn't there last time the bull came ashore and he behaved exactly as though it wasn't there this time either. One evening we were petrified by an enormous crash and the whole tent twanged and quivered as a large bull, roaring testily, snapped our guys like strings, to rid himself of their annoying entanglement. Even when the tide was such that sea lions were feeding in the first few hours of darkness, they came slithering up into the bushes in the small hours, ready for a few hours' sibilant sleep a few inches from our heads. One night, I tried several times to wake my loudly snoring wife; just a baby sea lion with its noisy head against her side of the tent. Or maybe a baby would start yelling for its mum like a lost lamb and a cow–pup duet ensued. The bulls took hours to settle down and usually gave a few bellows first. This invariably brought the master charging up the beach, roaring in reply, upon which the intruder kept quiet till things had settled down – and then roared again. Sometimes chases and fights, with the most frightful snarling and roaring, went on just outside the tent.

The effect in the blackness of the night may easily be imagined. We lay rigidly in our sleeping bags, waiting for the tent to collapse with a rib-cracking bull sea lion or two on top of us. Sometimes, in desperation, I crawled out with a torch and anything that came to hand – once the detachable alloy table legs which ever after were crazily twisted. The torch blinded them while a few whacks on the backside bewildered and sent them crashing off through the bushes. Then there was peace for a while until a newcomer arrived knowing nothing of humans who dazzled and belaboured sea lions. But morning always found a few sea lions sound asleep near the tent. More in hope than expectation we tried to keep them out with a barricade of boxes and cans, but their circus instincts led them triumphantly over all obstacles.

The harem in our rock garden numbered about 30 cows, and there were two more similar groups just along the beach, all within about 300 yards. Each had its master who patrolled back and forth just offshore, calling monotonously and progressing in a series of smooth, slow dives typical of patrolling bulls – head out, roar, blubbing noise as the head goes down, hindflippers appear elegantly apposed, and slide smoothly under, head reappears, roar and submerge again. They sometimes patrol for hours and then rest, perhaps on their backs in the shallows, great foreflippers folded neatly on their chest, or maybe flat on the sand, like a great mound of rubber. Sometimes they slept in this position underwater, blowing streams of bubbles and occasionally lifting their heads to breathe. Elsewhere, elephant seals do exactly the same, and the act of rising to breathe seems fully automatic.

Bulls, besides being much bigger than cows, are enormously thicker in the neck and shoulders and have very steep, high foreheads which give them an unmistakable profile. Individuals vary in this character and in colour, and often can be recognised even by a human observer. As in many other gregarious mammals, the 'ownership' of females is decided and maintained by fighting and the females have very little say in the matter; presumably one bull is as good as another to an oestrous female.

We were curious to know how long one master could keep his harem against the challenge of intruder bulls and kept records of all the encounters we saw. The results revealed a complicated series of coups, counter-coups and dictatorships of variable duration. First, it was obvious that there was a considerable surplus of challenger bulls. It could hardly have been otherwise if, as happens in most seals, equal numbers of males and females are born, and neither sex is much more likely to die before breeding age. We often saw three or four massive bulls lying out just a few yards beyond the limits of a bull's territory, and in one or two cases, we recognised unsuccessful challengers amongst them. The discrepancy is less than appears at first sight, since several bulls eventually serve one harem. Bulls look much fiercer when hauled out and dry; the fur fluffs up and gives them a strong facial resemblance to a wolf or husky. When wet and shiny, they look rather like old men with the formidably domed forehead of the intellectual.

It was quite common to see at least four scrimmages involving five different bulls in one day, all, of course, in the one territory. There was another complicating feature: territorial bulls used to slip away for half a day or more, presumably to hunt. In their absence, a conflict involving two or three bulls might be settled only to be thrown open again by the return of the old master.

The bull in charge when we arrived on Hood probably lasted about a month – certainly not more. He was replaced in late August by a bull that received a forehead wound on 9 September and disappeared on 13 September, on which date two new bulls scrimmaged before one took over the territory. It wasn't a real fight; after a galloping chase along the beach, the pursuer caught its rival, gave it one bite on the neck and then galloped straight on in pursuit of a cow that was taking its calf out to sea. He seemed more intent on cutting it off than chasing the other bull. He didn't last long in any case. Later the same day, a bull with a long neck wound drove him away.

This neck-wounded bull was a prominent character in ensuing events. He lasted until about the end of September during which time he occasionally left his territory, returned and drove away whoever had taken over in his absence. He seemed to have one long absence from 22–24 September. On the night of 21 September, there was a great fight full of blood-curdling sound and fury; next morning a bull was lying up in the bushes with a nasty wound – a deeply lacerated patch several inches square – on the lower back. There was nobody patrolling the territory, and the wounded bull eventually went to roll in the shallows. About midday, a large bull approached very purposefully from the open sea and made straight for him. The wounded one fled abjectly and was pursued out to sea.

This new bull remained in control till 24 September, driving away two or three youngish ones in the meantime, and we thought he was the new master. But at midday a bull approached from one side of the breeding beach. He swam steadily in and then stood up and gazed at the big bull who was rolling on his back in the shallows. The latter soon looked up, saw the newcomer and immediately moved menacingly towards him. Undaunted, the incomer moved forwards equally threateningly. At last, I thought, I shall see a battle royal! But after one lusty clash, with snarling and biting, the newcomer was victorious: it showed the long neck wound of our friend who had disappeared two days previously.

Two other bulls briefly held the territory but were displaced. On 26 September the wounded bull was back but now seemed rather spent, with the skin looser on his neck. Although still apparently able to drive off bigger and fresher bulls, he didn't last much longer, and we last saw him on 30 September.

Territorial clashes between males, though usually bloodless, are exciting affairs, partly because sea lions seem so human in many ways. They haven't much in the way of elaborate threat postures but show every subtle gradation of aggressive behaviour and are able to react appropriately without the need for the highly ritualised and distinctive postures shown by many birds. Indeed, there is a case for thinking that, in general, the more intelligent animals have less ritualised behaviour than the less clever ones.

Intruders are well aware of the risks they run and approach stealthily, low in the water and swimming gently, perhaps with long stretches underwater. They recognise the meaning of everything the master does. If he sits on his haunches, with his whiskered snout pointing vertically up in the air and wavering rather uncertainly, while uttering muted, half-finished calls, they know he is very sleepy and unlikely to notice them. Watched closely, he blinks owlishly, seems about to fall asleep where he sits and gives a (quite false) heart-warming impression of an old gentleman who is really not so fierce after all, but rather lovable. If, on the other hand, he is poised alertly on his flippers, head well back and up, or lying on the beach with his head supported by a convenient rock and gazing around at intervals, intruders know he is watchful, and often slide back out to sea as stealthily as they came, probably to haul out on a stretch of no-man's beach. If the bull is patrolling actively, they are lucky to get close inshore at all before they are spotted and chased.

The chase is an interesting sight, combining great power with marvellous athleticism. Accustomed to our own laborious progress through water, it seems almost impossible that such heavy and bulky creatures as sea lions can accelerate so smoothly and vividly. Usually the master did not set off in pursuit at full speed, but swam behind for some distance, keeping pace with the intruder. Then, as though galvanised into activity, they both surged forward, throwing up enormous waves. The intruder reacted so quickly that the two appeared to accelerate simultaneously. When swimming at full speed, sea lions brought their enormous foreflippers into full play and submerged their heads so that only the smooth curve of the humped back showed above water. A sinuous motion of the hindquarters and movements of the hindflippers in the vertical plane added further power, and the hurtling bulls shoved walls of water aside as though it were no more substantial than air. Often they chased in a series of dives, jumping clean out of the water in graceful arcs, leap for leap, as dolphins and occasionally even our own seals will do. The heavy bodies plunged into the sea, throwing up a cascade, and if the intruder was overhauled there was a turmoil for a few seconds as they leapt out of the water in contorted postures and bit savagely at each other. Then one broke away and the chase went on. A bite wound on the rump was a badge of ignominy.

If an intruder was seen trying to regain the sea, a special sort of contest followed in which the master used the curve of the bay to cut off his rival – keeping him penned in the shallows, knowing that ultimately he would have to make a dash for it. When he did, the master judged the angle so beautifully that he just intercepted the fleeing bull and got in a nip. Then the two went leaping and plunging out to sea for a few hundred yards before the master returned at a leisurely pace to resume his watchful patrolling and calling. Meanwhile, the females remained, supremely uninterested, yawning and scratching and snoozing as though this rivalry had no connection with them.

Bulls inspected females and youngsters entering and leaving the group, rushing up and thrusting a whiskery face at them to get a good sniff, for scent is their main identification cue. As the animals nuzzled, their heads moved excitedly and rather jerkily, with slight head shaking, conveying a clear impression of uncertainty and some hostility. This, and reclining the head with a pronounced swaying, were about all they essayed as behaviour apart from the easily interpreted overt hostilities and sexual behaviour. The masters sometimes chased and bit partly grown youngsters, presumably if they did not belong to the group; quite often they went right up the beach to sniff at the sea lions hauled out there. Occasionally the masters played with them just offshore, not too weighed down with their responsibilities to enjoy a gambol.

The beach master's social interaction with members of his group was a noticeable feature of its organisation and marks an important difference between this position's role in the sea lion compared to the equivalent of say the elephant seal or fur seal. The latter take no interest in the young, though they quickly resent any attempt by females to leave the harem. The sea lion's duties are not confined to mere fertilisation of females, and his discrimination between his 'own' group and young from another may be a valuable means of preventing his charges from becoming too numerous. Thus, one of the first things a new beach master does is become acquainted with the members of his group and they often reciprocate his interest. At least one valuable function of his guardianship is to prevent small youngsters from straying into shark-infested waters, and for this there must obviously be an optimal group size.

The group was constantly changing, some members coming ashore to sleep and others setting off to fish. Wet sea lions lolloped up to the ranks of nicely dry and sandy ones snoring peacefully in the sun and fell on top of them, dragging soaking bodies and flippers over the sleepers' warm dry fur, thereby causing much bickering, snarling and occasionally irritable snapping. Wet youngsters seemed to nuzzle and paw the others deliberately as though to get a reaction, rather than merely in an effort to find a nice spot amongst them.

It is hard to imagine anything more contented than a line of corpulent sea lions, fast asleep in the sun on a clean sandy beach. They breathe heavily, sigh with exquisite pleasure and occasionally scratch themselves delicately with the long nails of their flexible foreflippers or rub the flies off their faces. The sand forms rims around their eyes and adds a comical element of surprise to their soulful gaze. Once we crept up to one and scratched it gently; eyes closed, it lazily lifted a flipper for us to scratch in the angle, but one blink and with a sharp startled *woof* it scrambled madly down the beach, generating a wave of alarm. Another time we stole up to a sleeping bull, and gently lifting its enormous flipper, examined the five claws set in their little pockets of skin without rousing the animal. Its fat, scarred sides heaved and its whiskers twitched as it slept luxuriously on the warm, dry sand; a warrior at rest.

Despite the constant territorial activity of the bulls, I saw mating only twice. The first time, on 18 August, occurred around dusk in two or three feet of water. The female was underwater most of the time and kept rearing her head to breathe and bite the male. The huge weight of the bull seemed to pin her down and the supple curve of his hindquarters held her firmly; he didn't grip her with his mouth. When released, she fled over the rocks, dragging her hindquarters firmly along the ground. The bull chased her, even following her into the camp area. Eventually she lay down, but shifted and squirmed restlessly, and the bull retired to the sea.

We saw another mating on 28 August around midday; this time we also saw the preliminaries. A female was ambling along the beach in the ordinary way when the bull showed interest and came ashore, giving me the impression that his initial reaction had been olfactory; oestrous females of other seal species are known to stimulate males by scent rather than by performing precopulatory or 'soliciting' behaviour. The female fled and the bull followed without really trying to catch her. When she stopped at the edge of a jumble of boulders, he didn't approach her. This seemed to stimulate her; perhaps her flight had been sexual play, for she now gambolled up to him.

A long period of play followed, in which the male nuzzled her, particularly at the base of the foreflippers, which made her jump as though tickled. He often flopped his enormous bulk on top of her and she reared her head and firmly seized the skin on his throat or chest. The male seemed thoroughly good-tempered throughout, frequently sounding a subdued version of his aggressive patrol call. Eventually he managed to wrap his hindquarters round the female and complete the mating. He left her immediately after coition to chase a young bull that had meanly entered his temporarily unguarded territory. It seemed that the pressure of challenger bulls was so great that even momentary inattention to the territory, when the master was engaged in higher matters, encouraged trespass.

One wonders for how many successive seasons bull Galapagos sea lions maintain their reproductive activity but the likelihood is that it may only be a matter of a few weeks during a single season. Bull sea lions probably show a steep drop in survival rate once they reach sexual maturity, and if they are at all comparable to elephant seals in this respect, over 85 per cent of 'old' males (in the case of the elephant seals, eight years or more) die in any year. So, once big enough to survive shark attack, the bull sea lion has a carefree life for several years, with plenty of food, pleasant sunshine and soft, secluded beaches to laze away the day – up until the point that it is ready to charge for temporary supremacy and ownership of a harem of females.

The main pupping period on Hood was between August and October, when about 20 pups were born in the two nearest colonies to our camp. Baby sea lions are extremely attractive, rather like black Labrador puppies and about as long. Their heads are a bit too big for their bodies at first and their skin full of folds. The female gives birth either on sand or among rocks and leaves the placenta where it drops, granting lava lizards (and perhaps Galapagos hawks) a free feast.

Soon after birth the mother moves the pup away from the natal area, which is usually slightly apart from the main resting place of the harem and the playground of the pups. The mother grips the pup in her mouth by the scruff of the neck and may swim a considerable distance with it. The first time we saw this we felt sure the pup would drown, for the mother apparently made absolutely no attempt to keep it above the surface. At intervals it managed to poke its head out and bleat piteously before going under again – an altogether hair-raising baptism. However, when she brought her offspring ashore it seemed none the worse, though it stumbled and sneezed for a long time.

It is delightful to watch a bunch of youngsters playing in the sunlit shallows. They chase each other under the water, climb on to boulders and knock each other off whilst the old bull cruises restlessly up and down, roaring and keeping a wary eye on them – and occasionally even herding them back if they move too far out into waters patrolled by sharks. We once found a partly grown sea lion with the whole of one foreflipper and a great piece of the shoulder torn away, leaving a raw gaping hole; it looked like the work of a shark.

The pups also gambol ecstatically on the beach, falling flat on their faces and giving themselves sandy goggles and noses. Often they sleep with one foreflipper sticking vertically up in the air, which may be a way of losing body heat and thereby regulating their temperature. June briefly made friends with one new pup; after a wary start, it began to rub against her, lift its head to have its throat tickled, and seemed delightfully tame and affectionate. Unfortunately, its mother's fright reaction so alarmed the pup that it became distrustful again, this time for good.

Female sea lions find their young by a combination of sound and scent. When the female sea lion comes ashore she calls, and the pup recognises her voice and answers. It is amusing to hear the anxious bleating of the pup and the deeper calling of the mother gradually homing on to each other, and to watch the ecstatic greeting when they meet, the mother nuzzling the pup, which stumbles and falls against her. Unknown youngsters are bitten should they approach a newly arrived female.

Sea lions suckle their young until well advanced in the next pregnancy and it is common to see a great big youngster sucking noisily at its mother's teat for hours. Eventually she turns snappish and, I suppose, gradually slackens the maternal bonds, though there is nothing like the rapid fattening and sudden desertion of young shown by some other seals. By then the young sea lion is well able to look after itself and has even a place in the beach's companionable group.

Young males at least may wander extensively during this period, now virtually secure from predators because of their size and strength. The youngster can lie like a fat torpedo, side by side with others or perhaps join up with a bull, swimming with him and hauling out by his side. I never gained any information about the nature of this rather charming association, which reminds one of the 'squire' to 'master' stag relationship in the red deer – nor do I know if it has previously been recorded for the sea lion. In time the youngster becomes more and more solitary; finds a favourite hauling out place to which, probably, he regularly returns until he becomes fully mature. In due course, he may become one of the powerful young challengers for territory and a harem. No doubt he loses his first battles, but eventually he may find a spent old bull which has to give way. In his turn, the once-wobbly scrap of sea lion thus becomes an old tyrant and beach master.

The end probably comes peacefully. Spent old bulls often die comfortably, stretched out in one of their resting places, as shown by the huge skeletons we found. Maybe such remains are those of defeated and wounded bulls, but of the hundreds of encounters we observed, none was serious enough to kill.

On Tower, we soon discovered a small colony of 20 or 30 Galapagos fur seals on the east side of the bay at the foot of the cliffs. They differ from the larger sea lions, particularly when dry, by their blunter faces, thicker-set bodies and much longer fur, which, unlike the sea lion's, often hangs in wet spikes. This group was restricted to a jumble of rocks and caves at the base of a small stretch of cliffs. They loved dark recesses, from which they peered, whiskery faces flat against the rock. With large eyes, they feed mainly at night.

Breeding only on the archipelago, Galapagos fur seals were formerly heavily persecuted. From 1816–97, some 17,845 animals were taken, and the species vanished from several islands. In 1923 Beebe saw only two in the entire archipelago. The Tower colony marked a big increase over anything seen there for years. Nevertheless, it remains a rare and declining creature – its population being thought to have dropped by half over the past 24–35 years. El Niño, marine pollution and infectious diseases caused by the spread of dogs are thought to threaten the population. As a result, IUCN now lists the Galapagos fur seal as Endangered – a sorry (if not unfamiliar) state of affairs.

The sea lions constantly delighted us, and on Hood we felt to be sharing their beach and their bay. We were; sometimes too close for enjoyment. By contrast, we met the nocturnal fur seals only on Tower, mainly as distant blobs across Darwin Bay, sleeping away the day on their lava shelves. At closer quarters, from our rowing boat, they looked like bristly doormats, still boringly asleep. Even with all the difficulties they brought, we still preferred the sea lions.

16

HOOD: FROM WEEVILS TO ROYALS

JUNE

Despite benefiting from a break between our two islands, we didn't approach Hood with the same enthusiasm. Tower had handed us novelty, a perfect setting and idyllic weather. We had mostly revelled in our 200 days there. Yet that was a long stretch with few diversions, the challenge of poor food and Bryan's ailments, and we knew that Hood had a cooler climate with rough seas. At least we had less 'stuff' on Hood. The sun-bleached store tent, punctured by numberless bird feet, disintegrated as we dismantled it on Tower. We had eaten what seemed like most of our year's food or dispatched the truly inedible, such as bubbling chitterlings or inert, cardboard-tasting dried egg. Above all, we had abandoned the solar still. For those penultimate weeks on Tower I had spent far too much time inside it, trying to fix crab nibbles in the plastic lining, and coax it into producing more water. Once we calculated that we could manage with the drinking water in our containers, despite its nasty taste, I foreswore my daily Turkish bath with relief. By now we knew how much drinking water we needed, provided we were frugal, and, for Hood, organised enough, with a top-up via the *Beagle*, to last until we left. The still, made from odd pieces of washed-up wood, was bulky and awkward to pack, even when dismantled. The lining, a problem almost from the start, went with the rubbish, and the well-weathered Mylar might not even have survived re-erection. And anyway, the sparse sun on Hood would have produced a miserable yield.

Throughout our time in the Galapagos rarely a day went by without Bryan having some sort of ailment. They seemed to come especially thick and fast on Hood. Always a poor sleeper, any night sounds had him looking for danger. On Tower we got used to distant nocturnal arrivals from squawking red-foots. Rustling centipedes had him up for the machete but they didn't happen too often. Fortunately, most birds waited for dawn to squeeze inside or begin their noisy courtship outside.

Our arrival on Hood produced a different set of challenges. Almost as soon as we arrived, we discovered two giant centipedes in the tent which had Bryan at the ready for the rest of our stay. We also had no choice but to camp in a sea lion colony; Bryan sleeping amongst a posse of sea lions spelt disaster. I was tired so I slept. On the first night, Bryan slept fitfully, but after an intruder bull came galumphing past the tent on our second night, Bryan barely slept for the rest of our stay.

Bryan always needed more sleep than he got, and his health and mood suffered correspondingly. He battled throughout life with tension headaches and suffered them at least twice a week in the Galapagos. Cold sores or mouth ulcers constantly re-erupted. A sty irked him for over two weeks. Leg sores kept reappearing, as did swellings, rashes and itches. Boils on his bum meant that he couldn't sit, reducing him to kicking a Primus when it wouldn't light. One day he had backache and a groin pain. Stomach ache frequently plagued him and could last for days. It must have irked him that I, apart from the occasional stomach ache, seemed mostly to be a healthy peasant.

The weather hugely affected both of us and became our next biggest challenge. We knew Hood weather would be different but hadn't quite expected such a contrast with Tower. A lot was due to the time of year. A friend found working on Hood much more pleasant than on Tower, where mosquitoes plagued him. But for us, rain, cooler air and misty mornings made our days feel heavier. We were never too hot, though protested often about needing clothes to keep warm.

With our store tent abandoned in tatters, we had no option but to keep the fridge at the back of our main tent. This was a hazardous solution. Despite our concerted efforts we could not keep birds out, and they regularly rocketed round, extinguishing the flame of the paraffin fridge or provoking it to noxious fuming when the flame flared out of control.

Hair washing had been a problem on Tower, after all that immersion in seawater. Here, of course, our hair had grown, and now we had a fridge regularly spewing little black particles into our living tent. Having needed twice the usual amount of shampoo to wash out earlier stickiness, we had finished it. The only substitute I could find was the gritty paste meant for removing engine oil from hands, mixed with an old-fashioned, tough soap powder. Our drinking water would last only for drinking. The 'clean' water, saved in a polythene bottle, had turned bright green. Bryan said we smelt like a broom cupboard though I don't think even his golden locks turned green.

All our equipment was ancient and the Primus stoves particularly started playing up. One day we had to try three before managing to cook lunch, so Bryan replaced parts and cleaned them – and they sputtered on. The situation with the tilley lamp became desperate when, after just two hours, moths reduced our penultimate mantle to half, and we bestirred ourselves to find a solution. Having found the netting bag, by using a tin lid, wire and canvas we constructed an upper frame over which to drape it. No more fluttering moths could kill themselves or claim our final mantle.

Midway through our time on Hood, alarmed by our tattered clothes, I started knitting. First a pair of long socks. Next I unpicked the feet of another pair and reknitted them to eliminate all the mending. And finally Bryan's thin jumper had hugely darned elbows and albatross-oiled cuffs. As the wool ran out, the new sleeves fitted too snugly so Bryan could barely raise his arms, but this nevertheless compensated a little for the huge patches on his shorts.

Right from the start I had rationed some foods, but still we had been profligate on Tower. Now on Hood, where we were more in need of treats, I became a martinet. Of our treats we had merely enough for one pound of bacon, one of oats and a packet of cornflakes each month. Similarly with the rest of our tins, though after seven months we had quite lost interest in tinned fish and corned beef hash, even if curried.

By this time our flour had around 50 maggots or beetles per pound. Sieving with a spoon squashed the maggots and blocked the sieve; I had to use gentle fingers. Dried beans had three or four beetles per bean which left no bean. In spaghetti a black shadow meant beetle, a grey one maggot. It took a long time, breaking out each shadow, to make a meal. Both macaroni and rice had beetles – and tasted of sacking. Beetle protein should have been added to our diet.

One lucky day, a lobster boat brought us two huge, delicious fish. Treats like this made a big difference in a desert of monotonous, ill-tasting stodge. We carefully rationed the fish over four days and I managed four different ways of cooking it. On the first day we relished it fresh; fillets with crumbs, fried in butter. It was worth using a sliver of our precious butter just to produce that enticing aroma. Our salivating was rewarded by the delicious taste. A fish stew stretched my ingenuity, sieving out bits of onion and mushroom from the dried soup, a squeeze of tomato paste, a pinch of (by now pretty tasteless) herbs. As the odd-smelling steam rose from the pot, I felt very much like a witch around her cauldron. On the third day a few of our precious potatoes provided fish pie, enlivened with the anchovy paste that had proved so useless for fishing. We were surprised at our delight with humble fishcakes; crispy and scented with another raid on the dwindling butter.

Given such otherwise dire food, a huge compensation was the goats. Due to their impact on native vegetation, goats were scheduled for urgent removal from all small Galapagos islands. So eating them would arguably be helping conservation – and Hood's goats were all doomed anyway. But Bryan could rarely bring himself to kill anything: 'Think of the millions of years of evolution that have gone into producing that slug.'

Nevertheless, anxious to be prepared, Bryan had brought a shotgun to the Galapagos, and eventually we ate three goats. The first one we skinned and cut up on the beach, carefully preserving the skin for a rug. In his diary, Bryan notes that we earmarked a fine youngster for the pot:

'Every day he and his mother, a saddleback, wandered down to the tip of Punta Suarez, browsing as they went. Then they turned and came back past our camp at midday. All the goats followed fairly well-defined paths and time-tables like this, as a lot of animals do. When I tried to get really close they became wary and kept a respectable distance with a few shrubs as a shield.

One morning while watching blue-footed boobies I spotted saddleback browsing towards the point. I ran for the gun and began my version of stalking, though it was mid-morning and baking hot, not the weather for crawling under spiny shrubs and over uneven ground.

The goats were coming straight towards me so I waited five minutes before raising my head, only to see their distant backsides – an appropriate gesture. After a detour and more sweating I settled down again, but when I looked, saddleback was gazing straight at me, ears forward and head high. She couldn't see me and there was hardly any wind, but she was suspicious and took the kid away out to open ground. At the next abortive attempt, when I was scuttling along, bent double, a blue-foot exploded beneath my feet like a rocketing pheasant. It was most unusual to find a solitary blue-foot squatting unsociably amongst dense scrub and it made enough commotion to rattle the dry bones of the goat carcasses littering the ground, victims of previous campaigns to clear the island.

Eventually I got fairly close without being seen; saddleback and the kid settled down to rest under a dense *Cryptocarpus* canopy, within fifteen yards. When I stood up they both immediately rose and stood still, presenting a perfect target. But after all that I simply let them go, because I knew them too well.

The eventual victim had to be a complete stranger. Within an hour it had been skinned, cleaned and quartered and the succulent joints hung temptingly from the veranda roof. The mockingbirds got to work instantly and clinging, tit-like, with their strong feet and legs, hammered away with their serviceable beaks, tearing off strips of flesh. They were so intent that I easily plucked them off the carcass as they fed. That goat was really good, quite as good as young mutton and better than old.'

I became quite creative when cooking goat: steak, liver, kebabs, tasty shepherd's pie, numerous different stews, curried goat. Joints that had been in the fridge for at least a week were the most tender and juicy. A leg that smelt alluringly of roast lamb as it cooked, served with mint sauce, tasted of all our best-remembered meals rolled into one and cheered us incalculably. Even the ancient dried mint seemed to blossom, and we had a few potatoes left to roast with it. No wine, of course, unless we had pilfered the pure alcohol used for preheating the paraffin equipment. Not once did we fall for that.

By now the flour had deteriorated so badly that we tried various ruses to avoid eating the strange-tasting bread. Following one doleful breakfast of margarine and fusty bread, we decided next day just to skip breakfast and have brunch instead. Returning from a round of checks and weighings I struggled to think up something different to cheer us. We had goat with prunes. After a few meals of goat, we both insisted we felt more energetic.

One day the fridge refused to work, and the goat started smelling. Bryan noted that I refused to discard anything, saying that we must be prepared to eat carrion. For his next comment he wrote that his sty was returning and that a red rash with swelling had appeared on one leg. The next day the rash erupted on a different area. A week later we both felt unwell.

At the end of three goats we'd had enough. When the *Beagle* unexpectedly arrived, with the new director of the Charles Darwin Research Station keen to meet us and see Hood, we brightened at two invitations on board for a meal. We had to talk animatedly throughout dinner, however, when the plates arrived bearing yet more goat; there really was a concerted effort to clear them from the islands. And on the *Beagle*'s second invitation we were served tinned tuna. This was equivalent to visiting my parents after over a year away and being given tinned sardines. In those final weeks, desperate for a different solution to yet another tin of sardines, I'd tried frying them in batter; they were not too awful if you thought hard about something delicious. Food assumes great importance in restricted situations.

And although now sick of it – goat for brunch, goat and potato pie for supper – we definitely both felt chirpier; Bryan wondered whether we had been short of protein. One day I even reported 'feeling boisterous'. With sunny days our mood lifted markedly. But a return to cold mist brought us down again.

It was difficult to decide whether the sharp contrast in weather so adversely affected our well-being or whether, after seven months and with food markedly deteriorating, we had just had enough of desert islands. Usually it was much too miserable to go without clothes, and long days passed without swimming. We had no boat for fishing or fun days off and had long ago given up competing with the fit 18-year-olds in our magazine cutting. The thunderous wave that snatched our goggles eliminated underwater exploring for lobsters to cook on the beach. The evenings were too cold for dancing to Radio Belize (although we did enjoy Handel's 'Messiah' one evening). Add to that constant niggling ailments and fast-deteriorating food and much of Bryan's spark evaporated. In mid-August, for the first time, I admitted to wishing that we were going home. Six weeks later we agreed that were we given the choice whether or not to start this enterprise all over again, we would decline. That attitude shows just how low we had sunk.

Stomach ache could last for days; we did have some pretty degraded food by then. Looking back, I wonder why we didn't at least buy some fresh flour when we moved islands. Our fragile finances maybe, though one fewer sack from Guayaquil in December and a new one from Santa Cruz in August would have been more sensible. From our position of ignorance on the Bass Rock we had no idea what we might be able to buy on the Galapagos or how much more expensive it would be; perhaps it seemed safer to take everything. And I had no experience of ancient flour, particularly in South America. In mid-September I mournfully opened the final tin of sausages. Food was becoming grim; stocks of all tins were running out and we had eaten the last potatoes. With food so low we reluctantly opened a tin of squid: it tasted faintly fishy and had a horribly sloppy texture.

I'm not sure why, but at the end of September we had a spring clean, including moving the groundsheet. The resultant giant centipede went back to Britain in alcohol. As part of the clean I determined to do something about the sticking keys on my typewriter. Having finished all the typewriter oil, in desperation I had tried cooking oil. Normally I used the typewriter most days, but this time I had probably been too dispirited to use it for over two weeks and all the keys were totally gummed. It took hours to clean them with paraffin.

By October it slowly dawned on us that we would be off to Peru next month, to study the Peruvian booby on the 'guano islands'. The realisation concentrated our minds in several ways, and when grey days yet again foiled filming we used any spare time to begin packing. We had collected our usual assortment of dead objects, and several items we no longer needed, so the first box was soon completely packed. Three goatskin rugs had recently been added to our weird collection to try the patience of some poor customs official. We had found my favourite items, three seahorses, already cured on the lava of Tower. Nearly 50 years on, I still use them as earrings. On the same stretch of lava, we found a dried, hollowed-out iguana. And we couldn't possibly leave the albatross skull with its enormous beak; it sits on my bedroom window ledge next to a hyena skull from Jordan.

In mid-October we had a brighter spell of weather and once more our mood lifted. We both worked better, I embarked on some typing with my speeded-up typewriter and our meals improved. For the first time for ages I spent the whole day naked, saying I'd run out of clothes.

But then for eight days we again endured cloud, wind and rain. In hopeless conditions for filming, we cheered ourselves with a swim. Bryan developed another crop of mouth ulcers and remarked: 'Our last but one Saturday and I don't feel sorry.' Bryan's malaise was infectious; some days we felt we had accomplished little and this despite the glum realisation that we would soon be leaving and had much yet to do. We kept flogging but it often felt like a dead horse.

Despite feeling that we should be doing more, bulging notebooks testified to our industry. I calculated that we had carried out 3,216 weighings, often a stressful undertaking that involved scratches, hard pecks or being sprayed with excreta, oily vomit or stinking fish. Boobies and albatrosses had been ringed. And we had measured countless bills, wings and weights, and examined countless birds for moult. Many pages were filled with detailed descriptions of behaviour. Bryan had written and I had typed two papers; one for the journal *Auk*, the other on frigatebirds.

On a couple of partly sunny days, Bryan managed some photography and again our mood lifted a little. But true to my Yorkshire roots I had to find some downers and noted that we had hardly any butter, less than one tin of margarine, one spam, two sardines and some tuna – and neither oats nor cornflakes. Paraffin and alcohol were low, both chairs and my bed had broken, and our clothes hung in rags.

The December heat on Tower seemed a long time ago. Back then we were freshly arrived, excited by the island's welcoming wildlife, lagoon and fine coral beach – and a year on the 'Enchanted Islands' seemed an alluring prospect. But by mid-October on Hood we had become different creatures. This period marked the lowest point of our stay in the Galapagos. Our clothes were threadbare, our equipment disintegrating. We were beginning to feel anxious that time was running out and maybe we had not accomplished as much as possible. Bryan's endless ailments, our vile food and often miserable weather had reduced him to bouts of lethargy; a longer lie-in, reluctance to leave the tent, uncharacteristic lack of enthusiasm for writing. He still needed to film several aspects of booby behaviour. Yet each morning and evening when the light should have been good for filming, down came the mist or even rain.

How we needed cheer! And how we got it – because two superb feasts came our way. This fine dining would have been good by any standards; by ours at that time, after nearly a year on vitamin pills and sardines with the odd goat as a treat, they were the stuff of dreams.

The first meal came at the end of October in the dining room of the *Puritan*, a fishing boat under the command of an American (whose hobby, at which he was unerringly successful in every port, was collecting gold coins). We sat reverently at the table. The menu: fish soup; prime rib of beef served with potato salad, green salad, celery, kidney beans, rice and tomatoes; followed by fruit salad and ice cream.

The captain and chief engineer had lovely cabins with fitted carpets, television and private bathroom. The crew ate well too – food was their only pleasure – and, even in 1964, the cost of keeping such a boat at sea could exceed $1,000 a day (nearly $9,000 in today's money); fruitless voyages are costly for the two 950hp engines gulp fuel at a prodigious rate. Since the Ecuadorian government levied a fishing fee commensurate with the capacity of the boat (in this case the permit would have cost almost $10,000) it clearly behoved them to catch fish. In fact they almost always did, something they made sure of by staying at sea. The crew was paid on the basis of their catch; catching nothing meant no wage, although their keep was free. The skipper bore the main responsibility for success, for he decided where to go and, with powerful binoculars, did most of the scanning for telltale signs such as jumping fish and diving seabirds.

The *Puritan* had a tough-looking mixed seventeen-man crew from Portugal and Puerto Rico, plus American officers. The youngest member had a sullen expression and a head swathed in wrappings. Both were due to the enthusiasm with which his messmates had observed the ritual of crossing the Equator, and a crew member dressed as Neptune (god of the sea) had removed all his glossy black hair.

The feast aboard the *Puritan* made up for a lot of spam and sardines. Yet the following day I felt less than 100 per cent. We had become unused to a life of plenty.

Our time on the Galapagos was galloping to an end. After a year of so many highs and lows, we had ambivalent feelings about departure – relief coupled with regret. And then came the splendiferous finale to our stay.

A less strict regard for the truth might allow me to describe how, early one morning, a trim motor vessel slid snugly round the tip of Punta Suarez. A smartly lowered dinghy manned by immaculate sailors surged ashore. Hastily donning clothes, we went to meet it, when who should step ashore but Prince Philip. This came within an ace of happening – but fortunately Roger Perry, then the brand-new director of the Charles Darwin Research Station, had visited Hood some five weeks earlier and given us the news of this royal visit.

After almost a year of washing in seawater and drying in tropical sun, snagging on thorny scrub and being jabbed by horny beaks, our clothes were disintegrating. How to make our tattered selves presentable? Bryan had no option. The patched shorts streaked with seabird vomit, a stinking mix of oil and decaying fish, a thin sweater with reknitted tight sleeves, and bare feet would have to do. It hardly seemed right, Bryan wrote, to don the lounge suit which for some obscure reason mouldered in the bottom of a chest. Shorts, a beard and bare feet seemed not inappropriate. It didn't matter in the slightest, that he looked like a half-starved castaway, because he pretty nearly was one.

But what could I wear? My shorts seemed not quite so disgusting as his, but they suddenly looked so short. Think Jimmy Connors and John McEnroe from the 1980s tennis scene. Short shorts didn't seem at all suitable for the expected plush carpets and footmen. Desperate, I scrabbled in the bottom of one of our chests and, by some magic, surfaced with smart green ski pants, an entire black sweater and real footwear. The light, sleeveless summer top I had planned to wear would look silly with ski pants. Sweater and thick pants it would have to be, in spite of the heat. I had last worn them in November, en route to the Galapagos, when the *Queen Elizabeth* hove to in the mid-Atlantic in that Force 11 gale. No doubt the visitors would have tolerated a far more basic appearance, befitting the environment; had they arrived unexpectedly they would certainly have found one. Attire settled, it remained only to remove the inhospitable sea lion barricade and await the royal arrival.

The *Beagle* had been rendezvousing with the Royal Yacht *Britannia* at various points in the archipelago, with Karl Angermeyer as guide. At exactly 8am, as scheduled, the *Britannia* slid round Punta Suarez and the little *Beagle*, with Karl's brother Fritz at the helm, hastened in from the north after a rough journey from the other side of the Equator. With the *Britannia* still underway a rubber dinghy took to the water and circled the yacht. This was an unofficial visit to see and photograph the wildlife of the Galapagos, which was perhaps why we were included in the itinerary – though I suspect that the albatrosses and blue-footed boobies had the edge on us. And it was a momentous visit, the first time a member of the British royal family had set foot in the Galapagos, islands whose English names commemorate the Stuart line.

The late Duke of Edinburgh was justly admired for his realistic attitudes and genuine charm. Upon arrival, he quickly dispelled any awkwardness we may have felt about our unexpected looks. Indeed, my smart but sweaty garb obviously impressed since he remarks in his Foreword that when we first met on the beach June appeared 'as neat and tidy as the day she left civilisation'.

Major Aubrey Buxton, well-known naturalist and director of Anglia Television, was with the group, which also included Gerard Corley Smith, Her Majesty's Ambassador to Ecuador. Both were keen birdwatchers and with Prince Philip as interested as anyone, we spent four hours watching albatrosses, boobies and tropicbirds, and taking photographs under a grilling sun. The albatrosses even came out from the shade and performed their courtship dance as a Royal Command Performance. Normally they are sunk in lethargy at that time of day and loath to start even the tiniest ecstatic ritual. But Prince Philip got the works, including whoops, grunts, rattles and clunks and mad laughter. Corley Smith nearly fell over the cliff trying to photograph tropicbirds and Buxton stuck cigar stumps on the bushes at intervals to provide a back-trail.

Mockingbirds and giant centipedes seemed to figure quite prominently in our Galapagos year, but never together. Today, maybe they too craved royal attention, for part way through our tour of Punta Suarez a giant centipede trailed its ugly, red, chitin-clad 12 inches across our route, promoting a pantomime from the endlessly curious and bold mockingbirds. 'No, sir, we've never seen one in daylight. I think that's why the mockingbirds are behaving like that; they've never even seen one before.' The mockers circled the centipede warily and would not approach. And we all circled the mockingbirds, fascinated to know what would happen next. But the centipede scuttled beneath a rock and its audience dispersed, the mockers running off in their comical fashion rather than flying.

By this time we had reached our colony of blue-footed boobies. Prince Philip seemed not to believe Bryan's interpretation of their electrifying landing display, with the pair of large turquoise webbed feet raised skywards in an improbable salute just before touching down. As Bryan commented that this display was used by the male both to proclaim 'this is my patch' and to strengthen his bond with his mate, the Duke was heard to mutter, loudly: 'How does he know?'

Fortunately, Bryan got a chance to explain in some detail that we had been watching these birds for hundreds of hours, and by observing exactly what happened we could work out what their signals meant. Then the party watched in fascination as several males paraded around their sites flaunting these unlikely webs in a series of complex courtship displays, with Bryan explaining what they were doing. As an encore, we wandered round to the spectacular blowhole where huge jets of water constantly exploded 75 feet into the air.

Approaching 12.30 the party turned towards the *Britannia* and, as we'd 'feared', Prince Philip invited us on board for a meal. Fortunately it was lunch so at least our sartorial elegance would not be competing with the party's evening dress. I was already noticing that my outfit looked totally ridiculous beside the smart tropical kit of the Prince's entourage and the uniforms of the crew. And I smelt fusty.

I went first up the long ladder – and there stood the captain, telescope under his arm, saluting, flanked by two sailors, also saluting. We were taken to a luxurious guest suite for a wash, both barefoot as lava had shredded our island footwear. I had decided that clumpy winter walking shoes would just not do for such a visit. Bryan acquired a pair of sandals, but there was none for me. Maybe they had no smaller sizes; I was the only woman on board. Another steward then took us up to the cocktail lounge for drinks. The *Britannia* was beautiful inside – discreet elegance with the expected soft grey carpet, beautiful wide stairs, fresh flowers on the grand piano, huge windows and soft chairs everywhere.

The contrast with almost a year's Galapagos camping was extreme. We were inured to washing in seawater, eating weevily spaghetti and beetle-infested flour, using a sea-washed gully for latrine, and all the many tiny but somewhat sordid necessities of such a prolonged camp in tropical-island surroundings. And now we were ensconced within the magnificence of the *Britannia*'s suites.

The admiral awaited us in the cocktail lounge. I felt inappropriately dressed but relieved that my short shorts were in the tent rather than about my person. Prince Philip gave us a signed copy of his book of bird photographs. Then it was into lunch. Prince Philip sat at the head of the table, with me on his right and Bryan on his left; the ambassador was on my right, then the rest, with the admiral at the foot. Bryan surely presented the footman with the most ragged posterior he ever guided to a *Britannia* chair. Queues of stewards waited on us. I was served first for everything – beginning with goulash, noodles, potatoes and broccoli in sauce. Stewards offered us salad on the side. Cold meats then appeared but had no takers. After months with desserts such as horrible vanilla biscuits 'cooked' with dried fruit in the fridge, we talked for weeks afterwards about apple *millefeuille* and fresh cream. So close to the end of our stay in the Galapagos, with food in the tent strictly rationed, cheese, biscuits and coffee almost sank us, but provided a superb ending to the finest of dining.

Prince Philip was splendid. Most of the time he talked to me in a thoroughly informal way, joking about how crazy we were spending such a year. He even offered to take us to Panama if that would be any help in getting to Peru. It would have almost been worth going in the exact opposite direction to spend two days on the *Britannia*.

But there was a downside to having most of Prince Philip's attention. He ate quickly then turned to me. It would have been good to focus on this banquet, to simply gaze at it with relish, but politeness required eye contact with the Prince. Eating gracefully whilst composing answers to his interested questions and explaining our foibles needed deep concentration. Too many scurrying thoughts prevented me from savouring each delicious mouthful. We'd forgotten the taste of beautifully cooked, fresh produce; the sensations of delicate flavours; the different textures of real food. Amongst my turmoil I had a vision of those endless plates of bug-ridden spaghetti with sauce made from dried onions and mushrooms sieved from soup, mixed with the despised sardines. I left the dining room realising that I remembered the conversation vividly but had barely noticed or tasted the food.

And that meal was far from the total of our debt. We must add needles to repair ravaged clothes, razors to restore hirsute jowls to elegant smoothness and sandals to enclose lava-leathered feet – and had it not been for our unbelievable perverseness in having planned to leave Hood the next day, food would have been ours too. Above all, the *Britannia* kindly took notebooks and film safely back to England and the air conditioning of Buckingham Palace. On an expedition such as ours one always fears the loss of scientific material on the journey home, which in our case involved several transferences from boat to ship, with disaster conceivable at any point.

The Duke's visit was a fine and unexpected climax to our Galapagos venture. Whatever happens to the memories of a year's boobies and monotonous food, the fresh cream of the *Britannia* will aye endure.

17

FAREWELL GALAPAGOS

JUNE

One hundred and six days after our arrival on Hood, we were up at dawn. After hastily breaking camp with the ever-helpful crew from the *Beagle*, we sat on deck at 8.30am in a stiff breeze, watching our now much tidier campsite slowly vanish into the early morning, happy to be leaving and mainly satisfied with what we had achieved. This was virtually the end of our studies in the Galapagos.

We had had a kaleidoscopic year on the 'Enchanted Islands'. Let out of school, we joyfully embraced our time on Tower. Everything was new; well, apart from our ancient equipment from the Bass. The sun shone, we had energy, new subjects surrounded us, an idyllic camping spot captivated us every new morning, and we had salt water back and front that was always ready for a reviving swim. New friends on Santa Cruz had sent us off with well wishes, a good supply of freshly picked produce and promises of more. We felt the luckiest pair on earth. And we had so much to learn. We didn't care much for civilisation and, three years married, lived happily on our own, frowning when we noticed – too frequently – visitors invading 'our' desert island. Hood, with its inhospitable climate, didn't much attract them; there they would have been more welcome.

Looking back, I can trace how things deteriorated, alongside our food. At the time we didn't much notice, continuing our routine of trying to fit together the jigsaw of our subjects' lives, and exploring Hood. We were still enjoying many of our activities and overall it had not been a miserable year. Very much the opposite. Yet, inevitably,

I have been influenced by my letters and Bryan's descriptive diary, including grumbling details of our poor food and his sufferings. In his book they are insignificant. With hindsight, they loom large in mine. They were even more so by the end of our stay.

During those final taxing weeks we had several times rejoiced that soon we would no longer have to endure straitened times. And we could say goodbye to those mockingbirds. They were mainly lovable, especially on Tower, and we had enjoyed their antics – but with so many other things conspiring against us their sheer numbers, persistent curiosity and thievery wore us down. And with huge relief we could finally abandon our medieval prison fare. Lunch aboard the *Britannia* had reminded us of the alternatives.

Endings are always strange and usually ambivalent. We hoped to briefly revisit Tower and spend a while on Santa Cruz. We felt excitement; a new phase, with travel, people, totally different experiences on a new island off the Peruvian coast with new birds. We felt relief; life had become a struggle. Yet inevitably we felt regrets; had we wrung the last drop out of our privileged stay? We could have done more. Bryan's filming had been so curtailed by early and late mists and, unlike on Tower, we hadn't managed much fun. And we felt scared; for nearly a year we had spoken to very few people and lived a protected life. Could we cope with teeming Guayaquil, with once more having to make complicated arrangements in strange lands, with exotic travel on unusual transport, our first ever flight, and the demands of living cheaply in South America when we spoke virtually no Spanish? And all arrangements had to be made in person. No mobiles, no internet.

After leaving Hood on 5 November 1964, most of our time was spent rather uneventfully on Santa Cruz, though on the day of our return to the Station the Angermeyers invited us to one of their sparkling parties, with its inevitable morning ending. We slunk off early to bed around 2am. Our quick visit to Tower, to see what was happening after a four-month interval, had to wait for a leak in the *Beagle* to be repaired. This in turn meant waiting for the month's highest tide, which took about three weeks.

Roger Perry kindly invited us to eat with him, and we slept in one of the dormitories built recently for visiting scientists. We were inside a lot as the weather continued cloudy. Quite a few people invited us for meals – usually goat. Having recently eaten three, we didn't relish the appearance of more. But smoked goat was a different species. And we never tired of Galapagos fish or the local fruit and vegetables. After our recent dismal meals, almost everything seemed a feast, though we ate daintily, not wishing to challenge our shrunken stomachs too severely.

We went to yet another party, and one day trekked back up to the Santa Cruz hills. As during our first hike, heavy rain had produced incredible mud, and I travelled the last quaggy bit by horse. We had neither time nor even inclination for that gruelling slog up to the tortoises, which had been the original plan, but remembered our astonishment at their lumbering bulk, and our delight at emerging into such a fitting setting for them. Years later, hearing that hundreds had been returned to Hood gave us a glimmer of hope that much of the Galapagos could be restored. In the highlands, Mrs Horneman gave us her usual reviving lunch, and the ancient coffee grinder did its magic on home grown beans, launching us cheerily back down the slithering track.

Bryan describes how, on one of our final days, he and Roger explored an area north of Academy Bay:

'After about two and a half miles a great cave, which runs beneath the road, opened as a large hole only a few yards from the road. The entrance, however, lay in a subsidence jumbled with boulders, and unless you knew exactly where to look you could spend hours in the search. A few yards' error in the Galapagos can be as good as miles. At first the roof of the tunnel was comfortably high, and we saw a barn owl, but deeper underground it became low and narrow. After a long stooping journey it became so low that further progress meant squirming flat on one's belly until the cave ended where floor and ceiling meet. It was vaguely alarming to press on and on, squeezing through narrow slits in the absolute blackness, with an awful feeling that the earth which presses so insistently on all sides, was ready to slip. That would be nothing fresh in the Galapagos.

About three-quarters of the way along, a narrow chimney rises vertically towards a chink of sky. Roger wanted to climb the crack. The ascent was not difficult, but still the incident sticks in my mind. Roger is that hypothetical beast, the 'type' Englishman, dryly humorous, imperturbably well mannered and impeccably dressed (perhaps I should have written the Englishman's idea of the 'type' Englishman!). When duty or inclination indicate a visit to an outlying island Roger goes along as he went to his job with the BBC, in suede Chelsea boots, faultlessly creased trousers, long-sleeved shirt, bow tie and pork-pie hat; and of course, the pipe. The first time he came to Hood, dressed like this he placed one elegant foot on a block of lava and tied his shoelace in front of an interested and respectfully grouped audience of sea lions and iguanas. After his arrival in the Galapagos the islanders, amazed and, who knows, perhaps impressed, waited for the supply of shirts, bow ties, trousers and boots to dry up and the workday garb of the field naturalist to appear; in vain. Sartorial elegance was but a minor expression of his perfectionist nature. Serene among lava, cacti, sea lions and iguanas, Roger picked his precise way.

To return to the cave chimney – he climbed it without removing pipe or pork-pie hat and emerged into daylight amid the scrub and lava. To my deep regret no thunderstruck Ecuadorian was there to goggle as this impossible apparition squeezed up from the bowels of the earth and out through the tiny crack in the hot crust of lava, buried among the scrub and cacti. That way legends grow.'

Galapagos hospitality continued without cease. Any visitors staying for a while were eagerly welcomed by old-timers. Visiting scientists had special cachet. Long-time residents were intelligent, resourceful folk who knew their island and its life intimately. With no great urge to leave, they still welcomed news of the world, and particularly any update on findings about their own. We enjoyed an evening meal with Miguel Castro and his fascinating collection of photographs presented by Galapagos visitors. On spare evenings at the Research Station we chatted enjoyably to Roger about the BBC and travels, or listened to Galapagos adventures from Edgar Potts. He had filled many virtuoso roles and could tell a mean tale. And of course, we had to have a final evening with the Angermeyers. It began with coffee at 4pm on Karl and Margo's lava terrace; watching their iguanas feeding from a dish whilst listening to the slap of surf and swashbuckling tales. Karl looked like a pirate, with his gold tooth and craggy, burnished charm. He had been invited to Hollywood but the Galapagos always drew him back. More folk arrived then we all decamped next door to

Fritz and Carmen for smoked goat, delicious bread, more coffee and the usual late farewell.

At last the *Beagle* was ready and, with Skipper Karl, we left for Tower. I was never totally happy travelling on the *Beagle*. Viewed from the land, she was a beautiful craft, but down below was pretty sick-making in a swell. Getting up each morning was the worst; she was usually rolling and the cabin had become incredibly stuffy. Just sitting up in bed, even for a minute, made me feel sick. I dressed lying down, rolled off the bunk, then dashed aloft. It worked, but then came the problem of how long I could last without having to descend to the stinky loo; a lengthy job working pumps and taps.

Our first stop involved enquiring about our return to mainland Ecuador. Dreading a repeat rolling sail on the *Cristobal Carrier*, news of a possible flight presented a dilemma. Firstly, it would be our first ever flight and secondly, it would be in an ancient plane mostly used for transporting staff from the air base on Baltra. We were told that the flight leaving in four days' time was fully booked. However, the Station made sure that they had a good relationship with the air base, and we had taken presents. The helpful base commander and his wife invited us for coffee, but we left with little hope of tickets.

When Karl told us the pilot was the worst in Ecuador we began to haver. Maybe serendipity had decreed that there were no seats. Perhaps a five-day roll back to Guayaquil on the *Carrier* might be a better idea after all.

As compensation, we delighted in two days back on Tower and relived our joyful seven months in such an idyllic spot. Sleeping on the *Beagle* provided a poor substitute for our sturdy tent, its enticing verandas looking on to the lagoon and the sea, and a wake-up call from the swallow-tails. However, this was more than compensated for by being looked after, by the delicious freshly caught fish and Angermeyer vegetables, and especially by the swelling laughter. Those aboard the *Beagle* were entertaining companions – something we had missed during our exile.

Ashore, many of the young boobies, sporting 'our' colour rings, still sweltered on their disintegrating nests, and we learnt a lot more about Galapagos breeding cycles. Some of our ringed adults had started nesting again; was it their egg lying broken under the nest? Best of all we had the final joy of an excited Poppet on the beach to nip our fingers.

From Tower we returned to the air base on Baltra to learn that the plane had been delayed until the following day. There was still not much hope of seats, as capacity on the ancient plane was limited by the weight of its cargo.

The day before the flight unspooled a chaotic scene. Prospective passengers had to present themselves at the airport and were all milling around frantically having their baggage weighed. At the end of November, this was one of the last flights before Christmas, and airbase personnel had assembled a weird collection of Christmas presents. How about finding a bag of Galapagos salt in your stocking? One crate, of lava destined to decorate a garden, weighed 136lb. It seemed like us versus rocks. Eventually we were told that we could go so long as our baggage weighed no more than 50lb. Ridiculously, I abandoned my favourite green dress, and we sent rucksacks and tripod back to the Research Station.

For our very first flight we reluctantly rolled out of bed at 4.15am, only to encounter the usual Galapagos delay and then quite the experience. The worst pilot in Ecuador kangarooed on to Baltra. Excited Spanish chatter quavered with anxiety. Children screamed and ran; unknowing that they had drawn that human short straw. Muscles bulged as men strained at the crates and sacks, and the smell of sweat mingled with acrid fuel fumes in the dusty dry air. We could taste it.

Folk straggled reluctantly aboard, stumbling on the rickety steps, then blocked the entrance as they struggled to adjust to the gloomy grey interior. The twin-engined plane – very small, very outdated – was merely a hull with a long row of metal benches on either side, of which ours collapsed. The cargo, with its salt, rocks, dried fish and live lobsters, also included 17 passengers from the base.

The sight of parachutes being handed out did nothing to boost our confidence, especially when I got the last one and Bryan was instructed to share mine. Passengers then began hanging fragile, varnished lobsters from the wiring running the length of the plane; prize Christmas presents. Just to complete the picture, the base commander had a full-sized camp bed erected in the middle of the plane for his three children to play on. Our first flight looked set to be memorable and we held our breath. Most passengers were Catholic, crossing themselves as we took off. The plane, massively overloaded despite all that hassle with weighing cargo, seemed to be crawling, though very noisily, to the end of the runway, which happened to be the cliff edge. It felt as though we dropped off the end then, somehow, became airborne; rather like an albatross, but without continuing with their graceful flight.

However with our usual good fortune it all turned out to be worthwhile. In four and a half hours we were in Guayaquil for just £14 instead of spending five rolling days for twice the price on the terrible *Cristobal Carrier*.

Farewell Galapagos.

18

AFTERMATH

JUNE

The Galapagos were now of the past, and we were not too sorry to watch them dwindle. We had reached the stage where the future seemed more enticing.

After all the solitude, Guayaquil felt even more frightening than we had imagined. Hair-raising traffic had me clutching Bryan's arm; where would the next vehicle be coming from? Swarming crowds jostled us, and a speeding runner tried to grab my watch as he hurtled past. Endless harsh noise – quite different to booby harsh – with horns providing all the notes, and the smell of a tropical city on a muddy river, assaulted us. But at least it was familiar, and it felt good to know our way around and have contacts. We homed straight to the Pension Helbig, feeling happier after an excellent lunch and dinner. From a comfortable base, things seemed much easier.

After a sociable time with the folk we already knew in Ecuador, Consul Lacey and the Gilberts, at long last a haircut for me, and what must be the finest train ride in the world – into the Andes to Quito – we took our much less scary second flight to Peru. Flying over the mountains at dawn, we marvelled at range after range of arid, razor-edged hills; Galapagos lava looks fertile in comparison.

With more serendipity, a trip to the British Embassy in Lima provided an introductory letter to the Peruvian Guano Company. They enthusiastically welcomed us, and insisted on providing permission, passage, accommodation, food and even a taxi to the dock to get us to Guañape Norte and the Peruvian booby; our fourth study species nesting only on the guano islands of Peru.

With everything arranged on our first afternoon in Peru, we continued our cheering break, almost a conventional holiday, exploring Lima, and returning to the Andes to visit Machu Picchu. Then it was offshore again.

At which point things slid rapidly downhill. We ate with the *guardianes* on Guañape; warm, friendly men but without a word of English, and our Spanish, embarrassingly, had barely progressed. Of course, they were poor, and we ate in their grimy kitchen without windows. We were given the huge house built for the islands' manager, but now it was covered in guano dust and abandoned. Anybody who has lived on the Bass is inured to the stink of guano. There it is wet, acrid and mixed with rotten fish. On this dry island we barely noticed the smell but suffered its fine dust every moment of our stay.

Christmas dinner of lumpsucker and cabbage summed up the food. And without even decent meals to look forward to, our living quarters – with hard, narrow cots from which guano rose in clouds whenever we sat down – seemed even grimmer. Without any hint of green, ringing and weighing boobies on the island's glaring white expanse, in a quivering heat, exhausted us. Each night I lay in lonely misery fantasising about leaving Bryan, living with my godmother, and going to university.

But when we returned to take up our lives in Scotland, to meet friends, to the excitement of interviews, to more adventures, all that changed. Bryan and I lasted another 50 years.

In January 1965 we had a date at Buckingham Palace. Bryan's supervisor at Oxford University, Niko Tinbergen, lent us his new

Ford Cortina estate, and off we went to London to collect our scruffy box of notebooks and negatives. The duty police were expecting us, so in we went past the Queen's Guard in their busbies, then across the front of the Palace to the door of the Privy Purse. There were no royalty around, but we had a long chat with Prince Philip's aide and secretary. Our records were returned to us safely.

With so much writing and catching up to do, we felt quite helpless. Everybody wanted to see our slides, and almost every post brought media requests. The television programme *Tonight* wanted us to take a train from Scotland to London that afternoon, for a live interview. We decided we had better get back to the Bass Rock quickly before we had nervous breakdowns.

But the gannets had not yet returned, so no escape there, and we had a new Land Rover to collect (all of £650), ready for a visit to Norfolk to see Aubrey Buxton, who had accompanied Prince Philip on Hood Island. Aubrey went on to commission and produce a Galapagos film for Anglia TV. He would have liked to use Bryan's film, but of course Bryan scorned 'human interest', which made it useless for the *Survival* series. But we were invited to the film's premiere, shot by Alan and Joan Root, at London's Royal Festival Hall. Later Bryan introduced it to four branches of the Scottish Geographical Society, showing slides of the Galapagos and talking for about 45 minutes before the film. Over 1,000 people attended the event in Edinburgh's Usher Hall. Fred Marr, boatman for the Bass, caused great merriment when he delivered two hot crabs backstage.

After our visit to Aubrey in Norfolk, we several times visited his remote house in northwest Scotland. Following one, he asked to borrow our Land Rover for his next guest, Princess Anne. We could take his Bentley in exchange. A Bentley on Scotland's single-track roads was not a pleasant experience. We forgot to remind Aubrey that our jack lived behind the front seats. He had an embarrassing experience with a puncture. Maybe Princess Anne leapt out and offered to remove the tyre.

Prince Philip enjoyed several expeditions with Aubrey, eventually visiting his house in the Scottish wilds, and we once joined them (plus a detective and valet) there. 'Interesting' folk were invited for dinner or to join for the day. An excellent cook would normally drive several miles to prepare dinner for Aubrey's group but that same journey to prepare breakfast didn't make sense. Would I do it? I agreed, of course, but with some trepidation. The first breakfast involved fried eggs. Oh dear, I would be sure to break them. Would the detective mind cooking them? What a silly lack of confidence; mine would have been far superior to his overcooked offerings.

The valet knocked on my door in some consternation. He had forgotten the royal garters; plus fours without garters just don't work. Would I please sew some? Of course I wasn't allowed to measure the royal leg, but we managed between us. I could see the photograph of the Queen beside Prince Philip's bed whenever I passed his room.

Following a short row to a nearby seabird island, I was left on board to look after the dinghy. After some long time, and bored with singing to the fascinated seals, I tied up the boat and went for a walk. We all returned to the dinghy simultaneously. Prince Philip surveyed my efforts at a nautical knot and asked: 'And whose knitting is this?'

The highlight of the stay was a trip to Handa Island, famous for its seabirds. En route we came across two elderly women standing beside an Austin Mini that had ended up in a ditch. Prince Philip, driving the lead Land Rover, braked hard, jumped out, and organised the party to lift out the drunken car. Turning to leave, he wagged a finger at the open-mouthed owners: 'Now don't do that again.'

Getting to Handa wasn't straightforward. The poor chap with the outboard, started many times in preparation for the royal crossing, could not get the engine to start at the vital moment. Redder and more flustered with every pull, he eventually agreed we would have to wait a while.

Eventually though, we had a delightful day on the island, dive-bombed by skuas, with so many subjects for the camera, and eventually a swim in the loch. I had been led discreetly away by Aubrey, but I'm sure Prince Philip would have had no qualms about skinny-dipping with me. Bryan later reported that, as expected, Prince Philip dived in first. He came up clawing weed from his face. 'Be careful,' he spluttered. 'It's very shallow.'

Following Handa, it was time for an intense spell writing up the Galapagos data, continuing work on the Bass, submitting scientific papers and articles, and starting Bryan's first book – *Galapagos: Islands of Birds* – from which much text appears in this present volume. After this we were given the chance to see the two remaining species of booby, which nest on Christmas Island in the Indian Ocean. Appallingly, the jungle trees, sole nesting place of Abbott's booby, were being felled to mine phosphate. After our study there, Bryan asked Prince Philip to enlist Malcolm Fraser, the Australian prime minister, to declare Christmas Island a national park and save Abbott's booby – protection that was eventually formalised in 1980. Anglia Television showed Bryan's film about Christmas Island.

Prince Philip wrote the Foreword for Bryan's Galapagos book, and later the Queen presented Bryan with an MBE in recognition of his work helping Abbott's booby. During the investiture, she remarked that missing the Galapagos was one of the things she most regretted about her reign. I can sympathise; my life would have been totally different without our year in these remarkable islands. I wish that everybody in the world could spend at least a week there – although not all together! They might well leave with a totally different view of wildlife and how it should be treated. To even visit the Galapagos is truly special. To spend a year living and working in this laboratory of evolution was a privilege like no other. Granted we endured hardships, but our time there allowed us, among other delights, to savour the exceptional trust of Galapagos creatures. The world must not betray them. Our grandchildren – and their grandchildren – deserve the joy of watching these splendidly adapted creatures of the 'Enchanted Islands'.

APPENDIX I
FOOD FOR ONE YEAR

24 tins sausages

4 tins ham

24 tins bacon

200 tins butter

100 tins margarine

50 tins lard

2 tins cheese

12 cheeses

4 sacks flour

2 sacks sugar

12 packs icing sugar

24 packets cornflakes

24 tins oats

7lb oats

30lb spaghetti

30lb rice

7lb dried peas

21lb dried beans

6 large packets dried vegetables

Countless pounds of candied fruit sent in mistake for dried

12 tins chitterling (sent by mistake, and – bubbling – thrown away on arrival)

100 tins corned beef hash (sent in place of corned beef, and disgusting)

50 tins spam

24 tins salmon

50 tins tuna

50 tins sardines

60 tins milk

24 tins cream

10x5lb tins dried milk

7lb tea

24 tins coffee

2 tins cocoa

Hundreds of tins of fruit juice sent in mistake for fruit

14lb dried egg (ghastly mistake)

2 gallons corn oil

1 gallon honey

24 jars jam

24 tins tomato puree

12 jars pickle

2 jars salad cream

Stock cubes

36 jellies

24lb biscuits (ghastly)

12lb chocolate

24 packets mints

1 crate lemons

200 tins fruit

Misc. yeast, spices, etc

1 large sack salt

Many items on our original list were just not available in Ecuador.

Stolen during unloading in the Galapagos

24 tins stew

4 tins chicken

1 tin turkey

APPENDIX 2
SCIENTIFIC NAMES OF GALAPAGOS SPECIES MENTIONED

This appendix lists the vernacular and scientific names of Galapagos animals mentioned in the text (but not those from other parts of the world, other than northern gannet). It follows current taxonomy and nomenclature, which, in some instances, differs from that used during the 1960s.

Birds

albatross

    waved *Phoebastria irrorata*

booby

    blue-footed *Sula nebouxii*

    Nazca *S. granti*

    red-footed *S. sula*

dove

    Galapagos *Zenaida galapagoensis*

finch

    Genovesa cactus *Geospiza propinqua*

    Genovesa ground *G. acutirostris*

    large ground *G. magnirostris*

    mangrove *G. heliobates*

    warbler *Certhidea* spp.

    woodpecker *G. pallida*

flamingo
>American *Phoenicopterus ruber*

frigatebird
>great *Fregata minor*
>magnificent *F. magnificens*

gannet
>northern *Morus bassanus*

gull
>lava *Larus fuliginosus*
>swallow-tailed *Creagrus furcatus*

hawk
>Galapagos *Buteo galapagoensis*

heron
>great blue *Ardea herodias*
>yellow-crowned night *Nyctanassa violacea*

mockingbird
>Española *Mimus macdonaldi*
>Galapagos (Genovesa) *M. parvulus bauri*

noddy
>brown *Anous stolidus*

owl
>(Galapagos) short-eared *Asio flammeus galapagoensis*
>common (Galapagos) barn *Tyto alba punctatissima*

pelican
>brown *Pelecanus occidentalis*

penguin
>Galapagos *Spheniscus mendiculus*

phalarope
>grey *Phalaropus fulicarius*

shearwater
　　　　Galapagos *Puffinus subalaris*
storm-petrel
　　　　band-rumped *Hydrobates castro*
　　　　wedge-rumped *H. tethys*
tattler
　　　　wandering *Tringa incana*
tropicbird
　　　　red-billed *Phaethon aethereus*
turnstone
　　　　ruddy *Arenaria interpres*
warbler
　　　　American (Galapagos) yellow *Setophaga petechia aureola*
whimbrel *Numenius phaeopus*

Other animals

centipede
　　　　Galapagos giant *Scolopendra galapagoensis*
crab
　　　　Galapagos fiddler *Minuca galapagensis*
　　　　red rock (or 'Sally Lightfoot') *Grapsus grapsus*
crayfish (or Galapagos lobster) *Panulirus penicillatus*
deer
　　　　red *Cervus elaphus*
dolphin (Delphinidae)
flying fish *Hirundichthys* sp.
fur seal
　　　　Galapagos *Arctocephalus galapagoensis*
　　　　northern *Callorhinus ursinus*

        South American *Arctocephalus australis*
Galapagos mice (Cricetidae)
goat
        feral *Capra aegagrus*
iguana
        Galapagos land *Conolophus subcristatus*
        marine *Amblyrhynchus cristatus*
lava lizard
        Española *Microlophus delanonis*
mackerel *Scomber* sp.
mice
        Galapagos (Cricetidae)
mullet
        yellowtail *Minimugil cascasia*
pufferfish
        bullseye *Sphoeroides annulatus*
rat
        house (or black or roof) *Rattus rattus*
sand eel *Ammodytes* spp.
sardine
        Pacific *Sardinus sagax*
sea lion
        Californian *Zalophus californianus*
        Galapagos *Z. wollebaeki*
        South American *Otaria byronia*
seal
        elephant *Mirounga* sp.
shark
        blacktip *Carcharhinus limbatus*

whitetip reef *Triaenodon obesus*

snake

Ecuadorian milk *Lampropoeltis micropholis*

Española racer *Pseudalophis hoodensis*

tortoise

giant *Chelonoidis* spp.

turtle (Chelonidae)

whale

sperm *Physeter macrocephalus*

SELECT BIBLIOGRAPHY

Alexander, W.B. *Birds of the Ocean* G.P. Putnam's Sons, New York, 1928

Beebe, W *Galapagos: World's End* G.P. Putnam's Sons, New York, 1924

Colnett, J. *A Voyage to the South Atlantic and round Cape Horn into the Pacific Ocean, for the Purpose of Extending the Spermaceti Whale Fisheries, and Other Objects of Commerce, by Ascertaining the Ports, Bays, Harbours, and Anchoring Births* [sic]*, in Certain Islands and Coasts in Those Seas at which the Ships of the British Merchants Might Be Refitted* W. Bennett, London, 1798

Darwin, C. *The Descent of Man* John Murray, London, 1874

Darwin, C. *A Naturalist's Voyage Around the World* John Murray, London, 1890

Eibl-Eibesfeldt, I. *Galapagos* Macgibbon and Kee, London, 1960

Fosberg, F.R. 1965. *Natural bird refuges in the Galápagos.* Elepaio 25: 60–67

Lack, D. *Darwin's Finches* Harper & Brothers, New York, 1947

Nelson, J.B. *The Sulidae: Gannets and Boobies* Oxford University Press, New York, 1978

Nelson, J.B. *Galapagos: Islands of Birds* Longmans, London, 1968

Parker, E. *Oddities of Natural History* Seeley Service & Co. Ltd, Buckley (UK), 1943